GLOBAL INVESTING

GLOBAL INVESTING

A Practical Guide to the World's Best
Financial Opportunities

Darrin Erickson

WILEY

Published by John Wiley & Sons, Inc., Hoboken, New Jersey.
Published simultaneously in Canada.

For general information on our other products and services or for technical support, please contact our Customer Care Department within the United States at (800) 762-2974, outside the United States at (317) 572-3993 or fax (317) 572-4002.

Wiley also publishes its books in a variety of electronic formats. Some content that appears in print may not be available in electronic formats. For more information about Wiley products, visit our web site at www.wiley.com.

Library of Congress Cataloging-in-Publication Data

Names: Erickson, Darrin, author.
Title: Global investing : a practical guide to the world's best financial
  opportunities / Darrin Erickson.
Description: Hoboken, New Jersey : Wiley, [2023] | Includes bibliographical
  references and index.
Identifiers: LCCN 2022040333 (print) | LCCN 2022040334 (ebook) | ISBN
  9781119856665 (hardback) | ISBN 9781119856689 (adobe pdf) | ISBN
  9781119856672 (epub)
Subjects: LCSH: Investments, Foreign. | International finance. |
  International trade.
Classification: LCC HG4538 .E74 2023 (print) | LCC HG4538 (ebook) | DDC
  332.67/3—dc23/eng/20220909
LC record available at https://lccn.loc.gov/2022040333
LC ebook record available at https://lccn.loc.gov/2022040334

Cover Design: Wiley
Cover Image: © Yuichiro Chino/Getty Images
SKY10036841_101722

For Dawn
She walks in starlight

CONTENTS

vii

For those of us who have traveled extensively or lived abroad, we know how remarkable and expansive the world is in which we live. In the early days of 1977, not long before my eleventh birthday, my father took a job in Iran, where he helped design and construct a pulp and paper mill. As difficult as it was to leave my friends behind, I would not trade that experience for anything. My family lived there among the Iranian people, as well as other ex-pats from around the world, for a little over a year. Looking back, I realize now how this incredible adventure shaped the way I view the world as well as my views on investing. By the time I returned home at the age of 12 I had lived in a foreign country, circumvented the globe, and visited Great Britain, Thailand, the Philippines, Hong Kong, and Japan. By the spring of 1978 I was back home in British Columbia, but my curiosity about the world around me was ignited.

These early life experiences initially inspired me to pursue bachelor and master's degrees in international politics at the University of British Columbia. Diplomacy, arms control, and the reunification of Germany were central political events at the time, so in June 1990, I naturally jumped at the opportunity to join an academic tour of the European Community, NATO, and SHAPE headquarters along with stops in Berlin and Warsaw. The energy at the time was palpable as the Berlin Wall fell and visitors from East Germany flocked to the West. Merely one week before Checkpoint Charlie was dismantled, I was able to travel through the infamous crossing, chipping off pieces of the Berlin Wall along the way for my souvenir collection. As a visitor I could sense the excitement for the possibility of a new and brighter future. Tremendous changes were on the horizon.

Prompted by the immense economic and business implications of these events, I entered an MBA program, where I was introduced to the wonderful world of finance. My first job in the investment industry was as a currency trader, which, as you can imagine, is heavily influenced by global factors. It was at this time that my fascination with the global financial markets became an obsession. I came to view the financial markets as a mathematical version of the world around us and the engine that keeps our modern economy running. Powered by the interactions of nearly 7.8 billion people and a multitude of businesses, the infinitely complex workings of the world economy create tremendous wealth and a massive pool of investment opportunities.

Economic growth is a primary driver of new wealth creation. Over time, greater amounts of wealth should result in an increasingly developed equity market, since a portion of newly created wealth is invested in productive financial assets, such as stocks. It seems logical then that our views on where to invest our capital should consider expected long-term economic growth as a source of wealth creation and increasing stock market capitalizations. As the value of the equity market increases in size, it gains in importance to the local economy and greater efforts are made to help protect shareholder rights and maintain the integrity of the market. It should come as no surprise then that wealthier countries tend to have more developed financial markets and greater total stock market capitalizations.

By using wealth creation as our basis for investing, we are attempting to "follow the money." While the economies of developed countries are expected to grow their GDP by an average of 13% from 2022 through 2027, emerging and developing economies are expected to grow GDP by more than twice that amount at approximately 29%.[1] Viewing economic growth forecasts across the globe shows that the highest growth rates are expected in developing Asia, Europe, Africa, and Latin America. While developed market economies are not growing as quickly, they are home to a large number of leading global businesses, some of which derive a significant portion of their revenues from these same high-growth regions. Although the highest economic growth rates exist in emerging and developing economies, it is important to remember that the vast amount of wealth already accumulated in developed economies means that a significant percentage of new wealth will continue to come from these regions. Furthermore, even developed economies with slower long-term growth rates can experience short-term bursts of rapid economic growth.

Over any given time period the best-performing stocks will be spread across every region of the world. Although the relative performance of different regions fluctuates over time, the free flow of investor capital within and between geographic regions will ensure that money will move to wherever the best investment opportunities exist. Furthermore, with more than 55,000 companies listed on public stock exchanges worldwide, there are plenty of investment opportunities available to the global investor. In addition to this vast pool of investable businesses, there are new businesses coming to the market every day. There was a total of 1,388 companies newly listed on an exchange worldwide in 2020, with a total market value of $236.1 billion USD, and a majority of these businesses were located in emerging markets.[2]

Whether we acknowledge it or not, we live in a global economy, and we are subject to the forces that drive it. As an investor, do you need to own businesses from around the world to become wealthy? The answer is no. As you will see throughout this book, however, there are numerous benefits to investing globally. In response to the question, "Should you consider companies from around the globe in your investment process?," the answer is a resounding yes. Investing globally gives you access to a greater number of attractive businesses and the flexibility to take advantage of varying rates of growth around the world, and may also allow you to reduce the risk in your portfolio. The price you pay is hard work. Successful global investing requires you to be a voracious reader and to train yourself to see the big picture.

Building a great global equity portfolio requires you to think globally. To do this we have to shake off our natural tendencies and, in the words of Howard Marks, employ "second-level thinking" in our investment approach.[3] Frankly, this is much easier said than done. To accomplish such thinking, we have to overcome instincts developed over centuries that were needed to survive in hostile environments. The same instincts that helped us survive as a species often work against us as investors.

My goal as an author has been to produce a book that provides anyone who reads it with the ability to navigate the global equity markets successfully, regardless of where they reside. While many books have been written on investing, relatively few have taken a global perspective. I have tried to make this book truly global in nature by being politically neutral and avoiding any form of regional bias. I have also attempted to bring together two distinct disciplines in my writing, the study of international relations as well as the study of finance. The two are inextricably connected and I hope you find this somewhat unique perspective helpful. Additionally, my intention was to produce a book that all investors might find helpful in some way, especially those individuals who are new to investing. I have therefore tried to avoid industry jargon and overly complex financial concepts.

While there may be uncontrollable factors that prevent one from investing in a foreign country, perhaps the biggest obstacle to global investing is a lack of familiarity. Global investing may be unfamiliar territory, but it does not have to be scary. The same sound investment methods applied to investing in your home country can be applied to other regions as well, albeit with some additional work required on the part of the investor. If I am able to accomplish one thing with this book, it would be to help investors overcome their natural tendency to stick with what is familiar, and instead think globally when making investment decisions to take advantage of the best opportunities, wherever they may be.

There are numerous books from renowned investors that are worth their weight in gold, including writings from Warren Buffett, Ray Dalio, David Dodd, Charles Ellis, Benjamin Graham, Jeremy Grantham, Joel Greenblatt, Howard Marks, Charlie Munger, Jeremy Siegel, among others. Inspecting these volumes at the start of your investing career will greatly increase your odds for success. While I have not achieved the same financial success as these investing icons, I have persevered in an incredibly challenging career and have garnered a few gems of wisdom that I can pass along to the next generation of investors. My top recommendation to anyone who wants to invest on their own or better understand how their money is being invested is to read the works written by the authors noted above and heed their sage advice. Doing so will not prevent you from making mistakes, but it should protect you from disastrous investment decisions. My hope is that this book will build on what these authors have already shared with us by providing a complementary global perspective. I hope you enjoy the journey.

ACKNOWLEDGMENTS

I would first like to extend my sincere thanks to Adam Duncan for his incredible support, as well as the tremendous effort he devoted to reviewing this manuscript. Producing the plethora of graphs, charts, and maps used throughout this book involved incredible effort and creativity, and for this I thank graphic designer Mackenzie Clarke, with an added thank-you to Nicole Gortemaker and Tyler Burtniak for graciously aiding in that regard.

To my esteemed friends, Joseph Shaw, who generously took time from his busy schedule to co-author Chapter 18, and Joseph Zuiker, who in true form made a significant contribution through his efforts proofreading the manuscript, it was an honor to collaborate with you both.

For providing invaluable insights, which were instrumental in developing the global industry primers found in Part V, my sincere thanks to Carol Yeh, Ryan Grube, Carl Hamann, and Scot Atkinson.

For sharing their vast array of knowledge on select chapters, I wish to wholeheartedly thank my friends and colleagues: Robert Venable, Anil Tahiliani, Matthew Flynn, Finlay McKay, Steve Firman, Bill Sackley, Garry Steski, Dick Marshall, Phillip Sharkey, Geeta Kapadia, Deborah Kidd, Tim Skelly, and Lindsey Bauer.

To my fellow authors and friends, Antonella Puca, Carl Bacon, and Shamez Kassam, thank you all for your encouragement and indispensable advice.

I am eternally grateful for the people who took a chance and mentored me in the field of investing, including John Smith, Edward "Ted" Ransby, and Beverley Squair, as well as my thesis advisors and mentors back in my days studying international politics, namely professors Brian Job and Donald Munton. To the Value Partners Investments leadership team, Gregg Filmon,

Steve Norton, Paul Lawton, Dean Bjarnarson and Jim Lawton, thank you for your continuing support.

Thank you, Sheck Cho, Susan Cerra, and Samantha Wu, along with the production team at Wiley, for your guidance and support during the production of this book.

This book is dedicated to my beautiful wife, Dawn, whose unparalleled kindness and compassion acts as a source of inspiration and wisdom to me every day. Finally, I would like to thank my dad, Jerry Erickson, and my mom, Patricia Erickson (Robinson), for their love and support. Without the three of them this book would not have been written.

ACKNOWLEDGMENTS

Darrin Erickson, MA, MBA, CFA, is an accomplished equity portfolio manager with nearly three decades of investment industry experience. Over his career, Darrin has served as the lead portfolio manager for numerous equity mandates, including Global, North American, US large cap, US mid-cap, and Science & Technology, as well as long/short portfolios. Darrin holds a bachelor's degree in international relations and a master's degree in political science from the University of British Columbia, as well as an MBA from the University of Alberta. He holds the CFA charter and has served as a volunteer for CFA Institute in various capacities for more than 20 years. Darrin has made several television appearances, where he has shared his insights into the global financial markets.

Joseph Shaw, CFA, MSc RE, MBA, is a real estate investment expert with over 25 years of industry experience primarily focused on real estate transactions in the United States and Canada. Joseph also teaches at the Rotman School of Business and at Western University's Urban Development Program and has served as adjunct professor at both Johns Hopkins University and Ryerson University. He has lectured on real estate at Harvard University, for the Urban Land Institute, and for the Real Estate Property Association of Canada, consults as an expert witness, and is an active volunteer with CFA Institute.

Joseph Zuiker, CPA, CA, CFA, has extensive international experience in investments and fund services, banking, financial accounting, regulatory reporting, business leadership, and risk analysis. Joe joined the Bermuda Monetary Authority in 2019 as a senior member of the Regulatory Supervision team, which is responsible for the supervision, regulation, and inspection of Bermuda's banks, trust companies, investment businesses, investment funds, fund administrators, money service businesses, and corporate services providers, as well as the credit union and Bermuda Stock Exchange. Joe has served as a volunteer with CFA Institute.

Adam Duncan is a research analyst with over six years of investment industry experience ranging from retail to institutional portfolio management. Adam has exposure to a multitude of asset classes, including equities, fixed income, real estate, infrastructure, and money market. He holds a Bachelor of Commerce (Honors) degree with a major in finance from the University of Manitoba and is a CFA Level III candidate.

The purpose of this book is to help investors better understand the global financial landscape and how to best take advantage of the multitude of investment opportunities it provides. Although I have tried to make this book truly global and avoid any form of regional bias, I have referenced most data in US dollars throughout the book as a base currency due to its continued prominence in world finance.

Part One discusses why the most effective way to build wealth is through business ownership. In Chapter 1 we explore why actively selecting good, publicly traded businesses from around the world is the optimal way to obtain business ownership. We also touch on some of the greatest impediments to investment success and why thinking like a business owner can help you weather the toughest stock market environments. We conclude by sharing the characteristics that define a good business.

Part Two focuses on the global investment opportunity, including what is driving those opportunities and the implications for investors. Chapter 2 provides a history of the global economy and how we came to live in the digital age. We look at areas of the world where economic wealth is most likely to be created in the future and some of the spin-off effects of that wealth. Chapter 3 discusses world trade patterns, how trade is conducted, and what risks exist within the global supply chain network. Chapter 4 provides an overview of the world's financial markets and why they are critical to the global economy and everyday life for each of us. A special emphasis is placed on the world's stock exchanges and equity markets.

Part Three examines the key risks involved with investing globally, including market cycle risk, currency risk, and geopolitical risk, as well as how to manage those risks. Chapter 5 discusses how market cycles are driven by the economic cycle, the risks that market cycles pose for investors, and how to best manage these risks. We also examine bear markets and suggest some measures that may provide a warning sign to investors that a bull market is nearing its end. Of particular importance is how to prepare for the inevitable periods when share prices fall significantly. The reader will learn that for an investor who is prepared, these "bear markets" are beneficial because they provide an opportunity to build even more ownership in good businesses. Chapter 6 discusses the benefits and risks associated with investing in stocks denominated in a foreign currency. Chapter 7 reviews different forms of geopolitical risk, how those risks can impact your investments, and how to best mitigate those risks.

Part Four discusses how to analyze companies and identify good businesses. Chapter 8 provides a detailed process for analyzing potential investment opportunities by assessing their earnings sustainability, growth prospects, valuation, investment risk, and balance sheet strength. We also review how a detailed analysis of a company's profitability can aid investors in making better investment decisions, how to assess acquisitions made by the companies you own, and the importance of returning capital to shareholders.

Part Five provides the reader with a primer on each of the world's major sectors and industries. Chapters 9 through 19 provide an overview of 11 global sectors and 91 major global industries. Each chapter is focused on a single global market sector and its constituent industries, specifically communication services, consumer discretionary, consumer staples, energy, financials, healthcare, industrials, materials, technology, real estate, and utilities. Companies are grouped into sectors and industries based on common drivers of profitability and sales growth. We explore key trends affecting each sector and industry, provide examples of global companies operating in each industry, and describe how to evaluate and compare these businesses.

The last section of the book, Part Six, brings all of the previous material together and reveals how to construct a portfolio of great businesses from around the world. It also provides some helpful tools and resources that every investor should keep on their radar screen. Chapter 20 reveals how to construct a portfolio of great businesses that will help you build wealth over time as well as protect that wealth during times of market weakness. The Conclusion provides a recap of the most important lessons I have learned in the course of my investing career with the hope that they will help you prosper in yours. Finally, at the end of the book you will find some indispensable tools and resources to help guide you on your global investing journey.

BUILDING WEALTH THROUGH BUSINESS OWNERSHIP

Own Good Businesses

■ Business Ownership

The best way to build wealth is through business ownership. Think of some wealthy individuals. Most of them probably became wealthy by owning and operating a business. Even some of the most famous actors, singers, and athletes end up generating more wealth after their careers end by using their fame as a platform to start a business. Don't be concerned if you can't think of a lucrative business of your own to start. Become an owner of an already successful business that someone else founded! Owning shares in a company could potentially be as good as if you started the business yourself, but with significantly less effort. For anyone who has money to invest, share ownership (also referred to as stock or equity ownership) provides them with an opportunity to be a business owner. You may be surprised at how little money it takes to get started. This makes stock ownership the great equalizer when it comes to wealth creation. Accordingly, this book is focused on equity (stock) investing. If you start investing at an early age, owning good businesses for an extended period of time could be all you need to build significant wealth. Having a long time horizon makes wealth accumulation easier, but even if you only have a shorter time period the power of investing can still have a positive impact on your financial health. Financial securities that do not provide business ownership, such as bonds, are not addressed in this book, but it is important to note that these securities may have a place in your portfolio as well, depending on your personal situation.

■ Active versus Passive Investing

Even though they are popular among investors, we do not discuss index funds or exchange-traded funds (ETFs) in great detail. The reason for this is that index funds and ETFs are (primarily) passive investments that track the performance of a stock market index or sector with no consideration given to the quality of the underlying businesses. There are a number of actively managed ETFs available where the manager tries to own only good businesses, but I would urge investors to distinguish between active and passive investing and to fully understand the investment strategy being employed before investing.

While an index fund is a form of mutual fund, an ETF is essentially a cross between a mutual fund and a stock. Like a mutual fund, ETFs usually represent ownership in a group of companies from a specific region, country, sector, industry, or broad stock market index (such as the S&P 500, Nikkei 225 or MSCI World Index). However, while mutual funds tend to have higher fees and are bought and sold directly through a broker or the fund's manager, ETFs usually have low fees and are bought and sold on an exchange in the same way a stock is traded, making it easier and faster to buy and sell them. Today, there is an ETF for almost every type of investment imaginable, including bond indices, market sectors, commodities, and investment styles (like value or growth), as well as more obscure financial concepts, such as volatility.

The reason I exclude passive investments from this book is that they represent most or even all the companies in a specific group, which means you are buying the worst as well as the best businesses when you buy a passive ETF or index fund. Why would you want to invest any of your hard-earned money into substandard businesses if you do not have to? Active investment managers, on the other hand, try to separate stock market constituents into two baskets, the best opportunities and then everything else. In some cases, passive investments may be an investor's only option since investing in individual securities or an actively managed fund may not be possible or may be prohibitively expensive.

Furthermore, many indices, like the S&P 500, Euro Stoxx 600, or Nikkei 225, are market-capitalization-weighted, which means that a stock's weight in the index is determined by its size. The larger the company, the bigger it is as a portion of the index. ETFs that track these indices are therefore subject to concentration risk. As investors pile into an ETF, they force additional buying of the constituent companies, with most of the money (on average) going to the stocks with the highest market values. A rapid increase in the price of a stock can cause the stock's weight in the ETF to become excessive. This is okay as long as the stock's price keeps rising, but when it falls, look out below.

A prime example of concentration risk in an ETF involves GameStop Corp. During the global pandemic, GameStop reached a low of $2.57 on April 3, 2020, in part driven down by short sellers. A short seller is an investor who borrows shares in a company and sells them, with the intention of buying them back in the future at a lower price and returning the borrowed shares. The short seller thinks that the price of the stock is too high and that it will fall in the near future. However, GameStop became popular as a "meme" stock, and private investors aggressively bought the company's shares, driving up the price and forcing the short sellers to cover their short positions (buy back the shares they had borrowed) at higher and higher prices. Meme stocks are stocks that become popular on social media where investors share stories about stocks that are sometimes, but not always, based on fact. The combination of investors buying the shares to own them and short sellers buying to cover their positions can lead to a sudden surge in prices and trading volume, which is known as a "short squeeze." In the case of GameStop, the short squeeze caused the share price to jump as high as $347.51 when the markets closed on January 27, 2021. GameStop represented just over 1% of a popular retail sector ETF on April 3, 2020, but this rapid jump in share price increased the company's weight in the ETF to nearly 20% on January 27, 2021. A careless investor buying this ETF on January 27 would not realize that close to 20% of their money was being used to buy shares of GameStop at an incredibly expensive valuation.[1] This example also serves to highlight the growing importance of social media in investing and the risk of being short a stock that has the potential of experiencing a short squeeze. I discuss short selling more in Chapter 20, along with other advanced investment strategies, but would warn readers that short selling introduces new risks into your portfolio and should only be attempted after careful consideration by experienced investors.

Active investment management conducted in the manner described in this book can outperform passive investment strategies in the long run. Accordingly, this book is intended for investors who agree that the best way to build wealth is through ownership of good businesses, whether they invest for themselves, or they employ an active investment manager.

■ The Pitfalls of Investing

At its core, equity investing is simple: own good businesses in growing industries and buy them at attractive prices. This investment process, also referred to as "value investing," reflects the investment philosophies shared by many of the world's most renowned investors, such as Benjamin Graham, Warren Buffett, Howard Marks, Seth Klarman, Joel Greenblatt, and Jeremy Grantham. If we own businesses that are difficult to replicate, difficult to compete with, and that provide services and products that are difficult to live without, we can generate significant wealth over time and protect our portfolio from losses during periods of market weakness. Value investing does not restrict one to owning businesses that are not growing. Value investing refers to ensuring that you are not overpaying for the business and that you are getting good value for what you pay. Shares of companies that cannot grow are often inexpensive and will likely stay that way, earning them the nickname "value traps."

Investing in good businesses involves a straightforward process, but it is not easy. The reality is that investing successfully is a complex and time-consuming task. To understand the myriad factors that can affect the performance of an investment, investors must be voracious readers and pay close attention to market and industry developments. Not only are investors required to assimilate vast amounts of data but they must also quickly understand the context and implications of new information. This is what Howard Marks refers to as "second-level thinking" in his book *The Most Important Thing*. For the global investor who must monitor the entire world, the job of gathering and analyzing market data is significantly more challenging. Despite the work required, investors who are keen to take advantage of all the world's financial markets have to offer will find it to be a worthwhile endeavor. Whether we recognize it as individuals or not, we live in a global financial system. Businesses that we would consider domestic or local can be affected by developments that take place on the other side of the world. In this sense, any investor will benefit by staying informed of events that occur in other regions of the world. By thinking and acting globally, any investor will be better equipped to understand and mitigate risks in their portfolio, whether they invest globally or not.

Staying objective and having the ability to effectively filter out inconsequential information or "noise" when monitoring the global markets is an essential but difficult task for investors. All human beings are subject to certain instincts (commonly referred to as behavioral biases) that make the seemingly simple task of investing very challenging. As humans evolved as a species, we developed fixed patterns of behavior designed to ensure our survival. While these instincts help us survive, they can make us fail miserably at investing. A splendid example is our preference to be part of a larger group and follow the crowd; after all, there is safety in numbers. Wandering off on your own to hunt for food was risky for the earliest humans, a fact that led us to be hard-wired to associate with other people. It is psychologically challenging to invest in a way that you know is contrary to the crowd and goes against what you are reading and hearing from other investors. It is for this reason that truly contrarian investors are so scarce, and often so successful.

Confirmation bias is another instinct we need to overcome. It causes us to downplay facts that conflict with our existing beliefs about a company and instead focus on things that support what we already believe to be true. Part of the reason we do this is that we tend to believe that other people think the way we do. It is important to avoid making this assumption because people often do not think alike, and eventually business fundamentals will prevail. A company in a fast-growing industry may perform well for a while even if its technology or product offering is inferior to that of its competitors. However, a company's competitive positioning will eventually determine how its share price performs. Numerous examples of this occurred in the tech bubble. Many technology companies (including anything with a ".com" attached to its name) saw their share prices increase significantly in the late 1990s even though their longer-term business prospects were mediocre at best. Once investors came to their senses in the early 2000s and business fundamentals once again mattered, many of these companies failed.

Without exception, the noise investors are subjected to at market peaks is universally positive, which makes it difficult for them to sell stocks and lock in profits, exactly at the time it is most important to do so. Conversely, the commentary at market bottoms is universally negative, which makes it hard to buy stocks at precisely the moment you should buy aggressively. Of course, there are many other forms of behavioral biases. These include a reluctance to take a loss on an investment and the related desire to break even on a trade, which often causes investors to hold on to losing trades far longer than they should, eventually leading them to sell at an even greater loss. As people, we also typically prefer to invest in companies we are already familiar with, which results in a home bias. This means we tend to invest predominately in companies that we know and use on a regular basis and do not look further afield, even though better investment opportunities may be out there. This is not to suggest that you should invest in a business you do not fully understand, simply that you look beyond your immediate region when deciding which businesses to invest in. If this book can accomplish one thing, my hope is that it helps investors overcome their home bias and look objectively for the best investment opportunities from around the world.

In my experience, the most common mistakes made by investors (professional or otherwise) include an underappreciation of business risks, overpaying for a business, focusing on short-term share price movements instead of long-term earnings fundamentals, and not considering the full set of global investment opportunities available to them. Last, a lack of preparation and forethought that considers how businesses perform in various stages of the economic cycle, and how their share prices behave in various stages of the market cycle, can lead investors to react emotionally and make poor investment decisions.

The first step to beating the odds and overcoming these pitfalls is to train yourself to think like a business owner. Thinking of your investments as businesses, rather than numbers on a page, changes the way you respond to unwelcome events and will naturally allow you to take a longer-term view, improving your chances for success in the process. If you spent your lifetime building a great business, would you sell it in the midst of a recession at a "fire-sale price" if you were confident the business would fully recover and continue to grow? Definitely not. It is true that you would not have spent a lifetime building the business if you acquired ownership by buying its common shares, but the financial consequences would be similar. The simple fact that share prices can deviate significantly from the true value of the business is why public equity markets are indispensable for building wealth. When share prices fall to fire-sale prices, buy ownership in good businesses.

■ Characteristics of a Good Business

If someone asked you to define a "good business," what would you say? It seems like a straightforward question, but the more specific our answer needs to be the more challenging it becomes, and not everyone would answer this question in the same way. Furthermore, the most important business fundamentals vary significantly between different industries, so the characteristics of a good business will change depending on the industry in which it operates. This chapter is meant to provide the reader with a general overview of what attributes are present in all good businesses. Since there are many other success factors that vary by industry, we will elaborate on specific industries in greater detail in Chapters 9 through 19. This chapter provides an overview of what typically makes a company a sound investment regardless of the industry it operates in. What do I mean by a "good business"? Good businesses have the following common attributes:

1. Operate in a growing industry with relatively predictable pricing
2. Dominant and defensible industry position
3. Strong balance sheet
4. Astute management team
5. Positive image in society

Operating in a growing industry with relatively predictable pricing helps the management team plan effectively and provides a greater opportunity to grow the business. This does not mean that earnings cannot be cyclical (meaning they are dependent on where we are in the economic cycle), but we must have a sound understanding of how earnings are generated and have the ability to predict with some certainty what the company's earnings will be based on expected economic conditions. This trait is usually associated with stable political, regulatory, and competitive environments.

A dominant and defensible position within an industry is usually evidenced by a stable or growing market share and industry-leading profitability that is driven by a sustainable competitive advantage. This competitive advantage could come from a superior product or service, more efficient distribution channels, scale of operations, manufacturing knowledge, lower material costs, brand recognition, or a number of other factors. The best businesses have a distinct advantage that competitors cannot easily overcome.

A strong balance sheet provides financial flexibility, allowing for dividend increases and share buybacks, and also makes it easier for the company to borrow money, refinance, and pay back debt. It also provides protection in economic downturns and allows management to pursue growth opportunities more easily, including expanding into new geographic markets, acquiring other firms, or investing in research and development. Such investments can enable dominant companies to stay in a leading position far into the future.

The best management teams are made up of visionaries who understand their industry and function as good stewards of investor capital, including operating with good governance by employing sound policies and procedures designed to enhance decision making and risk management. They are also astute allocators of capital (they deploy the company's resources in an optimal way) who are able to navigate through tough times and seize opportunities as they arise to enhance shareholder value. Their interests are aligned with those of investors and society.

Having a positive image in society is another important attribute of good businesses. A company's image is no longer just about brand recognition. Corporate policies on social and environmental issues can influence how the company is perceived by consumers, other businesses, and government regulators. For example, having a reputation for being a bad polluter in one market could cause a company to lose customers in other markets. A company's governance structure (how it is governed and managed) can also have an influence on a consumer's decision to buy its products or whether other businesses will choose to engage with the company in business activities. Having business dealings with a company that has a bad reputation can cost a company customers and lost revenue.

Not all these attributes have to be present in equal measure for a company to be a worthwhile investment, but weakness in one or more of them should give you reason to pause and take a closer look. Breaking these five attributes down a bit further, we will take a closer look at the importance of company profitability, earnings sustainability, balance sheet strength, growth prospects, investment risk, valuation, and social factors in Chapter 8 when we discuss company analysis.

■ Own the Best and Leave the Rest

Given the vast number of publicly traded companies and the large amount of information you need to look at when analyzing them, it is essential that you optimize your time. Create your own process for analyzing a business, prioritizing items that are critical to you as an investor and that can be verified quickly. If these items appear satisfactory, then you can devote more time and delve deeper into the business. If the company does not meet an important criterion (e.g., it does not generate revenue), remove it from consideration and move on to the next opportunity.

There are so many good businesses available around the world that you should only own the best businesses available to you. Buy those businesses that you think have sustainable earnings growth and are priced attractively. If a company you own becomes expensive compared to its historical valuation ranges, versus its peers' or the market, reassess why you own it and consider switching into another business. Factoring in where we are in the market cycle can also help you make better decisions on when to exit an investment and move into the next wonderful opportunity. We will discuss the importance of market cycles in detail in Chapter 4. Now we turn to explore the global investment opportunity.

Chapter 1 Highlights

The best way to build wealth is through business ownership and for many people the best way to achieve business ownership is to buy shares in good businesses from around the world. Active investing involves owning only the best businesses available and should allow investors to outperform passive investments over a long period of time. Equity investing is straightforward but not easy, requiring diligence and hard work. The most important element of investment success is owning good businesses. Good businesses operate in growing industries with relatively predictable pricing, hold a dominant and defensible position within that industry, have a strong balance sheet, an astute management team, and a positive image in society. The most common mistakes made by investors include underappreciating business risks, overpaying for a business, focusing on short-term share price movements instead of long-term earnings fundamentals, not considering the full set of global investment opportunities available, and not considering how businesses perform in various stages of the economic cycle, or how their share prices behave in different stages of the market cycle. These mistakes can lead investors to react emotionally and make poor investment decisions.

PART II

THE GLOBAL INVESTMENT OPPORTUNITY

15

The Global Economy

■ Global Economic Evolution

If we go back only 20 years or so to the turn of the century, the total value of goods and services produced around the world (gross domestic product, GDP) stood at the equivalent of US$33 trillion. The world economy has tripled since then and is expected to exceed US$100 trillion in 2022.[1] That is an enormous increase, and it is even more impressive when you consider the fact that we suffered three global recessions during that time: the tech bubble, a global financial crisis, and a global pandemic. Admittedly, a majority of the growth in GDP has resulted from the seemingly endless liquidity provided by central banks around the world that has served to drive interest rates lower and help sustain economic growth. In fact, of the $67 trillion increase in world GDP since 1999, an estimated $44 trillion resulted simply from rising prices (inflation), whereas the remaining $23 trillion could be considered "real" economic growth coming from actual increases in production.[2] The infinitely complex workings of a world economy driven by the interactions of nearly 7.8 billion people creates a massive pool of investment opportunities, not to mention an equal number of potential hazards for an investor's portfolio. This chapter gives the reader an overview of the global economy, where it is going, and what the implications are for investors. As we look to the future and try to gauge where the global economy is headed, it is best to begin by looking at how we got to where we are today.

The history of the global economy has been marked by periods of extraordinary transformation and expansion. From time to time, the economies of different countries and regions around the world have benefited from human innovations that served to increase productivity and generate significant economic growth. The wealth and improvement in our quality of life that can be created in these periods is remarkable. While some of these transformations have been localized, others have encompassed much of the globe.

An early example of an economic transformation is the Agricultural Revolution, which began in Great Britain in the eighteenth century. The Agricultural Revolution resulted in increased crop yields through the introduction of better crop rotation methods, the use of nitrogen as fertilizer, and advancements in soil drainage. Greater food production meant that more people could be fed, leading to a dramatic increase in the population.[3] Another achievement during this time included improvements to infrastructure, such as roads, bridges, and inland waterways, which allowed for the more efficient transport of goods.

The Industrial Revolution, which occurred in the late 1700s to mid-1800s, involved the transition from making goods by hand to mass production using newly invented machinery and manufacturing processes. The Industrial Revolution was characterized by a wide range of smaller advancements that, taken collectively, resulted in what many consider to be the most significant economic transformation in history. Among these, the large-scale manufacturing of chemicals and textiles is notable, as was the switch from wood to coal as a source of heat, which allowed for rapid growth in iron production. Transportation networks also improved tremendously during the Industrial Revolution, with the introduction of the railway as well as further improvements to roads and inland waterways. The impact of this remarkable economic transformation was widespread and played a significant role in creating the world economy as we know it today. Over time, these advances led to improvements in our health, education, and overall quality of life, which helped accelerate gains in human productivity. In the words of Ray Dalio, "[h]uman productivity is the most important force in causing the world's total wealth, power and living standards to rise over time."[4]

■ The Digital Economy

Today, we are in what has become known as the technological or Digital Revolution. This transformation began with the invention of computing and the rise of the digital economy. Digitization continues at a rapid pace and is responsible for improvements in healthcare, education, finance, travel, the way we shop, and how we learn about the world around us. Blockchain is one example of a new digital technology that has the potential to transform many different industries. Blockchain is a special type of database that chains together blocks of data to form a sequential record of historical transactions. The data is stored in a way that makes it difficult or impossible to alter, which helps prevent fraud, and it is distributed across many computers, making it difficult for a single person or even group of people to control. While the primary focus of blockchain to date has been to create digital cryptocurrencies, such as Bitcoin, there are many potential applications for the technology that have yet to be explored.

Similarly, some innovations can have dramatic effects on individual industries. In these situations, the impact could be felt globally or limited to a single country or region. For example, innovations or regulatory changes can significantly change the profitability of a specific industry or make a country's entire economy more competitive on the world stage. Conversely, these changes can also make an economy less competitive or less attractive for foreign investment. The global investor must stay alert for new developments that can change business dynamics and create new financial opportunities or risks. The most conscientious investors will take note of these early on, understand their implications, and invest accordingly.

Not all periods of economic transformation are the result of technological innovation. Political upheaval or changes to government policy can also have dramatic effects on the rate of a country's economic growth. A remarkable and more recent economic phenomenon that resulted partly from policy changes is the rise of China. Renowned political scientist Graham Allison explains that "[m]illennia of Chinese dominance ended abruptly in the first half of the nineteenth century when the Qing Dynasty came face-to-face with the power of an industrializing, imperial Western Europe. The following decades were marked by military defeat, foreign-influenced civil war, economic colonization and occupation by outside powers—first by the European imperialists and later by Japan."[5] At the end of this period China's economy was in tatters, with the vast majority of its population living on less than $2 per day.[6] In 2010, Robert Zoellick, then president of the World Bank, noted that "[b]etween 1981 and 2004, through a variety of measures, China succeeded in lifting more than half a billion people out of extreme poverty. This is certainly the greatest leap to overcome poverty in history."[7] Assuming China continues to improve the productivity of its workforce, the math is simple. According to Allison, "[i]f over the next decade or two [Chinese workers] become just half as productive as Americans, China's economy will be twice the size of the US economy. If they equal American productivity, China will have an economy four times that of the US."[8]

China's economic transition benefited greatly from existing technological know-how in other parts of the world. However, as China's economy has advanced, it has been able to increasingly contribute to the world economy with technological breakthroughs of its own. In fact, according to the World Intellectual Property Organization (WIPO), a specialized agency of the United Nations, China was the worldwide leader in patent applications in 2019 after receiving around 1.4 million applications. The United States was second with nearly 600,000 patent applications, while Japan was third with almost 308,000 applications. WIPO estimates that Asia received 65% of all patent applications filed in 2019 worldwide.[9] While the United States, Japan, and Europe will undoubtedly continue to be leaders in technological innovation, countries in other regions of the globe are also making significant advancements in terms of technology and productivity.

It is important to remember that economic revolutions or transformations are not merely a thing of the past. We can only guess when the next major technological advancement will occur, but it will probably be met with some initial skepticism and take time to develop. Astute investors recognize the importance of critical innovations at an early stage. Since economic transformations usually take place over extended periods of time, it is often only with hindsight that we can see how significant the events of the day truly were and the extent to which they proved to be a generational opportunity to create wealth for investors. Obviously, not every innovation that comes along is going to change the world. Distinguishing between game-changing innovations and fads is one of the many difficulties the global investor must contend with. A healthy dose of skepticism is required and is an attribute of the most successful investors.

■ Economic Growth Rates

Most investors regard the world economy as being divided between developed and developing (or emerging) economies. A developing economy is often viewed as one that is dominated by agricultural production but increasingly moving toward modern industrial production. However, the line between developed and developing economies has become blurred, as many countries still referred to as "developing" have made significant advancements and no longer have "backward," agrarian-based economies. The labels "emerging" and "developing" also imply a high degree of risk that may not accurately reflect the realities of investing in a particular country. Rather than concern myself with labels that may be misleading, I prefer to focus on the size and growth rate of a country's economy, the level of political stability, and the degree to which its capital markets have been developed.

According to the International Monetary Fund (IMF), 27 countries around the world generated GDP greater than US$500 billion in 2019. By the year 2026, it is expected that number will grow to 38. In addition, the combined GDP of the top 50 economies is expected to grow from US$87 trillion in 2019 to more than $122 trillion in 2026. This is a cumulative increase of $35 trillion or 40%. Approximately 3% of the annual increase is expected to come from inflation while the remaining 1.9% would represent a real increase in annual global production. In dollar terms, the largest incremental gains in GDP in the period 2019 to 2026 are expected to be led by China, with an increase of nearly US$9.8 trillion, followed by the United States, with an increase of around US$6.2 trillion. This is followed by Japan, Germany, India, and the United Kingdom, which are each expected to grow their economies by more than US$1 trillion by the year 2026.[10]

Economic growth is subject to unforeseen events that can have a dramatic effect on the world economy. As a result, it is extremely difficult, if not impossible, to forecast economic growth with any accuracy. The 2020 global pandemic is a prime example of an event that few forecasters predicted, at least in terms of its timing as well as the impact it would have on the world economy and global financial markets. Some might call it futile, but despite our limited ability to accurately predict future events and economic growth rates, economic forecasts remain useful when we try to determine where we are in the economic cycle and where to focus our efforts when we search for businesses in which to invest.

The creation of economic wealth is the engine that will drive future investment returns. To begin our analysis of global economic trends and wealth creation, we can assess with a high degree of certainty the current state of the world and regional economies. Figure 2.1 shows the 10 largest economies in the world as measured by GDP in US dollars. Not surprisingly, the United States and China stand out as the world's economic powerhouses, with Japan, Germany, and India running a distant third, fourth, and fifth, respectively.

While this serves as a starting point, looking at current levels of GDP is essentially looking in the rearview mirror and shows what has already happened. Instead of concerning ourselves with what occurred in the past, our

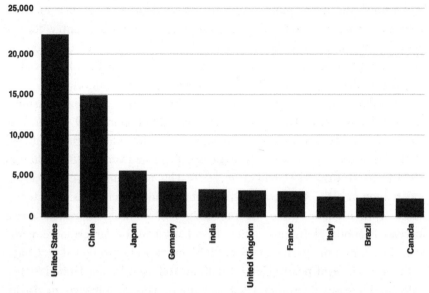

FIGURE 2.1 The World's Largest Economies (2019 GDP in Billions USD)
Source: International Monetary Fund, World Economic Outlook, April 2021, https://www.imf.org/en/Publications/WEO/weo-database/2021/April, accessed July 17, 2021.

goal is to capture future incremental economic growth and, in the words of Wayne Gretzky, to ". . . skate to where the puck is going to be, not where it has been." To do this we must also consider the rate at which different regions, countries, and industries are expected to grow in the future. Naturally, actual economic growth rates are likely to deviate meaningfully from expectations. There are many variables that affect economic growth, such as central bank monetary (interest rate) policy, demographic trends, advances in productivity, exchange rate fluctuations, and government fiscal (spending) policy. While basing one's investment decisions solely on these macroeconomic expectations is inadvisable, we can view economic growth rates as tendencies and therefore get an idea of where economic profits are most likely to be generated in the future. With this knowledge in hand, the global investor can increase their odds for success and find industries and geographic regions where economic profits, and therefore wealth, are most likely to increase.

Unfortunately, many of the fastest-growing economies are not easily accessed by foreign investors. Many of the fastest-growing economies have underdeveloped capital markets or restrictions on foreign investment and therefore investment opportunities may be limited or even nonexistent.

Still others may not be safe to invest in when you consider the protections afforded to investors. Simply put, some countries may not provide adequate protection of shareholder rights, potentially exposing investors to unnecessary risks, including corruption, poor accounting practices, political instability, or even the nationalization of businesses or entire industries. We discuss these risks in greater detail in Chapter 7, but in the interest of both protecting our capital from unnecessary risks and best allocating our most precious resource, time, we will focus exclusively on investing in markets that have developed capital markets and a regulatory environment that protects shareholder rights for all investors regardless of where they reside.

While economic growth is an important driver of wealth creation, it is only one of many factors we need to consider as investors. With high rates of economic growth could come elevated levels of inflation, which erode the value of money and may turn otherwise attractive investments sour. Other considerations include the level of political and economic stability in which these businesses operate. The price we pay for a business is also critical to determining whether an investment is profitable. You may invest in the highest-quality, fastest-growing business on the planet, but if you pay too much for it you can still lose money on your investment. Balancing what you pay with what you get is challenging and a shrewd investor will walk away from most potential investments. Owning businesses that operate in growing industries and economic regions is preferable to owning those that are in stagnant or declining industries or regions. Simply put, when investing I prefer to "swim downstream with the current" rather than upstream where there may be greater business risks lurking below the surface.

■ Wealth Creation

When making our decisions on where to invest capital, we should consider expected long-term economic growth. Over time, faster economic growth leads to greater wealth creation, which should result in a more developed equity market. As the value of the equity market increases in size, its importance to the local economy also increases and greater efforts are made to help protect shareholders and thereby enhance the integrity of the market. When we look at stock market capitalization as a percentage of GDP, wealthier countries tend to have more developed financial markets and greater total stock market capitalizations as a percentage of GDP. We discuss these issues in more detail in Chapter 4.

From a regional perspective, there is a large gap between expected economic growth rates. The International Monetary Fund (IMF) currently estimates that developed economies will grow their GDP by an average of 13% from 2022 through 2027, while emerging and developing economies are expected to grow GDP by more than twice that amount at 29%.[11] Viewing economic growth forecasts across the globe shows that the highest growth rates are expected in developing Asia and Europe, Africa, and Latin America, as shown in Figure 2.2.

To some degree, the higher economic growth rates in developing countries can be attributed to more favorable demographics. For example, a younger population combined with higher birth rates forms a strong backdrop for economic growth in Southeast Asia. To compensate for lower birth rates and an aging population, the world's developed countries must either expand immigration, incentivize their citizens to have more children, increase exports, or improve productivity. If they do not do any of these things, they will eventually struggle to grow their economies.

As a result of their higher growth rates, emerging and developing economies are slowly but surely becoming a bigger piece of the world GDP pie, and now represent a majority. Figure 2.3 shows how developing countries have grown from 40% of world GDP only 40 years ago to around 60% today, and this trend is expected to continue for the near future.

Combining the current size of the world's economies and adjusting them by their expected growth rates offers investors a glimpse of the future global economic landscape. In other words, if we take the world's economies as they are today and apply a reasonable growth rate to each region, we can get an idea of what the global economy might look like in the future. Of course, this process is highly subjective, and forecasts are prone to being wrong. It is difficult to accurately predict how fast an economy will grow next year, let alone over the next decade. Despite this fact, trying to figure out where and how wealth will be created in the future remains a valuable exercise when thinking about where to invest your capital. As noted earlier, the main reason we want to track economic growth is because it is a primary driver of wealth creation. Greater wealth in turn drives increased demand for goods and services and it forms a growing monetary base that can be invested in real assets (such as real estate), as well as financial assets (like stocks and bonds). By focusing on wealth creation, we are trying to follow the money. Therefore, we can begin by looking at investable assets by region and try to estimate to what level they are likely to grow in the future.

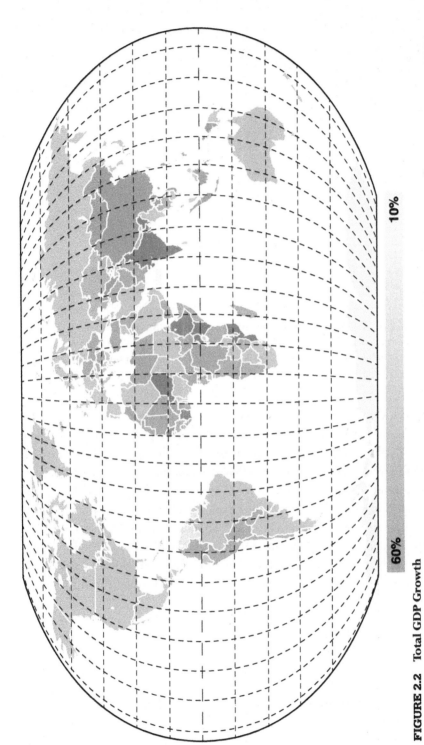

FIGURE 2.2 Total GDP Growth

Source: International Monetary Fund, IMF DataMapper, https://www.imf.org/external/datamapper/NGDP_RPCH@WEO/OEMDC/ADVEC/WEOWORLD, accessed July 23, 2021. Based on purchasing power parity (PPP) in constant 2017 US dollars.

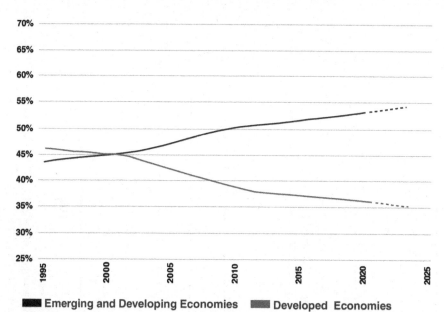

Emerging and Developing Economies **Developed Economies**

FIGURE 2.3 **Emerging and Developing Economies Share of World GDP**
Source: International Monetary Fund, World Economic Outlook, April 2021, https://www.
imf.org/en/Publications/WEO/weo-database/2021/April, accessed July 22, 2021. Based
on PPP in constant US dollars.

Boston Consulting Group (BCG) estimates that the worldwide total of
investable assets (such as stocks and bonds) grew 8.3% to a record-high
US$250 trillion in 2020, and that investable wealth will grow to US$315
trillion by 2025. They expect the US$65 trillion increase through 2025 to
come primarily from North America ($25 trillion), Asia ($22 trillion), and
Western Europe ($10 trillion). Real assets (such as precious metals, land,
and real estate), which tend to be more prominent in developing economies
where financial markets are not as well established or where the local currency may be more volatile, add another $235 trillion to global wealth. BCG
also notes that high-growth economies are expected to see a shift from real
assets to financial assets.

> *Over the next five years, however, a combination of greater
> financial inclusion and growing capital market sophistication
> will change the wealth composition in growth markets. In Asia,
> for example, financial asset growth is likely to exceed real
> asset growth (7.9% versus 6.7%). In particular, investment
> funds will become the fastest-growing financial asset class,*

with a projected CAGR [compounded annual growth rate] of 11.6% through 2025. This spike comes as more individuals embrace viable alternatives to investments in traditional real assets.[12]

Although the highest economic growth rates are expected to occur in developing economies, it is important to keep in mind that the vast amount of wealth already accumulated in developed economies means that a substantial percentage of new wealth creation will continue to come from more advanced economies. Furthermore, even economies with slower growth rates can experience short bursts of growth that can exceed the levels of growth experienced in high-growth economies. Demographic and other structural issues generally prevent these situations from being sustained in the long run, however, and will eventually cause a mature economy to revert lower to its long-term average growth rate.

■ Effects of Wealth Creation

As the world's economies grow, a part of the wealth that is created will be invested in the local equity market, helping to drive better long-term stock market returns. High-growth economies should have the joint benefit of higher levels of investable wealth as well as an increasingly well-developed stock market in which to invest. Wealth creation is self-perpetuating, as businesses and individuals look for ways to deploy the wealth they have accumulated. Over time, greater spending and new business formations will lead to greater numbers of listed equities and, ultimately, greater capital market sophistication and regulation. Figure 2.4 shows the current amount of financial assets by region.

As a country grows its economy it creates wealth, which in turn can be reinvested in local businesses or spent on goods and services. Subsequently, there are several beneficial side effects of economic growth that create opportunities for global investors.

One such side effect of economic growth is increased healthcare spending. As countries grow their economies, they tend to spend a greater percentage of their GDP on healthcare products, facilities, and services. As of 2019, the average high-income country spent 12.5% of GDP on healthcare, while the average for low-income countries was 4.9%. Figure 2.5 shows how much countries around the world spend on healthcare as a percentage

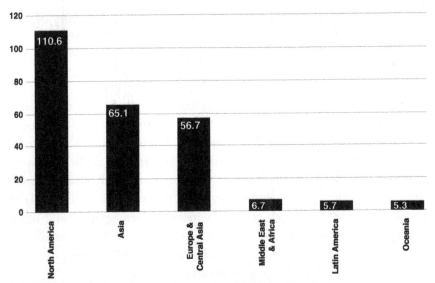

FIGURE 2.4 Financial Assets by Region (Trillions USD)

Source: Boston Consulting Group, "Global Wealth 2021: When Clients Take the Lead," https://web-assets.bcg.com/d4/47/64895c544486a7411b06ba4099f2/bcg-global-wealth-2021-jun-2021.pdf.

of their GDP. Near the higher end of the range is the United States, which spent around 16.8% of its GDP on healthcare in 2019. The worldwide average for healthcare spending is close to 9.8% of GDP, whereas the average for the least developed countries is only 3.9%.[13] As a country's economy grows, not only does the pie become larger, but the size of the healthcare piece becomes larger as a percentage of the total, providing a strong tailwind for the businesses that operate in the healthcare sector. While it currently ranks near the bottom of the list in terms of healthcare expenditures as a percent of its GDP, India is a great example of a country that is benefiting from high levels of foreign and domestic investment in its healthcare industry.

Another side effect of high rates of economic growth is an increase in the number of wealthy individuals. This has created strong demand for luxury goods. Louis Vuitton Moet Hennessy (LVMH) and other luxury goods retailers are seeing extraordinarily strong demand from Asia as newly minted millionaires look for ways to spend their money. Similarly, rapid wealth creation will create strong demand for wealth management services. BCG estimates that wealth management services in Southeast Asia will grow at a compound annual growth rate (CAGR) of 11.6% from now until 2025.[14] A company like Zurich-based UBS (the world's largest wealth management company) may be

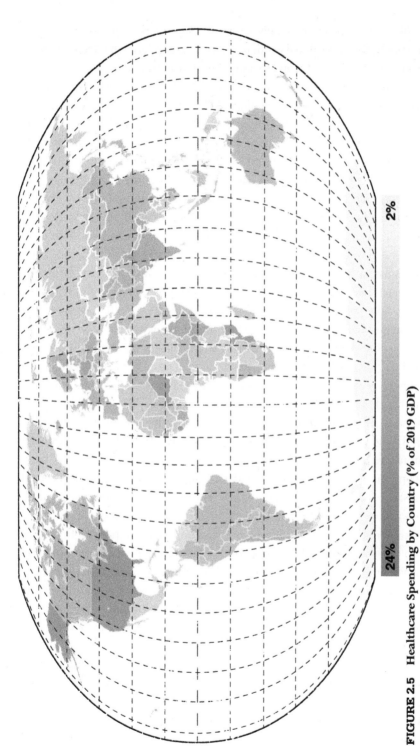

24%

2%

FIGURE 2.5 Healthcare Spending by Country (% of 2019 GDP)

Source: World Bank, World Bank Data Bank, https://databank.worldbank.org/reports.aspx?source=2&series=SH.XPD.CHEX.GD.ZS&country=, accessed May 1, 2022.

THE GLOBAL ECONOMY

particularly well-positioned, given its leading market position in Asia. Interestingly, the 2020 global pandemic served to accelerate the trends toward the accumulation of wealth and increased healthcare spending.

It is often suggested that investors can gain adequate exposure to high-growth economies simply by owning large, developed-economy businesses that sell into those markets. In reality, while there are exceptions, the average company located in an advanced economy generates only a small portion of its revenue from developing economies. A study completed in May 2021 by Morgan Stanley Research showed that North America–based companies generated an average 29% of their revenue from foreign sources, but after excluding the 15% of revenue coming from Japan and Europe only 14% was derived from emerging markets.[15] They also found that technology and materials businesses tended to have the highest exposure to emerging markets, at 56% and 48%, respectively. This suggests that North American investors may be able to get adequate exposure to rapid growth in those sectors globally by simply investing "domestically." However, to gain exposure to other segments of developing economies, investing in a foreign company will likely be necessary. The same study found that while European companies derived close to 30% from emerging markets, the companies that generate the most revenue from developing economies are the businesses headquartered in those markets, where the domestic economy generates an average of 72% of revenues. The implication of this is simple: to obtain the maximum benefit from localized areas of rapid economic growth, investors are often better off investing directly in businesses located in those regions.

Economic growth rates and trends are important considerations for all investors, especially those who see the entire world as their playground. Growth rates in emerging and developing economies are expected to be significantly higher than for developed economies and so maintaining exposure to those regions is likely to pay off for years to come. Keep in mind that these higher growth rates may come with greater risk, a fact that we address later in Part Three, where we discuss the risks of investing globally.

Naturally, great investment opportunities are not limited to high-growth economies. Certain industries within slower-growing, advanced economies can experience prolonged periods of above-average growth. As you can see from Figure 2.6, the semiconductor industry is a terrific example of an industry with an elevated level of sustained growth. Based on worldwide billings, the industry grew at a CAGR of 8.6% globally from 1986 to 2020,[16] while advanced economies as a whole grew at only a 4% rate over the same period.[17]

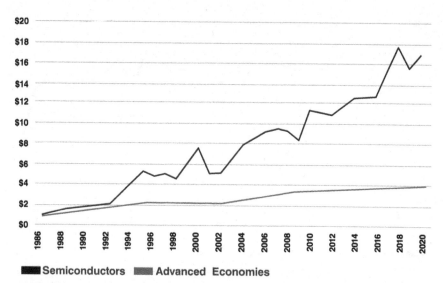

FIGURE 2.6 Semiconductor Industry Growth versus Advanced Economies
Source: International Monetary Fund, World Economic Outlook, April 2021, https://
www.imf.org/en/Publications/WEO/weo-database/2021/April, accessed September 9,
2021, and the Semiconductor Industry Association at (https://www.semiconductors.
org), accessed September 9, 2021.

Investors should watch the relative growth rates of industries and remain
alert for new developments that could cause the growth rate to change.
Whether this news will have a positive or negative impact on a company's
earnings is not always immediately obvious. Occasionally, stock prices will
react to news in the opposite manner from what you would expect. In some
cases, there may be mitigating or offsetting factors that affect how investors
view new information. Sometimes good news can be construed as bad and
at other times bad news can be seen as good. In these situations, good news
may be not good enough and prices fall, or bad news may be so bad that
investors believe things can only get better and prices rise. This reaction is
not easy to predict and can be difficult to decipher by the most experienced
investors, even with the benefit of hindsight.

■ Global Scope Provides Flexibility

Although the various segments of the world economy tend to move in a
synchronous fashion, they do diverge from time to time. Figure 2.7 shows
how the economic cycle in select regions can differ meaningfully from one
another, especially over shorter periods of time.

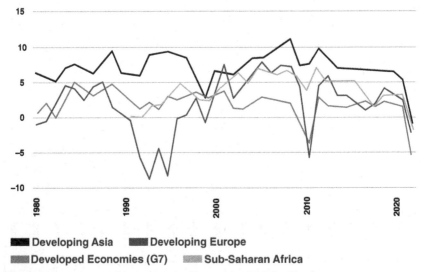

▬ Developing Asia	▬ Developing Europe		
▬ Developed Economies (G7)	▬ Sub-Saharan Africa		

FIGURE 2.7 Annual Percentage Change in GDP by Region

Source: International Monetary Fund, World Economic Outlook, April 2021, https://www. imf.org/en/Publications/WEO/weo-database/2021/April, accessed September 9, 2021.

As you can see, regional economies do not always move in tandem. During the reintegration of Eastern Europe in the early 1990s, for example, developing Europe showed weak or even contracting economic growth while developing Asia continued to grow. Then in the mid- to late 1990s developing Europe grew strongly while developing Asia was in decline. Whereas the global financial crisis of 2008 had a relatively muted effect on developing economies in Asia and Africa due to their limited exposure to subprime mortgage-backed securities, economies in other regions contracted significantly. Extenuating circumstances may cause one region to lag the world economy for a period only to catch up and accelerate above the worldwide average later. This provides global investors with a potential advantage over investors who limit themselves to their own region or local market. The fact that different regions of the world economy diverge from one another occasionally provides the global investor with greater flexibility, but it also poses a risk, a fact that we discuss in more detail in Chapter 5.

Keep in mind that economic growth does not always translate into corporate earnings growth. Jeremy Siegel noted that "[t]he reason that economic growth does not necessarily increase [corporate earnings] is because economic growth requires increased capital expenditures and this capital does not come freely."[18] That said, earnings growth is more difficult for companies to achieve without underlying economic growth. If your local economy is expected to grow at a below-average rate for an extended period, consider "going global" and diversify into higher-growth economies. At any given point in the economic cycle, differing rates of growth around the world mean that a greater number of investment options are available to those investors who are searching the entire globe for opportunities. No matter what part of the world you live in, taking a global view when assessing sources of growth and wealth creation provides more opportunities to you as an investor.

Chapter 2 Highlights

Our modern global economy is the culmination of centuries of periodic, revolutionary gains in productivity driven by human innovation. These improvements in productivity cause remarkable periods of economic expansion, generating immense wealth in the process. Real, long-term economic growth (which excludes the effects of inflation) is a primary focus for global investors, since this newly created wealth is diffused throughout the economy, improving overall quality of life for people, and generating countless investment opportunities for investors. Naturally, actual economic growth rates are likely to deviate meaningfully from expectations. There are many variables that affect economic growth, such as central bank monetary (interest rate) policy, demographic trends, advances in productivity, exchange rate fluctuations, and government fiscal (spending) policy. The economies of different countries and regions do not grow at the same pace or at the same time, providing investors who have the flexibility to invest outside of their home country with an advantage. Greater wealth drives increased demand for goods and services, and it forms a growing monetary base that can be invested in real assets (such as real estate) as well as financial assets (like stocks and bonds). By focusing on wealth creation, we are trying to follow the money. Taking a global perspective also provides investors with an edge, by gaining a better understanding of both the opportunities and the risks all businesses face.

Global Trade

■ Advancements in Global Shipping

As consumers in today's global economy, we cannot help but compete with others from around the world when we wish to travel or purchase a good. The ease with which goods (and people) can be transported overseas means that we are all competing to maintain our relative purchasing power at a global level. You may find it difficult to buy the house of your dreams if purchasers from other regions have benefited from higher levels of wealth creation and are able to bid up prices beyond your ability to pay. Whether you realize it or not, you live in a global economy. The same is true for operating a business. Unless government regulations prevent new entrants from entering your market, a bigger, stronger foreign business can come along and threaten your company's existence. The more profitable your business is and the easier it is to enter your market, the greater the threat from potential competitors, especially if the competitor benefits from a lower cost structure.

As the global economy has grown, the trade in goods and services between countries has expanded immensely. Siegel notes that "[f]rom the 1950s to the latest global economic crisis, the growth rate of international trade was almost consistently twice that of economic activity as a whole."[1] Most of the goods traded internationally are transported around the world via a combination of truck, rail, air freight, and marine shipping containers. On average, nearly one-quarter of all trade worldwide is between countries sharing a common border. This form of trade can primarily be conducted using road and rail transportation. For most global trade, however, transporting goods by ship or air is needed to get items where they need to go. The introduction of increasingly larger and faster cargo ships, as well as the expansion of air freight capacity, has caused the transportation of goods to become faster and less expensive. In the 1700s, it took an average of about seven weeks to cross the Atlantic Ocean by ship. Ship building knowledge experienced several marked improvements over the years and by the mid-1800s most merchant ships were larger and faster, being able to cross the Atlantic in as little as two weeks.[2]

Global trade began a massive transformation in the mid-1960s with the proliferation of the shipping container. The invention of the "roll-on, roll off" (roro) vessel in the 1930s had already created the ability to drive and stow vehicles and heavy equipment either safely inside or externally on the ship's deck. However, many products were still packaged and transported loosely, which often resulted in damaged and lost goods. The invention of the shipping container in 1956 changed all of that. The World Shipping Council explains that "[b]efore the container, products were shipped loose or packaged and bundled in ad-hoc ways. Crates, sacks and barrels had to be manually carried off the ship, and waste and damage was high."[3] Most shipping containers are of a standard size, measuring 20 feet × 8 feet × 8.5 feet, and are referred to as "twenty-foot equivalent units," or TEUs. The benefit of using a standardized container to ship goods is that they can be quickly unloaded from a ship onto a train or tractor-trailer and transported to almost any destination on the planet. The container also protects the goods while they are being shipped and can allow for perishable goods to remain refrigerated as they are transported over great distances.

Significant advancements in shipping have continued since then at a steady pace. In 1980 the largest container ship was the *Neptune Garnet*, which had a capacity of 4,100 TEU.[4] Today, the largest ships can carry more than 20,000 shipping containers and are appropriately referred to as Ultra Large Container Ships (ULCSs). Furthermore, despite their massive size these ships are fast, being able to cross the Atlantic Ocean in as little as 10 days. As of 2021, the largest container ship in the world, the HMM *Algeciras*, has close to six times the capacity of the *Neptune Garnet* at just under 24,000 TEU. To put this into perspective, compared to the merchant ships of the early 1800s, container ships today can cross the Atlantic Ocean with more than 500 times the amount of cargo and travel four to five times the distance each year. Undoubtedly, ships will continue to evolve, becoming either larger, faster, or more fuel-efficient, and hopefully thereby more environmentally friendly. This is becoming critical in light of growing concerns over climate change and the increasing importance of environmental factors, which we discuss in Chapter 8. Larger cargo capacity and shorter transport times have in turn driven down the cost of shipping goods around the globe significantly.

Quickly recognizing the benefits of container shipping, ports around the world were eager to adapt themselves to container shipping and today this is how most goods are transported globally, with an estimated 90% of everything we buy transported by ship.[5] Of course, ships cannot reach every corner of the globe and so combining ships with rail and road transport is necessary. This movement of goods via a combination of ship, rail and road is known as intermodal transport, with container ports serving as the critical junction points connecting land and sea. In 2019 the top ten container ports in the world, shown in Figure 3.1, handled nearly 250 million TEU arriving and departing by both land and sea.[6]

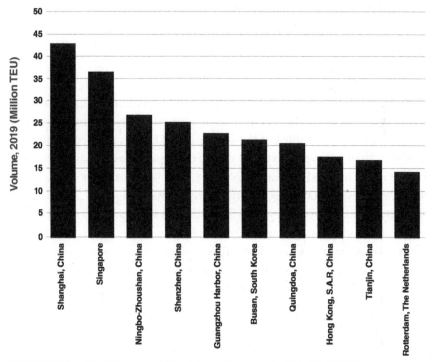

FIGURE 3.1 **The 10 Largest Container Ports in the World (2019)**
Source: World Shipping Council, "The Top 50 Container Ports," https://www.worldshipping.org/top-50-ports, accessed December 26, 2021.

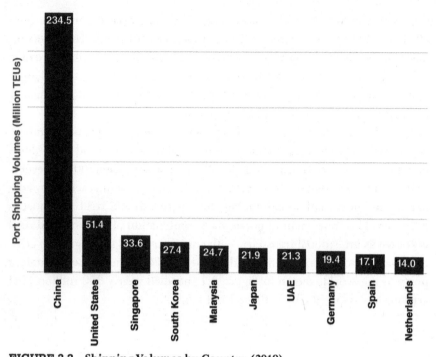

FIGURE 3.2 Shipping Volumes by Country (2019)

Source: The World Bank, https://data.worldbank.org/indicator/IS.SHP.GOOD.TU, accessed December 26, 2021.

With an average loaded weight of 10–12 tons per container,[7] these ports collectively managed the safe transit of approximately 2.5 billion tons of cargo and nearly one-third of the 795 million TEUs in total container port traffic in 2019.[8] Disruption in any one of these ports has the ability to affect the delivery of goods around the world. You will note that many of the world's busiest container ports are located in Asia. Figure 3.2 shows total shipping volumes by country, with five of the top 10 countries located in Asia.

What is readily apparent from Figure 3.2 is that Chinese ports have become a critical component of the global supply chain. Due to an imbalance in trade, where more goods are shipped from rather than to Asia, many containers leave Asian ports full but must be returned empty to meet future shipping needs.

■ Air Freight

If time is of the essence, air freight can bring the time needed to transport goods around the world down to mere hours. Higher transportation costs prevent air freight from being a larger portion of global trade, but it is still very significant, with approximately 57.5 million tons of cargo carried in 2020. Most air freight shipping occurs between North America and Asia (26.9% of the worldwide total), Asia and Europe (20.8%), and Europe and North America (12%). Air freight volume between the Middle East and Asia is also significant at 6.8% of the total.[9] The World Bank estimates that air freight is priced four to five times that of road transport and 12 to 16 times that of sea transport. These higher costs combined with the limited size of cargo planes has a direct impact on the types of goods that are shipped by air. "Commodities shipped by air thus have high values per unit or are very time-sensitive, such as documents, pharmaceuticals, fashion garments, production samples, electronics consumer goods, and perishable agricultural and seafood products. They also include inputs needed to meet just-in-time production and emergency shipments of spare parts."[10] Air freight is therefore critical in manufacturing processes since companies frequently exchange samples and technical drawings. Another limiting factor for air freight is the inability of planes to safely transport certain hazardous materials.

■ Trends in Global Trade

Faster speed of transport and reduction in per-unit shipping costs over the years has served to create deeper and more complex connections between businesses in different countries. In addition, increasing levels of global economic development have resulted in a greater number of manufacturers capable of producing high-quality, technologically advanced components. Where a company might have previously had no choice but to secure the supply of a critical part locally to guarantee availability, lower cost, and speed of delivery, it may now be more economical to source the component from an overseas supplier. Increasing wealth at the global level has also played a role, allowing consumers to reach further around the world to buy the goods they most desire. These trends can be seen in Figure 3.3, which shows the growth in worldwide exports from 1988 to 2019.

Despite downturns in 2009 and 2014–2016, global trade has continued to expand, with worldwide exports totaling US$20.5 trillion in 2019.[11] Although not reflected in Figure 3.3, the 2020 global pandemic caused global trade to weaken and resulted in calls for increasing domestic

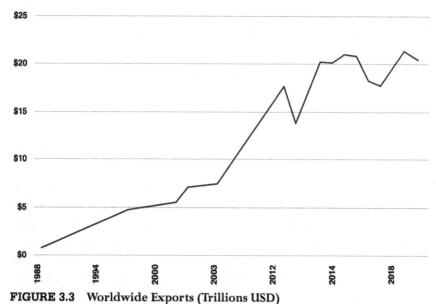

FIGURE 3.3   Worldwide Exports (Trillions USD)

Data source: World Integrated Trade Solution, https://wits.worldbank.org/CountryProfile/
en/Country/WLD/Year/2016/TradeFlow/Export/Partner/all/Product/Total.

production to ensure supply of critical components like semiconductors. Of course, any such changes to the supply chain would likely come at the expense of global trade. Even with this potential setback, however, it is very likely that international trade will continue to expand well into the future.

■ Global Trade Routes

Most goods are transported between countries along specific routes around the world. Whether by rail, road, air, or sea, these trade routes tend to be made narrow, either by man or nature, and are therefore subject to bottlenecks. As noted earlier, the majority of global trade is conducted by sea, with geographical constraints causing most ships to follow specific routes, which are subject to bottlenecks, or "chokepoints," as they are also known. These are typically the shortest or safest route between two points. These chokepoints are therefore of strategic importance to countries and represent significant risks to global trade as they are vulnerable (to varying degrees) to accidents and acts of aggression. Avoiding rough seas and pirates are among the obstacles shipping companies need

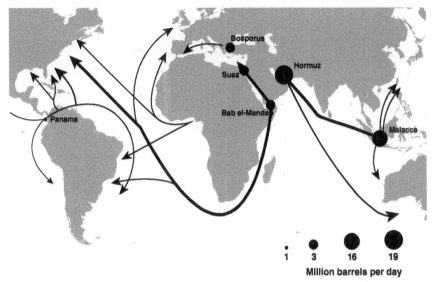

FIGURE 3.4 Major Petroleum Shipping Routes

Source: Energy Information Administration, as of 2017, adapted from https://www.eia.gov/todayinenergy/detail.php?id=330 and https://www.eia.gov/todayinenergy/detail.php?id=32292.

to overcome when transporting goods. These routes are heavily trafficked, which means they can become blocked, and the consequences can be costly. The key global shipping routes for oil and petroleum are shown in Figure 3.4.

> **The world's major shipping bottlenecks include the Danish Straits, the English Channel, the Strait of Malacca, the Panama Canal, the Suez Canal, the Strait of Hormuz, the Turkish Straits, and the St. Lawrence Seaway.**

The Danish Straits

The Danish Straits (Figure 3.5) consist of the waterways connecting the Baltic Sea to the North Sea and thereby the Atlantic Ocean. In addition to significant container shipping traffic, approximately 3.2 million barrels of oil was shipped per day via the Danish Straits in 2016.[12] Both the Danish and Turkish Straits are key access points for trade with Russia and are therefore critical to Europe's energy supply and its economies.

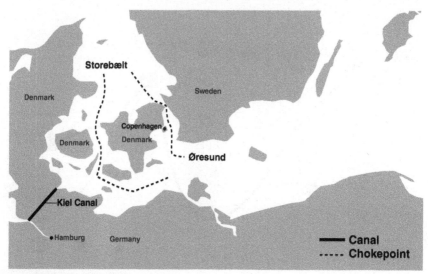

FIGURE 3.5 The Danish Straits

The English Channel

At 350 miles (563 km) long, the English Channel (Figure 3.6) separates Britain from France and connects the Atlantic Ocean with the North Sea. With 500–600 vessels passing through the English Channel each day, it is the busiest shipping route in the world and is critical to European trade. The English Channel connects major ports in Northern Europe (among the busiest in the world) to the rest of the globe.

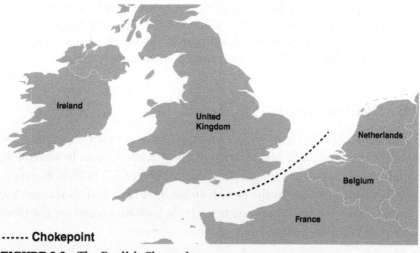

FIGURE 3.6 The English Channel

The Strait of Malacca

A 580 mile (933 km) long stretch of water between Malaysia and Indonesia, the Strait of Malacca (Figure 3.7) is the shortest sea route between China and India. At its narrowest point, the Strait of Malacca is only 1.7 miles wide and it connects the Pacific and Indian Oceans via the South China Sea. Energy products transiting the Strait of Malacca reached 16 million barrels per day in 2016, making it the second-largest oil trade chokepoint in the world after the Strait of Hormuz.[13] It facilitates trade within Asia as well as between Asia and Europe.

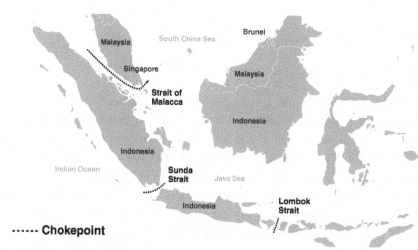

FIGURE 3.7   The Strait of Malacca

The Panama Canal

Completed in 1914, the Panama Canal (Figure 3.8) consists of three locks that allow ships to transit between a 65 km (40 mile) wide strip of land between the Caribbean Sea and the Pacific Ocean via Gatun Lake, which sits 85 feet above sea level. The journey takes between 8 and 10 hours and saves the vessel from having to circumvent the hazardous waters off Cape Horn at the southern tip of South America, a trip that could add two weeks and significant costs to the journey. The Panama Canal manages close to 12% of American seaborne trade.[14]

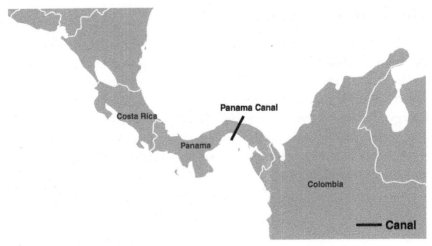

FIGURE 3.8   The Panama Canal

The Turkish Straits

The Turkish Straits (Figure 3.9) are made up of the Bosporus and Dardanelles Straits, which link the Black Sea with the Mediterranean Sea and then the world's oceans. "Only half a mile wide at the narrowest point, the Turkish Straits are among the world's most difficult waterways to navigate because of their sinuous geography. About 48,000 vessels transit the Turkish Straits each year, making this area one of the world's busiest maritime chokepoints."[15] Approximately 2.4 million barrels of crude oil and petroleum products were transported through the Turkish Straits per day in 2016.

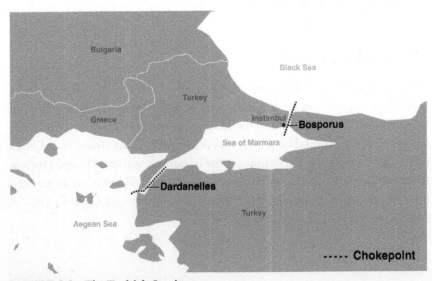

FIGURE 3.9   The Turkish Straits

The Suez Canal and the Strait of Hormuz

Completed in 1869, the Suez Canal offers the fastest sea route between the Indian Ocean and the Mediterranean Sea and, by extension, the Atlantic Ocean (see Figure 3.10). The Canal is narrow and cannot support two-way traffic, causing the 120-mile journey to take about 16 hours to complete. It is estimated that nearly 19,000 ships and over 1 billion tons of cargo passed through it in 2019, making it a critical chokepoint in the global supply chain network.[16] If ships could not use the Suez Canal, they would have to either wait for the passage to clear or circumvent the Cape of Good Hope at the southern tip of Africa, which would add significant delays and fuel costs to their voyage. This occurred in March 2021 when one of the largest container ships in the world, the 242,500-ton *Ever Given*, became stuck in the southern portion of the Suez Canal. The *Ever Given*, with a length of over 1,300 feet and capable of carrying more than 20,000 shipping containers, blocked hundreds of other vessels from passing through the Canal for a period of six days. With around 12% of global trade moving through the Suez Canal, it is estimated that this accident cost the global economy close to US$10 billion per day.

Located between Iran and Oman in the Persian Gulf, the Strait of Hormuz is strategically important because it is home to one-third of all seaborne-traded crude oil, making it the most important passageway for oil transportation worldwide.[17] With an average flow of 21 million barrels per day, the Strait of Hormuz handled close to 21% of global petroleum liquids in 2018. An estimated 76% of crude oil moving through the Strait of Hormuz was destined for Asian markets, principally China, India, Japan, South Korea, and Singapore.[18]

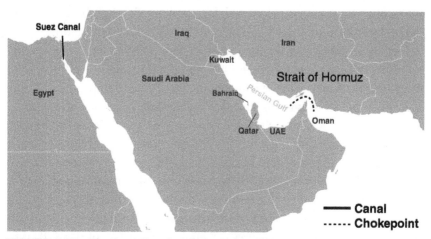

FIGURE 3.10 The Suez Canal and the Strait of Hormuz

The St. Lawrence Seaway

The St. Lawrence Seaway (Figure 3.11) runs 2,300 miles between Canada and the United States and is comprised of the St. Lawrence River, St. Lawrence Seaway, and the Great Lakes. The Seaway connects the industrial centers in the midwest United States and Canada to the Atlantic Ocean.

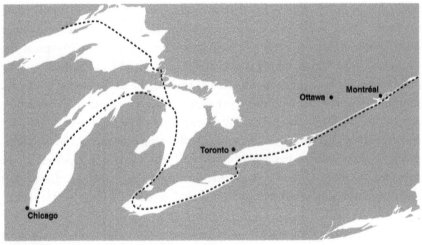

FIGURE 3.11   The St. Lawrence Seaway

The Baltic Exchange Dry Index

As with most products and services, shipping costs vary based on supply and demand. One indicator of the strength of global trade is the Baltic Exchange Dry Index (BDI). This index was created in January of 1985 for the purpose of tracking the average price paid for shipping dry bulk goods by sea. Figure 3.12 illustrates how shipping costs can fluctuate significantly.

Periods of strong global economic growth tend to result in higher shipping costs since demand for goods increases, but the supply of available ships also plays a critical role in determining the price paid to ship goods. As with many other business and economic factors, shipping costs have an automatic self-correcting mechanism. Increased demand for goods drives up shipping costs, which increases profitability for shipping companies. Shipping companies then invest in more ships to meet the higher level of demand, thereby increasing the supply of ships. At the same time, the manufacturers whose products are being shipped experience a drop in profitability due to the higher shipping costs they must pay. In response, manufacturers increase the price of their goods, which causes consumers to buy less of them, thereby reducing demand for goods. The reduction in demand for goods combined

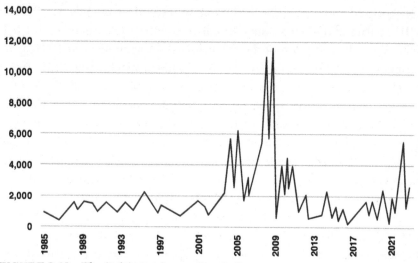

FIGURE 3.12 **The Baltic Exchange Dry Index**
Data source: Bloomberg, as of April 30, 2022.

with the increased supply of ships causes shipping prices to fall and the entire process starts over. This type of cycle is seen across many aspects of the global economy and is discussed in more detail in Chapter 5.

■ Trade Agreements

Another factor that has contributed greatly to the growth in global trade is the propagation of regional trade agreements and free trade zones. Free trade agreements have proliferated in recent years, growing from only 50 in 1990 to more than 280 in 2017.[19] While certain agreements are focused on specific areas of trade and commerce, others are broad-based. Designed to promote regional trade and economic cooperation, these agreements go beyond simply reducing tariffs, often addressing issues such as competition policy, intellectual property rights, and rules concerning government procurement. Mechanisms for dispute resolution are also key elements of most trade agreements. Broad-based trade agreements, which the World Bank refers to as deep agreements, increase goods trade by more than 35% and trade in services by more than 15% on average.[20] In some cases, these deep trade agreements cover a specific geographic region, creating what is referred to as a free trade zone. The most noteworthy free trade agreements are summarized below.

The United States–Mexico-Canada Agreement (USMCA) is a free trade agreement covering a population of nearly half a billion people. Formerly the North American Free Trade Agreement (NAFTA), the trade deal was renegotiated and signed in 2018, coming into effect on July 1, 2020. In 2019, trilateral trade between these three countries exceeded US$1.1 trillion. Since the inception of the original NAFTA agreement in 1994, merchandise trade between the three countries has grown by over 250%.[21]

The European Union is a political and economic union of 27 member states, which includes Austria, Belgium, Bulgaria, Croatia, Cyprus, Czechia, Denmark, Estonia, Finland, France, Germany, Greece, Hungary, Ireland, Italy, Latvia, Lithuania, Luxembourg, Malta, Netherlands, Poland, Portugal, Romania, Slovakia, Slovenia, Spain, and Sweden. The EU economy accounts for approximately 15% of the world's trade in goods, with total GDP of €16.4 trillion in 2019 (when the UK was still part of the EU).[22]

The Association of Southeast Asian Nations (ASEAN) Free Trade Area (AFTA), signed in 1992 in Singapore, now includes Brunei, Cambodia, Indonesia, Laos, Malaysia, Myanmar, Philippines, Singapore, Thailand, and Vietnam and is one of the largest free trade areas in the world. ASEAN later signed free trade agreements with Australia, New Zealand, China, India, and Korea, as well as the ASEAN-Japan Comprehensive Economic partnership. The ASEAN free trade area is home to more than 661 million people and generated GDP of nearly US$3 trillion in 2020.[23]

The Southern Common Market (Mercosur) agreement is designed to promote trade as well as economic and political cooperation in South America. Its members include Argentina, Brazil, Paraguay, Uruguay, and Venezuela. Bolivia is in the process of joining Mercosur. Mercosur member states are home to more than 295 million people and produced GDP of approximately US$4.6 trillion in 2019.[24]

The Common Market of Eastern and Southern Africa (COMESA) is designed to promote economic cooperation between its 21 member states, which have a joint population of over 583 million and produce total GDP of more than US$805 billion. Its member states include Burundi, Comoros, Democratic Republic of the Congo, Djibouti, Egypt, Eritrea, Eswatini, Ethiopia, Kenya, Libya, Madagascar, Malawi, Mauritius, Rwanda, Seychelles, Somalia, Sudan, Tunisia, Uganda, Zambia, and Zimbabwe.

The Regional Comprehensive Economic Partnership (RCEP) is a free trade agreement among 15 countries, including the 10 ASEAN member states of Brunei, Cambodia, Indonesia, Laos, Malaysia, Myanmar, the Philippines, Singapore, Thailand, and Vietnam, plus China, Japan, South Korea, Australia, and New Zealand. RECP member countries account for nearly one-third of the world's population and approximately 30% of world GDP.[25]

The Asia-Pacific Economic Cooperation is a cooperative, multilateral trade and economic forum comprised of 21 member countries, including Australia,

Brunei, Cambodia, Canada, Chile, China, Indonesia, Japan, South Korea, Malaysia, Mexico, New Zealand, Papua New Guinea, Peru, the Philippines, Russia, Singapore, Taiwan, Thailand, the United States, and Vietnam.

Negotiations for the Trans-Pacific Partnership (TPP) Agreement began in 2015 and continued to progress toward ratification until 2017 when the United States withdrew from the agreement. The TPP was subsequently replaced by the Comprehensive and Progressive Agreement for Trans-Pacific Partnership (CPTPP), whose signatories include Australia, Brunei, Canada, Chile, Japan, Malaysia, Mexico, New Zealand, Peru, Singapore, and Vietnam. To date only Japan and New Zealand have ratified the agreement.

■ Intergovernmental Organizations

In addition to the impact of individual governments and businesses on world trade, several intergovernmental organizations exist whose objective it is to facilitate global trade. Foremost among these is the World Trade Organization (WTO), whose fundamental goal is to improve the welfare of people around the world by fostering global trade. Agreements between the 164 members of the WTO outline the global rules of trade between those countries and are designed to ensure that trade flows as smoothly and freely as possible. WTO agreements cover a wide range of trade issues, including goods, services, and intellectual property rights, and provide countries with a mechanism for resolving trade disputes.[26]

The Organisation for Economic Co-operation and Development (OECD) fosters international cooperation to improve economic performance and create jobs, improve education standards, and fight international tax evasion. The OECD's 38 member countries represent about 80% of world trade and investment.[27]

The United Nations Conference on Trade and Development (UNCTAD) is part of the UN Secretariat and has the goal of ensuring that developing countries can effectively share in the benefits of the globalized economy. UNCTAD was established in 1964 and has 195 member states. It operates as a think tank where the goal is to tackle critical issues facing the global economy.

Another key organization that helps indirectly promote global trade is the Bank for International Settlements (BIS), whose purpose is to promote global monetary and financial stability and to function as a bank to the world's central banks. The BIS is owned by 63 central banks from around the world that together account for about 95% of world GDP. It was formed in 1930 and is headquartered in Basel, Switzerland, with offices in Hong Kong SAR and in Mexico City, and has Innovation Hubs around the world.[28]

The World Bank, while not explicitly designed to promote global trade, still has an indirect role to play as it strives to reduce poverty and promote sustainable development. Collectively, these agreements and institutions have shaped the modern global supply chain system.

■ Supply Chains

When investing in a company it is important to understand its business relationships and how the company may be dependent on other firms for components or services. The sources used by a company to obtain the goods it requires to operate its business are referred to as its supply chain. Information about a company's supply chain is often available in the company's regulatory filings under the section that details business risks; however, if this information is not disclosed, investors can usually contact the company's investor relations department directly to obtain this information.

From a business perspective, the global economy has become much more intertwined than it was only a couple of decades ago. Many businesses around the world depend on foreign sources for components used in their products. In some cases, goods are transported back and forth between different regions several times before becoming a final product that is sold to the end customer. The 2020 global pandemic served to highlight the interconnectedness of the world economy, not to mention the fact that supply chain shortages have the potential to cause inflationary pressures, as manufacturers from around the world ran short of everything from semiconductor chips used in automobile production to aluminum used to make beverage cans.

The best businesses are good at managing their supply chain, but for a major global company the supply chain can become extraordinarily complex. Apple Inc., for example, has more than 600 suppliers globally.[29] Complicating matters further, most businesses try to diversify between suppliers to avoid the risks associated with obtaining necessary components from a single source. If an important supplier were to suffer an environmental disaster, like an earthquake, it could fail to meet customer requirements. Similarly, manufacturing or quality control issues could mean the supplier delivers a part or service that is not useable or creates a defective product. A delay in delivering a $50,000 automobile to a customer caused by the shortage of a $5 semiconductor chip is a fitting example of how vulnerable a manufacturer can be to disruptions in the supply of key components.

The timing of component or service delivery is also important to consider. While inventory requirements vary by industry, the best businesses are generally able to minimize the amount of product they keep on hand. This is especially true in industries where assets depreciate quickly, such as technology. If a component is kept too long in storage, its value can go down and it can even become obsolete. In the meantime, the company is tying up cash unnecessarily by holding excess inventory. Striking the right balance is critical, as low inventory levels make the business more dependent on the prompt arrival of components to keep the manufacturing process going. Similarly, holding excessive amounts of inventory is not productive and inefficiently ties up working capital. While each industry is unique with some requiring few or no external suppliers, maintaining low levels of both components and finished inventory using secure and stable sources of supply is the structure most businesses strive to achieve.

The extreme interconnectedness of the global economy and business supply chains has made globalization inexorable and creates both opportunities and risks for the global investor. Although there is a long way to go until all of humanity shares in the prosperity that has resulted from globalization, the needle is at least moving in the right direction. If nothing else, globalization creates a dynamic whereby countries are more likely to seek amicable solutions to their differences.

Chapter 3 Highlights

Global trade has grown at approximately twice the rate of the world economy, supported by faster and less expensive shipping, and the propagation of regional trade agreements. This has led to increasingly deeper and more complex connections between businesses in different countries. Where a company might have previously had no choice but to secure the supply of a critical part locally to guarantee availability, lower cost, and speed of delivery, it may now be more economical to source the component from an overseas supplier. Most goods are transported between countries along specific routes around the world. Whether by rail, road, or sea, these trade routes tend to be made narrow, either by man or nature, and are therefore subject to "chokepoints." These chokepoints represent significant risks to global trade as they are vulnerable to accidents and acts of aggression. This makes understanding a company's supply chain critical for investors who are keen to fully ascertain risks associated with investing in the business.

The Global Financial Markets

■ Global Financial Markets

Developments in the global economy, including trade, manifest themselves in the global financial markets. The financial markets are essentially a mathematical version of the world around us, and they are the engine that keeps our modern economy going. The world's equity and debt markets provide capital to the businesses that power the global economy that in turn creates jobs and generates wealth. Efficient stock and debt markets are therefore a vital part of a country's continuing economic development. These markets should be structured and governed in a way that allows capital to flow easily to its most productive use. Regulations must exist and be enforced that protect shareholder rights and ensure that the use of investor capital is adequately rewarded. Also, if foreign capital is needed to allow domestic businesses to flourish, the rights of foreign shareholders must be protected on par with domestic investors. Trust in a country's financial system, the rule of law, and the manner in which business is carried out, is essential for sustainable economic growth in the long run.

Economic growth and development is an aspiration: it is a mechanism to alleviate poverty, to give opportunity to those who do not yet have it, to foster equality, and to create a bet-

ter society. Well-functioning exchanges enable economic growth and development by facilitating the mobilisation of financial resources—by bringing together those who need capital to innovate and grow, with those who have resources to invest. They do this within an environment that is regulated, secure, transparent and equitable. Exchanges also seek to promote good corporate governance amongst their listed issuers, encouraging transparency, accountability and respect for the rights of shareholders and key stakeholders.

Nandini Sukumar, CEO, the World Federation of Exchanges

All businesses require the reinvestment of capital to survive. The way companies fund their operations often involves using profits generated by the business itself. However, some businesses do not generate sufficient profits to meet their reinvestment needs, whether on a short- or long-term basis. This may be a new business that is growing quickly and needs money in order to fund its growth, or a more mature business that is experiencing a temporary downturn in revenue and needs access to capital to fund operations until the business environment improves. A business requiring an infusion of cash may turn to a bank or private investors or partner with other companies. When these avenues are not an option, however, companies turn to the capital markets for funding. In these instances, the business might borrow the money by issuing debt (bonds) or they might sell ownership in the business by issuing equity (shares). Each of these has different implications, for both the business and the investor.

Debt and equity each represent a claim against the assets and/or cash flow of a business. Debt represents a promise of interest and repayment of one's principal but offers no ownership stake in the business. Conversely, equity represents an ownership stake in the business with no promise of repayment. Shareholders therefore risk the loss of their capital in the event the company falls on hard times, but they also participate more fully in the profits generated by the company. Debt investors are afforded greater protection of their capital and face a lower risk of loss, but they do not participate in the wealth generated by the company to the same extent as shareholders. Both debt and equity provide capital to businesses around the world and are referred to here collectively as the capital markets. Figure 4.1 compares the relative size of the world's equity and bond markets.

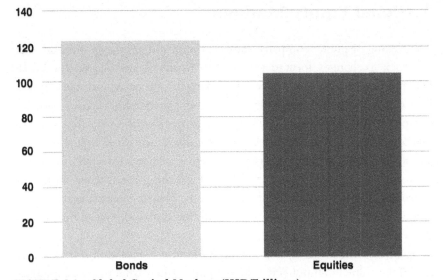

FIGURE 4.1 Global Capital Markets (USD Trillions)

Data source: The Securities Industry and Financial Markets Association (SIFMA), "Capital Markets Fact Book, 2021," https://www.sifma.org/resources/research/fact-book/, accessed November 14, 2021.

At the end of 2020, the global bond market consisted of approximately US$123.5 trillion in outstanding debt. Slightly smaller, but still massive, the world's stock markets ended 2020 with a total market capitalization of US$105.8 trillion.[1]

Much larger than either the debt or equity market are the currency and derivative markets. The Bank for International Settlements estimates the average trading volume to be the equivalent of US$6.6 trillion per day in the foreign exchange (currency) market, which is discussed in detail in Chapter 6. The derivative market is more challenging to quantify, partly because it depends on what is considered to be a derivative. In general terms, a derivative is a financial security whose value or price movement is "derived from" (based on) another asset, such as a currency, bond, stock, index, or commodity. Another challenge to estimating the size of the derivative market is that many derivative products are traded privately, making them exceedingly difficult to track. It is for this reason, as well as their complexity, that Warren Buffett famously referred to derivatives as "financial weapons of mass destruction." As noted earlier, the best way to build wealth is through business ownership, and the most effective way to build business ownership is through the world's public equity markets.

■ Global Equity Markets

The trading of public company shares is transacted primarily on more than 80 stock exchanges located around the world. According to the World Federation of Exchanges, "[a] stock exchange is an organised marketplace, licensed by a relevant regulatory body, where ownership stakes (shares) in companies are listed and traded. Listing happens in the so-called 'primary market,' where a portion of a company's shares are made available to the public. The company often uses the listing to raise funds through issuing new equity shares. Investors can then buy and sell these listed shares in the so-called 'secondary market.' While listing in the primary market may result in a flow of funds from investors to the firm, the trading between investors in the secondary market does not."[2]

The Securities Industry and Financial Markets Association (SIFMA) estimated the value of all publicly traded equities (their total market capitalization) to be $120.4 trillion (USD) at the end of June 2021. Roughly 43% of that total was based in the Americas, 33% in Asia Pacific, and 24% in the EMEA region (Europe, the Middle East, and Africa). From 2000 to the second quarter of 2021, the highest increase in total market capitalization came from the Asia Pacific region, which grew at a rate of 9.9% annually. In fact, since 2000 emerging economies have grown their share of total global market capitalization from 7.7% to 27%. This rapid growth in market capitalization for the Asia Pacific region was driven in part by an increase in the number of listed companies. Of the roughly 55,000 companies that are listed globally, the Asia Pacific region is home to 57.3% of them, EMEA 23.2%, and the Americas 19.5%.[3] With a greater total market capitalization and fewer listed companies, businesses based in the Americas tend to be larger than those in other regions. However, there are large, globally focused businesses to be found in every region of the world and excluding them from investment consideration simply because you are not familiar with them can be a costly mistake. Figure 4.2 shows how the 100 top-performing stocks over the past one, two, three, four, and five years are dispersed by region even after adjusting for currency movements.

Whatever time period you consider, there are stocks in every region of the world that turn out to be among the best performers in any given year. While the relative performance of different regions fluctuates over time, the free flow of investor capital within and between geographic regions will ensure that money will move to wherever the best investment opportunities exist. The growing number of companies listed on stock exchanges, combined with higher average share prices, have caused the dollar volume of

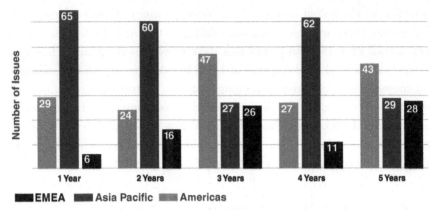

FIGURE 4.2   100 Top-Performing Stocks by Region

Data source: Bloomberg, as of December 17, 2021. Data set includes the largest 3,000 companies globally that have return data available for the stated period. Returns are based in USD.

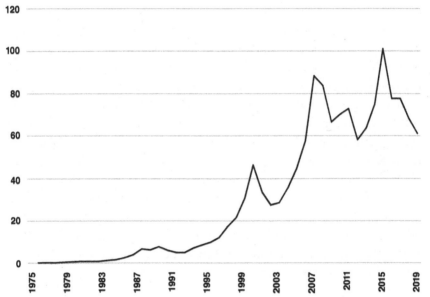

FIGURE 4.3   Annual Worldwide Equity Trading Volume (Trillions USD)

Data source: World Bank, https://data.worldbank.org/indicator/CM.MKT.TRAD.CD, accessed November 14, 2021.

shares traded to increase steadily over the years as shown in Figure 4.3, and this trend is likely to continue.

Figure 4.3 shows how significantly the global equity market has grown over the past few decades. With more than 55,000 companies listed on public stock exchanges worldwide, there are plenty of investment opportunities available to the global investor. In addition to this vast pool of investable businesses, there are new businesses coming to the market every day. There was a total of 1,388 companies that were newly listed on an exchange in 2020, with a total market value of US$236.1 billion. A majority of these businesses were located in emerging markets.[4] A tremendous amount of wealth can be created for owners when a company initially lists on an exchange and becomes publicly traded. When a company first decides to make the move from being privately owned to publicly owned, it goes through a process known as an initial public offering (IPO).

■ Initial Public Offerings

One obvious benefit to taking a company public is that it provides a way for the owners of the business to benefit financially from all the hard work required to build the company. It also enhances the company's profile, provides the company with access to a larger pool of capital, and disperses the ownership of the company among a larger group of investors. The downsides to going public are higher costs as well as greater regulation and scrutiny of the company's operations. Private companies can control who is able to invest in the firm, whereas public companies generally cannot.

Since so much wealth can be realized in the IPO process, it can be difficult for the average investor to take part in an IPO. Demand for shares is often multiple times the number of shares being sold by the company. This means that most of the shares sold in an IPO go to larger investors that are perceived as being more important to the firm that is underwriting (managing) the IPO. Company IPOs that are particularly attractive tend to be in greater demand and therefore are even outside the ability of most institutional investors to participate in to a meaningful extent. All is not lost, however, as there are many companies that continue to grow and create economic wealth long after they go public.

■ Financial Market Interaction

It is important for investors to understand how different segments of the financial markets interact and can affect one another. Developments in the global bond market, for example, can have a significant impact on equity markets. This means that equity investors must watch the bond market closely. The relative movement of stocks and bonds at any given point in time depends on market conditions and where we are in the market cycle (discussed in Chapter 5). However, in very general terms, when economic conditions deteriorate, bonds tend to outperform equities, and when economic conditions are improving, equities tend to outperform bonds. Watching activity in the bond market can therefore provide valuable insights for you as an equity investor.

Two important things to watch in the bond market are changes in interest rates and changes in credit spreads. Bond prices are heavily influenced by changes in interest rates, which are primarily determined by expectations for economic growth and inflation. Decisions affecting the level of interest rates are made by a country's central bank, and are referred to as "monetary policy." If the bank is reducing interest rates, the monetary policy is called "accommodative" or "dovish," and if the bank is raising rates, the monetary policy is referred to as "contractionary" or "hawkish." As noted earlier, when a central bank wants to generate higher levels of economic growth it lowers interest rates, and when it wants to slow economic growth it raises interest rates. The most influential central banks include the Federal Reserve in the United States, the Bank of England, the Bank of Japan, the European Central Bank, and the People's Bank of China. In extreme circumstances like the global financial crisis of 2008, the world's central banks will act in a coordinated fashion to resolve problems faced by the global economy and global financial system.

You may wonder why a central bank would ever want to intentionally reduce economic growth, but the reason is quite simple. Sustaining elevated levels of economic growth may eventually lead to inflation, which can be very damaging to an economy since it erodes the value of most assets and can adversely affect spending decisions for both consumers and businesses. To prevent high levels of inflation, central banks may deliberately try to slow the rate of growth and create a "soft landing" for the economy, which is characterized by a gradual reduction in economic growth. This can be a challenging task for the central bank. If the central bank raises interest rates too slowly, inflation may increase suddenly and become difficult to control. On the other hand, if the bank raises interest rates too quickly, it could create a rapid drop in economic growth and perhaps even cause a recession (defined as two or more consecutive quarters of negative economic growth).

It is important to note that it is changes in inflation and interest rate expectations that drive the financial markets. That is to say, market participants respond to changes in interest rate and inflation expectations, rather than to what the current economic data is showing. Although falling(rising) interest rates are generally good(bad) for equities, economic circumstances may cause investors to react in a seemingly irrational manner. For example, while falling interest rates are generally good for stocks, if a central bank were to unexpectedly announce a decrease in interest rates in an already strong economy, this could be regarded as inflationary and stock prices could actually fall instead of rise. Conversely, a gradual increase in interest rates can be construed as positive for the equity market in cases where economic growth is strong and the risk of inflation is slowly rising.

■ Credit Spreads

Credit spreads are also important to watch. A credit spread is the difference between the interest rate paid on a corporate bond and the interest rate paid on a "risk-free" government bond with the same term to maturity. For example, a five-year bond issued by a company would typically be compared to a five-year bond issued by the country where the company is located. The difference in the interest rate being paid on the two bonds is called the "spread." Corporate bonds typically pay a higher rate of interest than government bonds in order to compensate investors for a higher level of risk. In this instance we are referring to default risk, which is the possibility the investor will not receive all of the expected coupon (interest) payments or repayment of principal (the par value of the bond). Government bonds are regarded as risk-free because the chance of default is (usually) exceptionally low, although there have been instances of governments defaulting on their debt. Bonds issued by companies that are perceived to be more likely to default must of course pay investors a higher rate of interest and therefore have higher spreads compared to their lower-risk peers. These bonds are often referred to as high-yield or junk bonds.

Credit spreads are excellent indicators of investor psychology. When investors are confident that they will get their money back, credit spreads fall since investors are willing to take on more risk and lend money at lower rates. However, as the economy weakens and the risk of lending grows, investors will demand higher returns and the spread will increase. Figure 4.4 shows how credit spreads behave in periods of economic stress, measured as the mid-point of US corporate Baa-rated bonds.

Figure 4.4 illustrates that credit spreads are not constant, but rather change significantly over time. As investors become fearful, credit spreads increase, and as investors become more optimistic, credit spreads fall.

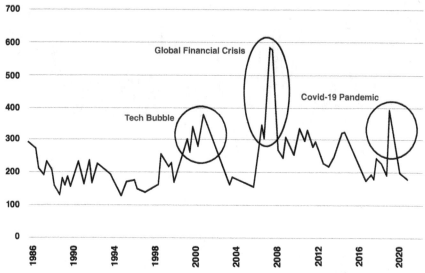

FIGURE 4.4   US Corporate Baa-rated Bond Spread (basis points)
Data source: Bloomberg, as of December 12, 2021.

Periods of fear and risk aversion are very apparent here, evidenced by the spike in credit spreads in the tech bubble, financial crisis, and the early days of the 2020 global pandemic.

Higher spreads result in higher financing costs for businesses, which causes companies to reduce spending and for go projects that otherwise might have been profitable with lower financing costs. The impact of changes in interest rates on business activity is therefore ultimately reflected in the equity market. Higher rates eventually reduce business investment and corporate profitability, while lower rates encourage investment, which spurs economic growth and generates additional corporate profits. Naturally, higher expected profits will drive share prices up, while lower expected profits will drive share prices down. The inverse relationship of credit spreads and equity prices is shown in Figure 4.5, which overlays the year-over-year change in the S&P 500 Index price level with the figure on credit spreads presented in Figure 4.4.

As Figure 4.5 shows, credit spreads tend to move in the opposite direction from stock prices, and in fact changes in credit spreads can be a leading indicator for the equity market. The bear markets that began in 2000 and 2007 were both preceded by rising credit spreads. In the case of the 2020 bear market, credit spreads rose only as the market sold off, so they did not function as an early warning sign for equity investors. However, the fact

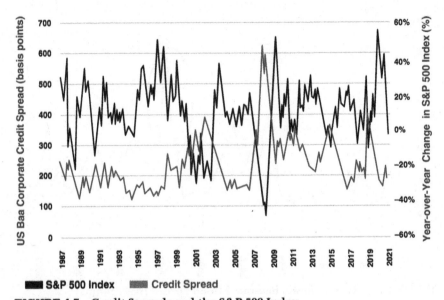

FIGURE 4.5 Credit Spreads and the S&P 500 Index

Data source: Standard & Poor's Financial Services LLC, sourced via Bloomberg, as of May 5, 2022.

that spreads began to narrow again in late March 2020 supplied some indication that the worst was behind us and that the stock market had already bottomed.

■ Currency Markets

Currency markets also affect equity markets and are therefore important for investors to watch. There have been instances where a rapidly declining currency has spelled serious trouble for local, regional, and even global equity markets. In extreme circumstances, currency crashes can cause equity market corrections. An example is the Asian Financial Crisis that began in 1997, when Thailand decided to no longer peg the Thai baht to the US dollar. The uncertainty and loss of confidence that ensued brought about the devaluation of several regional currencies as well as a subsequent drop in the regions' stock markets. Actions taken by the International Monetary Fund and the World Bank ultimately helped to restore confidence in the region, but not before fear gripped global equity markets and stocks fell around the world, including significant declines in Europe and the United States.

As discussed in Chapter 6, it is best to avoid investing in countries that have excessive levels of external and domestic debt compared to their ability to service that debt. Inflation reduces the value of debt, and so countries with elevated levels of debt have often used inflation to help reduce their debt burden.[5] In general, high relative levels of inflation will cause a country's currency to depreciate, so any investment made in that country will most likely fall in value over time based on currency movements alone. However, studies have consistently shown that investing in a basket of different currencies helps to reduce portfolio risk over a long time period. This is clear in Figure 4.6, which shows the degree to which the top 10 currencies in the world fluctuated over a 27-year period compared to an equally weighted basket of all 10 currencies.

Taken individually, the top 10 traded currencies in the world have experienced greater variability in their returns compared to an equally weighted basket of all 10 of the currencies. The reason is fairly simple: the relative price changes of the currencies are not correlated. This means that currencies move in opposite directions at times and therefore owning securities

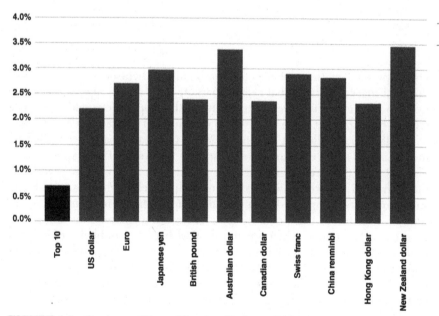

FIGURE 4.6   Currency Diversification Reduces Risk
Data source: Bloomberg, as of January 11, 2022. Top 10 currencies referenced are: the US dollar, euro, Japanese yen, British pound, Australian dollar, Canadian dollar, Swiss franc, China renminbi, Hong Kong dollar, New Zealand dollar.

denominated in a mix of foreign currencies will help investors overall and is one of the principal benefits of investing globally. From a US investor perspective, Roger Ibbotson and Gary Brinson found that "unhedged foreign currency exposure provides a buffer against the effects of unexpected changes in U.S. inflation relative to that of other countries."[6] This suggests that investors can protect their portfolios from domestic inflation by maintaining exposure to foreign currencies. Investors can gain exposure to foreign currencies by owning shares of companies domiciled in those countries, either by buying the common shares or a depositary receipt, discussed in greater detail in Chapter 20. The risks associated with investing in foreign currencies and how to manage those risks are discussed in more detail in Chapter 6.

There are tremendous opportunities made possible by the evolutionary nature and machinations of the modern economy, as well as by the always-evolving and interconnected global capital markets. However, with greater rewards comes greater risk. In Part Three we take a close look at the primary risks faced by global investors, namely market cycle, currency, and geopolitical.

Chapter 4 Highlights

Developments in the global economy manifest themselves in the global financial markets. The global capital markets provide the capital businesses need to reinvest in themselves to maintain their operations and grow. The global equity market is massive, with a total market capitalization estimated to be US$105.8 trillion at the end of 2020. Company shares are traded on more than 80 stock exchanges found around the world. There are stocks in every region that are among the best performers in any given year. With more than 55,000 companies listed on public stock exchanges worldwide and many more being listed each year, there are plenty of investment opportunities available to the global investor. Although a tremendous amount of wealth can be created when a company first becomes publicly traded in a process known as an initial public offering (IPO), there remains ample opportunity for investors to participate in wealth created by the business long afterward. Both the bond market and currency market play an important role in business activity and therefore can affect equity markets and provide clues as to stock market performance. Investing in a basket of different currencies helps to reduce portfolio risk over a long period.

PART III

RISKS
OF INVESTING
GLOBALLY

CHAPTER 5

Market Cycle Risk

I n an ideal world, investors and policymakers would have perfect foresight, enabling them to accurately predict future events. Central bankers would predict the actions of consumers and businesses and proactively implement fiscal and monetary policy that generated a steady level of economic growth while keeping inflation contained. Business leaders would anticipate changes in demand for their products and services and adjust output accordingly to grow their earnings at the highest possible rate. Investors would precisely forecast future corporate earnings and thereby accurately determine the fair value of each company.

Unfortunately, reality is nothing like this. No one can predict the future with any certainty. At best, we can make educated guesses of what may come, where the probability of being correct is hopefully greater than 50%. Even the most rational decision-maker is subject to the whims of the infinitely complex world we live in. In the words of Howard Marks, "[t]he reason for this—as I've harped on repeatedly—is the involvement of people. People's decisions have great influence on economic, business and market cycles. In fact, economies, business and markets consist of nothing but transactions between people. And people don't make their decisions scientifically."[1] Does not being able to foresee all possible events or know the probability of events occurring or the eventual impact they will have on our investment portfolio mean that trying to manage risk is hopeless? Not at all. What it does mean is that as investors, we need to accept that there is a high degree of uncertainty when investing and, to the best of our ability, strengthen our understanding of the risks we face and plan for potentially negative outcomes. It is at the extremes, when discipline matters most, that our instinct to panic kicks in and leads us astray. Having a game plan in advance of these moments is a critical ingredient of investment success.

The market cycle is characterized by periods of expansion and contraction in company valuations, driven by rising and falling profitability coinciding with peaks and troughs in investor sentiment. By definition, investor sentiment reaches an extreme high at the peak of stock market valuations and an extreme low at the trough of stock market valuations. Failing to understand how market cycles work and how we should respond as investors is perhaps the most common cause of investment losses.

■ Economic Cycles

Economies are comprised of people, making them subject to the same behavioral biases discussed earlier, resulting in bouts of extreme optimism and pessimism. Taken as a whole, this causes countries to experience recurring periods of expansion and contraction in economic output, a phenomenon referred to as the economic, or business, cycle.

Economic cycles are self-perpetuating, meaning that the conditions that create an economic boom inevitably cause an economic bust that in turn leads to another boom. As the cycle repeats itself, each iteration takes on distinctive characteristics, which ensures that the exact duration and extent of every cycle remains unpredictable. The cycle occurs in part because of our inability to predict the future. When the economy is growing, jobs are plentiful and home prices tend to rise, creating wealth for consumers, and leading them to become increasingly optimistic. During these times, consumers begin to spend more on goods and services and businesses respond by increasing supply to meet this heightened demand. This leads to more jobs and accelerates wealth creation even further. At some point in time, however, there are not enough people in the workforce to fill all job vacancies and businesses must increase wages to attract the employees they require. In addition, demand for raw materials needed in the production of goods increases, eventually causing prices of those inputs to rise. The combination of these factors causes the cost of goods produced to rise, forcing businesses to raise the prices they charge consumers and thereby causing inflation.

As inflationary pressures build and threaten the economy, central banks intervene to slow economic growth by raising interest rates. As noted earlier, higher interest rates lead businesses to cut back on production, thereby reducing employment. This causes the overall level of demand to fall as consumers become less optimistic. As the demand for goods falls, prices begin to decrease, causing businesses to slow production and reduce employment. As unemployment levels trend higher, house prices begin to decrease, causing consumers to become increasingly pessimistic and save rather than spend their money. This reduction in demand causes businesses to cut back even further on production and to for go or delay projects that would otherwise have aided economic growth. If the central bank is successful in creating a soft landing, the rate of economic growth will slow down but remain positive while inflationary pressures decrease.

When it is clear that economic growth is likely to weaken below an acceptable level, central banks try to stimulate the economy by lowering interest rates. This increases the amount of money in the financial system, enticing businesses to invest and consumers to spend. These lower interest rates will again cause businesses to anticipate stronger future demand and resume hiring, thereby leading to an improvement in consumer sentiment and spending. Almost without fail, the corporate sector overinvests and adds too much capacity when times are good and reduces capacity too much when times are bad. This process exacerbates the swings in overall levels of supply and demand across the economy and forms a cycle as the process repeats itself.

Central bank intervention combined with longer-term population and economic growth mean that economic expansions tend to last longer than contractions. According to the National Bureau of Economic Research, the average economic expansion in the United States has had a duration of approximately 64 months while the average economic contraction has averaged approximately 10 months.[2] As previously mentioned, two or more consecutive quarters (six months) of negative growth is considered to be a recession, while prolonged periods of extreme economic weakness are referred to as depressions. In modern times, a depression has only occurred once, beginning in most countries in 1929 and lasting well into the 1930s. By the time the economy in the United States bottomed in 1933, the Great Depression caused real GDP in the United States to fall by 30%, and the wholesale price index to fall by 33%.[3] It was so devastating to the world economy that the effects of the Great Depression were felt as late as the end of World War II in some countries. The global financial crisis of 2007–2009 was milder by comparison, with US GDP falling by only 4.3%, but the world economy still lost millions of jobs, with unemployment almost doubling to 9.5%.[4] In both cases, the economic weakness that followed led to a period of austerity, where both businesses and individuals were able to strengthen their finances and reduce their debt levels. As well, the market selloffs that resulted from these periods of financial turmoil brought stock valuations once again to attractive levels and created the conditions for a new bull market to emerge.

■ Market Cycles

The term "market cycle" refers to a recurring pattern in the general level of stock prices that are the direct result of the economic cycle and therefore display a similar sequence. The reason is that the same forces driving the economic cycle impact corporate profitability. As the economy improves, corporate earnings increase, and share prices appreciate. As the economic outlook deteriorates, share prices fall in anticipation of weaker corporate earnings in the future. Since the financial markets are always forward-looking, share prices and actual earnings do not peak and trough at the same time. Instead, share prices usually peak before earnings start to fall and rise before earnings begin to recover. In fact, stock markets usually peak and trough six to nine months before the economy. Figure 5.1 provides a simplified representation of the full stock market cycle.

As with economic cycles, market cycles can be broken down into distinct periods, each with unique characteristics. The most basic distinction to be

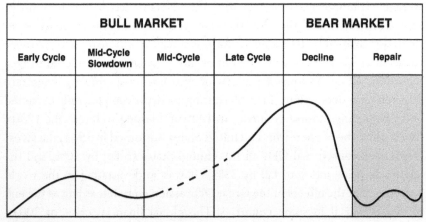

BULL MARKET				BEAR MARKET	
Early Cycle	Mid-Cycle Slowdown	Mid-Cycle	Late Cycle	Decline	Repair

FIGURE 5.1 The Stock Market Cycle

made is between a bull and a bear market. A bull market refers to a period when share prices in general are rising, whereas a bear market exists when share prices in general are falling. More specifically, a bear market is typically considered to be a period in which share prices fall by at least 20%. A drop in share prices of less than 20% is referred to as a bull market correction. For the purposes of this book, I have classified severe bull market corrections as bear markets, even though they are not generally regarded as such. Examples of severe bull market corrections include the market selloffs that occurred in 2011 and 2018, during which stock prices fell by more than 20%, but which did not coincide with an economic recession.

Since bull markets are associated with strong or improving economic environments and bear markets coincide with weakening economic environments, bear markets tend to be shorter in duration than bull markets, each averaging 370 and 1,446 calendar days, respectively. Bear markets are often followed by a repair phase, in which the market rallies but then retests the earlier lows before entering a new bull market. However, there have been cases where the market formed a V-shaped bottom, rising quickly off the low, essentially skipping the repair phase of the cycle. One example of a V bottom is the 2020 bear market, when markets rallied strongly and did not retest the previous lows. On average, it has taken the stock market 717 calendar days to fully recover to its previous high following a bear market.

Bull markets can be broken down further into an early, mid-, and late cycle. The beginning part of a bull market cycle is known as the early cycle and it refers to the period when share prices have reached a bottom and are beginning to recover. The late cycle refers to the later stages of a bull market when share prices are reaching a peak. The mid-cycle is the period between the early and late stages of the market cycle. While the middle stage of the market cycle tends to be characterized by steady economic and earnings growth, there are usually one or more pauses that are referred to as mid-cycle slowdowns. These pauses may manifest themselves as a temporary slowdown in the rate of earnings growth and a mild drop in share prices (typically between 5 and 10%). Long-running bull markets may have more than one mid-cycle slowdown. The table in Figure 5.2 provides a summary of bear markets experienced by the S&P 500 Index since 1927, including how long they lasted and how much share prices fell in each instance. Again, this list includes all market corrections in which share prices fell by 20% or more.

While the average bear market caused stocks to drop approximately 36% and last 370 days, some were much shorter in duration. Market analysts

Start Date	End Date	S&P 500 Return	Length of Bear Market (Days)	Recovery Period (Days)	Length of Preceding Bull Market (Days)
February 19, 2020	March 23, 2020	−35.4%	33	103	422
October 3, 2018	December 24, 2018	−20.2%	82	83	2556
July 21, 2011	October 4, 2011	−20.2%	75	86	867
October 11, 2007	March 6, 2009	−57.7%	512	1030	1827
September 1, 2000	October 10, 2002	−49.8%	769	1161	694
July 20, 1998	October 8, 1998	−22.5%	80	33	2839
July 16, 1990	October 11, 1990	−20.4%	87	85	1000
August 25, 1987	October 20, 1987	−35.9%	56	446	1842
November 28, 1980	August 9, 1982	−27.3%	619	53	2248
January 11, 1973	October 3, 1974	−48.2%	630	1461	961
November 29, 1968	May 26, 1970	−36.1%	543	451	784
February 9, 1966	October 7, 1966	−22.2%	240	143	1324
December 12, 1961	June 26, 1962	−28.0%	196	299	1512
July 15, 1957	October 22, 1957	−20.7%	99	227	2954
June 15, 1948	June 13, 1949	−20.6%	363	142	393
May 29, 1946	May 19, 1947	−28.5%	355	765	1492
October 25, 1939	April 28, 1942	−43.5%	916	553	573
March 10, 1937	March 31, 1938	−54.5%	386	938	1743
September 16, 1929	June 1, 1932	−86.2%	989	5571	N/A
Average		−35.7%	370	717	1446

FIGURE 5.2   A History of Bear Markets and Severe Bull Market Corrections

Data source: Standard & Poor's Financial Services LLC, sourced via Bloomberg, as of January 15, 2022.

typically focus on the size and duration of the drop in share prices; however, what is really important is the impact a bear market has on investor psychology. There are several market selloffs that are not listed in Figure 5.2 because they do not quite meet the somewhat arbitrary 20% minimum threshold for a bear market. And yet because of the time frame in which they occurred, these selloffs had the effect of wiping the slate clean and removing enough excessive optimism to allow the market to continue higher, thus prolonging the official bull market. The bear markets with the most profound effect on investor psychology, and that therefore take longer for investors to recover from, are those that are both deep and long lasting, such as the bear markets of 1929 to 1932 and 2007 to 2009.

Investors should also note that bear markets often contain strong temporary rebounds in share prices that are referred to as bear market rallies. Similar to bull market corrections, these are temporary but sometimes violent reversals in the underlying trend that have the potential to entice investors into buying stocks even though the bear market has further to run.

Market corrections and bear markets present opportunities. They are a necessary part of the market cycle that provide the foundation for continued growth, and they provide investors with the opportunity to buy great businesses at discounted prices. These moments are when it is most important to remain objective, and the best way to do that is to have a plan laid out before they occur. In this manner you can invest your money in a way that protects your portfolio from the negative impacts of market selloffs, while still allowing you to take advantage of the opportunities that are created by them.

Knowing approximately where we are in the market cycle can provide you with a tremendous advantage as an investor. Different asset classes and businesses perform well or poorly, depending on where we are in the market cycle. This knowledge can be a powerful tool when it comes to managing risk in your portfolio and seizing opportunities when they arise. To be clear, market timing is not the goal. As we noted earlier, it is impossible to know exactly when the market will turn from a bull to a bear market and vice versa. Regardless, if you are aware they exist and are looking for them, there are signs that should help you determine what part of the market cycle we are currently in with a reasonable degree of accuracy. To do this, though, we need a better understanding of the various stages of the market cycle and what underlying forces are at work in each stage.

Early Cycle

The early stage of the market cycle refers to the period instantly following a bottom in share prices for the broader stock market. It is important to look at the broad stock market because not all company share prices will reach a low at the same time. Certain businesses will have already started to improve by the time the stock market bottoms, while still others will see their earnings (and share prices) continue to fall.

Consider the early stage of an economic expansion. The economy has just gone through a period of weakness. Unemployment levels have increased, and interest rates have most likely been reduced by the central bank to encourage spending and spur economic growth. Businesses begin to expect a recovery in demand and start to hire back employees they previously laid off. If business leaders are less certain of the sustainability of the economic recovery, they may choose to hire temporary workers initially, with plans to hire permanent workers once they have greater confidence in the economic recovery. Under these circumstances, certain types of businesses will perform better than others. Also, investors will begin to invest in cyclical businesses as a new bull market emerges, since these businesses are more levered to economic growth, and they benefit the most when economic growth improves. Depending on what caused the preceding bear market, the early stages of a new bull market may be dominated by a strong rebound in the share prices of companies that suffered the greatest losses in the downturn. A notable example is found in the immediate aftermath of the 2020 pandemic-driven bear market, when the share prices of energy companies, one of the worst-performing sectors during the crisis, were among the strongest short-term performers once the market correction ended.

Mid-Cycle

As the economic recovery takes hold and it becomes clear that economic growth will be sustained, the bull market enters the middle part of its cycle. This mid-cycle stage can be long in duration and is characterized by broad-based strength in stocks. Mid-cycles typically experience one or more temporary slowdowns or pauses in economic growth, at which time stock prices either fall modestly (5–10%) or go sideways for a time. At these junctures, the market often experiences some degree of rotation out of stocks that have performed well into stocks that had been lagging. This process improves the state of equilibrium within the market and helps to create the conditions necessary for the market to advance once again. As the economic expansion progresses, however, prices start to rise as wages and other input costs go up, raising the specter of inflation. The prospect of higher inflation causes market participants to begin to predict higher interest rates, at which point the stock market enters the late stage of the cycle.

Late Cycle

The late-cycle stage of a bull market is characterized by a peak in corporate earnings and profitability. At this point in time the underlying economy has grown considerably, and businesses have generated significant profits and invested heavily in their operations to add to their productive capacity. Jobs are plentiful and companies must increase wages in order to hire and retain employees. Commodity prices have increased due to stronger demand from businesses and consumers. Stronger demand drives oil and gas prices higher and helps the shares of energy companies, causing them to outperform in the late stage of the market cycle. As the general level of prices begins to rise, however, central banks begin to increase interest rates to contain inflation. In turn, higher interest rates affect businesses differently. Banks, for example, typically benefit from modest increases in interest rates because their net interest margin (NIM) expands. NIM is the difference between the interest banks must pay on savings accounts and the interest they receive from lending money. NIM expansion makes banks more profitable and so they tend to perform well during the initial stages of an interest rate–tightening cycle. Shares of high-growth, high-valuation companies that generate little or no earnings, on the other hand, tend to perform poorly as interest rates move higher. The reason for this is simple: rising interest rates reduce the value of earnings and cash flows by a greater amount the further out into the future they are expected to occur. The process of adjusting future cash flows in this manner is referred to as "discounting," which we discuss in greater detail in Chapter 8.

Gradually, as economic growth begins to slow, investors are inclined to shift assets away from cyclical businesses to those that are more defensive, such as those within the utility and healthcare sectors. The term "defensive" refers to companies that have consistent earnings, regardless of whether the economic environment is weak or strong. This stable earnings profile provides downside protection, causing the share prices of defensive companies to fall less in bear markets. Toward the very end of the market cycle, credit spreads typically start to trend higher and may even increase rapidly, although they do not "blow out" except in the event of a credit crisis. Rising credit spreads serve as a sign of heightened risk in the stock market.

Sector Rotation

As noted earlier, the market cycle is marked by what is commonly referred to as sector rotation. Sector rotation is created when investors collectively shift their funds from one market sector to another in response to expected changes in economic conditions. As the economic cycle evolves, various sectors and industries will perform better than others. This creates smaller industry- or sector-level cycles within the broader market cycle. One method for identifying sector rotation is to monitor business news flow. While the normal condition is for companies to respond favorably to good news, as good news is absorbed by market participants and businesses become more expensive versus the broader market, share prices stop responding favorably to good news. This can be an early sign that all good news has been factored into current share prices and that businesses in the sector have become fully valued (or overvalued) and are likely to underperform in the near term. At this point it may be best for the investor to reassess those holdings in light of the current stage of the market cycle and consider whether it is prudent to take profits in those businesses and reallocate the capital to better opportunities. The same is true when the share prices of businesses in a sector stop reacting poorly to unwelcome news. It is at this point that all unwelcome news could be priced into those shares, and they may be due for a recovery.

■ Market Contagions

Weakness in one segment of the global financial markets has the potential to infect other areas of the market that are otherwise performing well. This phenomenon is known as a market contagion. It is difficult to predict whether a particular area of weakness may affect other segments of the global equity market. What might seem to be a significant event could turn out to be contained at the regional or country level, while something seemingly inconsequential could grow into a serious problem.

A number of the bear markets listed earlier in Figure 5.2 were the direct result of market contagions. While it started off as a regional crisis, the 1997 Asian Financial Crisis is a notable example. Currency devaluations in South Asia caused regional stock markets to fall, but eventually fear spread to other parts of the world, impacting the United States in October 1997 and causing the S&P 500 Index to fall 13% from its peak. This is shown in Figure 5.3, where the crisis in Asia took several weeks to affect European and North American equity markets.

Once it was clear that the situation in Asia had stabilized, equity markets around the world began to recover at approximately the same time. Unlike the Asian Financial Crisis, the global financial crisis, which began in the United States in October 2007, very quickly reverberated throughout financial markets, causing most of the world's equity markets to enter a bear market at the same time. Other examples of market contagions include the 2012 European debt crisis, and the Long-Term Capital Management crisis of 1998.

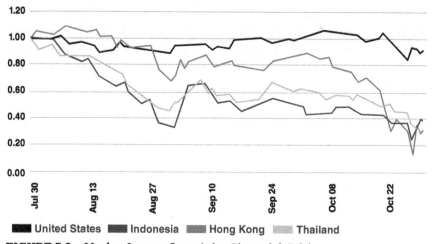

FIGURE 5.3   **Market Impact from Asian Financial Crisis**

Data source: Standard & Poor's Financial Services LLC, sourced via Bloomberg, as of January 30, 2022.

■ Bear Market Warning Signs

Any number of factors can cause an equity bull market to end, highlighting the importance of monitoring signs that may provide an early warning of market turmoil. Being aware of the potential for a banking crisis is paramount, in which inflated housing prices can play a significant role. Economic professors Carmen Reinhart and Kenneth Rogoff explain that "[f]or banking crises, real housing prices are nearly at the top of the list of reliable indicators, surpassing the current account balance and real stock prices by producing fewer false alarms."[5] An extended period of housing price increases has been behind many banking crises in the past, especially when they have resulted from easy lending standards and artificially depressed mortgage rates.

In fact, changes in the general level of asset prices may hold clues as to when the next financial meltdown will occur and how severe it will be. Extended periods of share price appreciation combined with historically high valuations, abnormally low credit spreads, and easy lending conditions, along with widespread apathy to potential risks and a general feeling that the good times will just keep going, are all warning signs that the stock market is vulnerable to a correction. The longer these conditions last and the more extreme they become, the deeper and more prolonged the market selloff is likely to be.

Another important statistic to monitor is the amount of margin debt in the financial system. Margin debt is the amount of money investors have borrowed to buy stocks. Margin debt helps support the stock market as investors continue to borrow and buy shares, but it is detrimental for the market when investors must sell those shares to repay the loans. Most margin debt exists in brokerage accounts and bank loans, and these monies must be repaid regardless of how well the equity markets perform. If stock prices were to fall beyond a certain point, margin debt may be "called" by the lender, forcing investors who borrowed the funds to sell stocks at the lower prices to repay their loans. This is known in the investment industry as a margin call, and enough of them occurring at the same time can increase selling pressure and cause share prices to fall even further. High rates of growth in margin debt are a sign of excessive investor optimism and should be a warning sign for you as an investor. Figure 5.4 shows the year-over-year change in margin debt in the United States.

Periods of large increases in margin debt preceded every major bear market since 1998. Although this data is not available in all countries, the prominence of the US equity market allows us to use this data to gauge the overall amount of leverage in the global financial system.

As noted in Chapter 4, the bond market can also hold clues to the future of equity markets, with credit spreads being a crucial factor. Rising credit spreads can point to growing aversion to risk and a tougher lending

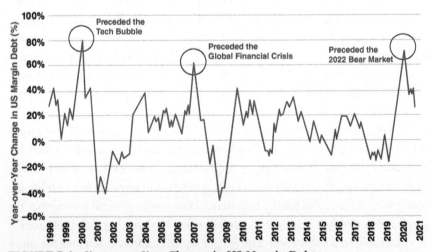

FIGURE 5.4 Year-over-Year Change in US Margin Debt

Source: The Financial Industry Regulatory Authority Inc. (FINRA), https://www.finra.org/investors/learn-to-invest/advanced-investing/margin-statistics, accessed January 16, 2022.

environment and are a potential red flag for equity markets. Without a large corresponding increase in credit spreads, market selloffs will most likely be short-term corrections rather than the start of a bear market. In a study completed in 2018, Morgan Stanley Research noted that "credit in general tends to be the first to 'crack,' providing a bearish market signal 3–12 months in advance, with government bond yields, on average, peaking about three months before [the MSCI] ACWI [Index] and S&P 500 [Index] do."[6]

In addition, changes in the level of interest rates play a key role in the future earnings power of companies. Rising interest rates may place equity markets at risk, depending on their level and the rate of increase. From exceptionally low levels and when economic growth is strong, moderate interest rate increases are often viewed as being positive for equity markets. The reason is that it shows that central banks believe that economic growth will continue at a healthy pace, and that inflation will remain contained. If interest rates rise quickly on the other hand, it could be a sign that inflationary pressures are mounting and that the central bank will have to raise rates to slow economic growth, thus dampening corporate profits. Monetary tightening by central banks is another sign that a bull market is in the late stages of an expansion.

Last, the relative performance of industry sectors can provide clues as to where we are in the market cycle. As the cycle nears an end, defensive businesses start to outperform the broader stock market. Then, as the market reaches a bottom or trough, cyclical businesses such as technology, financials, discretionary, industrials, and materials start to outperform.[7] In a related fashion, value stocks typically start to perform better than growth stocks, and safe-haven currencies like the US dollar, Swiss franc, and Japanese yen begin to outperform emerging market currencies at stock market peaks. In addition, Japanese and European equities usually begin to outperform US and emerging market equities at market peaks.[8]

Taken together, rapid interest rate hikes by central banks, widening credit spreads, improving performance of defensive company shares versus cyclical company shares, value indices outperforming growth indices, a recent period of excessive growth in margin debt, in combination with inflated stock and housing prices, should set off alarm bells for investors. Keep in mind, though, that no two market cycles will be identical. In fact, the exact same point of progression will differ in meaningful ways between two distinct market cycles. Simply put, the warning signs just listed may not all be present at the start of a bear market. However, an abundance of these red flags should allow you to mentally brace yourself for a market correction or bear market by figuratively "putting on your crash helmet." Let us assume for a moment that the previously mentioned warning signs are present, and you believe that a bear market is imminent. What should you do? The answer lies in the past—what you have done leading up to this point. The type of businesses you have invested in and the way you construct your portfolio are the best way to protect yourself from a bear market. If you have prepared yourself and your portfolio for these moments, as we outline throughout this book, you will see bear markets as opportunities and look forward to them rather than fear them. Don't fear the bear, stay calm and outsmart it.

■ Bear Market Bottoms

Bear market bottoms are often marked by a rapid reduction in interest rates by central banks, falling credit spreads, low equity valuations, and waning relative outperformance of defensive sectors in the market. Investors should monitor central bank statements closely to gauge potential inflection points. Signs that a bear market has ended include the outperformance of small-cap versus large-cap stocks, as well as high-beta versus low-beta stocks. Although the definition of small and large cap varies by country, in the United States small-cap stocks are generally regarded as companies with a total market capitalization (value) of less than US$2 billion, while large-cap stocks are those with market capitalizations greater than US$10 billion. The term "beta" is discussed in more detail in Chapter 8, but it essentially refers to how much a company's share price moves in relation to the overall stock market, with high-beta stocks being more leveraged than low-beta stocks to price changes in the stock market.

Trading volume and market breadth also play a key role in identifying market bottoms. One useful measure is the Arms Index, which investors also refer to as the TRIN. The market's TRIN is measured as the ratio of advancing to declining stocks, divided by the ratio of advancing to declining volume, and can be calculated as follows:

$$\frac{\text{Number of stocks trading up on the day} / \text{Number of stocks trading down on the day}}{\text{Total volume of stocks up on the day} / \text{Total volume of stocks down on the day}}$$

A TRIN reading above 1 is usually associated with a decline in the stock market, driven by a proportionally high level of selling volume. Conversely, a TRIN reading below 1 is associated with a rising stock market since there is a proportionally greater volume going into advancing stocks. A high TRIN reading (above 2) followed by a low TRIN reading (0.50 or less) may indicate capitulation selling followed by a volume thrust and is often associated with bear market bottoms. This may be especially relevant when followed by a breadth thrust, which is another sign that a market recovery is likely to continue. There are different variations or definitions of a breadth thrust, but one useful approach is to identify when most stocks in the market are trading at new 65-day highs. This is particularly relevant when these new highs occur after market breadth collapses, signaling capitulation on the part of investors. I highly recommend following Jeff deGraaf and the team at RenMac on social media for timely insights into many of the factors used to identify bear market bottoms. Particularly when markets have already fallen significantly (20–30% or more), it is at these moments that you should begin putting more money back to work and buying shares of the companies you want to own.

■ Managing Cycle Risk

The biggest risk for investors stemming from market cyclicality is selling when share prices have already fallen significantly. Conversely, buying after share prices have appreciated considerably also poses risks and has the potential of reducing forward investment returns. Focusing on the future earnings power of the business and the price being paid for those earnings will alleviate both pitfalls. This discipline will keep you from selling when other investors are panicking and share prices are bottoming, and from buying when investors are exuberant and share prices are peaking. Share prices peak when the last buyer buys and bottom when the last seller sells. It is therefore the absence of buyers that causes stock markets to peak, rather than a sudden surge in selling. Similarly, it is the absence of sellers that allows stocks to finally reach a bottom.

The good news is that there are some simple steps that investors can take to manage cycle risk in their portfolio. First, own good businesses. The high-quality businesses that were described briefly in Chapter 1 can withstand economic downturns better than their weaker competitors. These companies can keep their leadership position when times get tough and can generate a more consistent level of earnings. They may also be able to take advantage of a crisis by taking market share or buying companies with good assets that are more vulnerable to economic weakness and find themselves in distress. Diversify your portfolio by industry. Remember that the share prices of companies in the same industry tend to move in tandem. Owning several companies in the same industry will therefore not protect you as much as owning businesses in a variety of industries. In addition, owning businesses whose shares are denominated in different currencies can further help reduce portfolio risk. The topic of portfolio construction is discussed in more detail in Chapter 20.

Remain focused on being an owner of a business, rather than an owner of shares. This is an important psychological factor during bear markets. In some cases, the share price of a company may drop in a market correction while its earnings remain steady. Figure 5.5 shows how the earnings for Microsoft remained fairly consistent or continued to rise despite large drops in the share price during the tech bubble of 2000–2002 and the financial crisis in 2008. By focusing on the company's earnings and its ability to withstand tough economic times, you will be better able to look past temporary share price volatility.

Investors will be well-served remembering that nothing in the investing world is definite, and that rules are made to be broken. Ted Ransby, one of

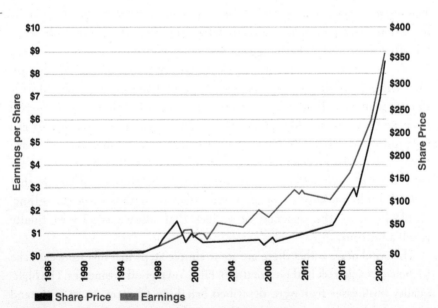

FIGURE 5.5   Microsoft Earnings versus Share Price
Data source: Bloomberg and Yahoo Finance, as of February 6, 2022.

my early mentors in the investment industry, described the stock market in this way: "[T]he market will bend the rules just enough to push investors past their breaking points." Ted aptly described the capitulation stage of the market cycle, where investors cast aside fundamentals and logic and react based purely on emotion. The fact that no two cycles are identical is crucial to the perpetuation of the market cycle process. It is only when the majority of investors are fooled into thinking the current trend will not end and they finally give in to buying or selling that markets peak or trough. Remember that markets peak when the last investor buys and bottom when the last investor sells. You do not want to be either of those investors—buying at the peak or selling at the bottom.

That leads us to the next point, which is to buy more of the great businesses you like when they become less expensive. Ownership positions are on sale at this point so why not take advantage of that? Another possibility is to consider shifting some money into businesses that you really like but that you felt were too expensive to buy previously. If you can do this effectively, you have succeeded in flipping conventional thinking on its head, and view falling share prices as an opportunity rather than a threat.

One final technique used to limit market cycle risk worth mentioning is to rebalance your portfolio on a regular basis. Rebalancing requires you to sell a portion of the stocks you own that have done especially well and use the proceeds to add to those that have lagged. Sticking with this consistently will help you reduce risk by redistributing money away from more expensive stocks to those that on average are less expensive. This approach is based on the concept of mean reversion, where valuations will tend to revert back to their long-term average. Stocks trading below their long-term average valuation will eventually rise until they reach it, while stocks trading above their long-term average valuation will eventually fall back down to it. The topic of portfolio rebalancing is discussed in more detail in Chapter 20.

This chapter provided a brief overview of why market cycles occur, what these cycles mean for you as an investor, and how you can manage the risks that arise from this cyclicality. For a more in-depth and insightful discussion on market cycles, I strongly recommend that you read *Mastering the Market Cycle* by Howard Marks. We now consider the risk that foreign currencies bring to global investing.

Stock market cycles are a direct result of economic cycles since economic factors impact corporate earnings. Economic expansions tend to last 64 months on average, while economic contractions typically last 10 months. Similarly, the average bear market lasts approximately one year, while bull markets last an average of four years (when we consider both bull market corrections and bear markets). Economic and market cycles are self-perpetuating since the factors that lead to periods of economic and market strength set the foundation for their own collapse and renewal. Cycle peaks and troughs are marked by extremes in investor sentiment and stock valuations, providing an opportunity for astute and patient investors. Rapid interest rate hikes by central banks, widening credit spreads, improving performance of defensive company shares versus cyclical company shares, value indices outperforming growth indices, a recent period of excessive growth in margin debt, in combination with inflated stock and housing prices, suggest that a bull market could be nearing its end. The key to withstanding periods of stock market weakness is to own good businesses and properly diversify your portfolio, as described in Chapter 20.

RISKS OF INVESTING GLOBALLY

CHAPTER 6

Currency Risk

■ Currency Market Overview

Currencies as we know them today are termed *fiat* currencies since their value is based on government decree. Most currencies are therefore controlled by the actions of a single government. Currency trading is what enables global trade and facilitates financial transactions of all kinds. In fact, the currency market is considered the largest and most liquid financial market in the world. Daily trading volumes are estimated to be the equivalent of US$6.6 trillion, far surpassing the combined dollar value of all stock and bond trades each day. Figure 6.1 shows the most widely traded currencies in the world as of 2019, including spot and derivative transactions. The term *spot* transaction refers to trades that are for immediate (typically next day) settlement, while *derivative* transactions are for settlement at some future date. Keep in mind that each transaction involves a pair of currencies and therefore Figure 6.1 shows double the actual total daily trading volume.

■ Exchange Rate Dynamics

Like most other assets, the exchange rate between two countries is determined by supply and demand. Demand is generated by trade and investment flows between a single country and all other countries that interact with it. For example, a US company building a manufacturing plant in Japan would

Currency	Daily Average	Currency	Daily Average
US dollar (USD)	5,824	Singapore dollar (SGD)	119
Euro (EUR)	2,129	Norwegian krone (NOK)	119
Japanese yen (JPY)	1,109	Mexican peso (MXN)	114
British pound (GBP)	844	Indian rupee (INR)	114
Australian dollar (AUD)	447	Russian ruble (RUB)	72
Canadian dollar (CAD)	332	South African rand (ZAR)	72
Swiss franc (CHF)	327	Turkish lira (TRY)	71
Chinese renminbi (CNY)	285	Brazilian real (BRL)	71
Hong Kong dollar (HKD)	233	Taiwan dollar (TWD)	60
New Zealand dollar (NZD)	137	Danish krona (DKK)	42
Swedish krona (SEK)	134	Polish zloty (PLN)	41
South Korean won (KRW)	132	Other currencies	447

FIGURE 6.1　The World's Most Traded Currencies (Daily Trade Volume in Billions USD)

Source: Bank for International Settlements, https://www.bis.org/statistics/rpfx19_fx_annex.pdf, accessed January 15, 2022. Data is as of April 2019.

need to convert US dollars to Japanese yen in order to pay the local construction firm. It may also need to purchase euros to buy equipment from Germany that will be used in the new factory. Similarly, an investor in the United Arab Emirates may want to buy a bond issued by the government of France, requiring them to convert UAE dirham into euros. Even an individual on vacation in a foreign country becomes a part of this equation.

As you can imagine, there are a vast number of currency transactions taking place every day. However, certain types of transactions tend to be much larger in scope and have a greater impact on the final level of demand for a particular currency, the most significant being investment-related currency transactions. Many factors affect investment-related currency transactions, but the most important is the level of real interest rates in each country. The "real" interest rate is simply the interest rate minus the rate of inflation. The currencies of countries that pay a higher real rate of interest on government bonds will likely be strong. Since investors are constantly in search of higher returns, the prospect of future currency appreciation or depreciation is an important consideration. Like most other financial instruments, currency exchange rates have a built-in self-correction mechanism. As a country's currency rises in value, goods produced by that country become increasingly expensive to foreign buyers. This will eventually cause them to import fewer goods from that country, reducing demand for the currency and causing it to fall in value. The opposite is also true—as a country's currency weakens, foreign demand for the country's exports will increase, thus increasing demand for its currency.

■ How Currencies Affect Investment Returns

As noted in Chapter 3, holding investments denominated in a basket of different currencies is beneficial to investors over the long run. At a minimum it should reduce the overall volatility of your investment returns. Part of the reason for this is that currencies behave differently under varying market conditions. As previously mentioned, some currencies are thought of as safe havens, and investors will often flock to those currencies when crises occur. Safe haven currencies include the US dollar, Japanese yen, and Swiss franc, as they tend to strengthen as global equity markets fall, thereby acting as a natural hedge or "shock absorber" for your portfolio. This was clear in 2008 and at the outset of the global pandemic when, in the first quarter of 2020, the US dollar, Swiss franc, and Japanese yen rallied against most other currencies.

Currency movements, especially in the case of the US dollar, can also affect other asset prices. Since most commodities are traded and priced in US dollars, a stronger US dollar tends to reduce demand for commodities and causes commodity prices to fall. Conversely, a weakening US dollar is generally positive for commodity demand and pushes prices higher. Higher commodity prices in turn will be construed as positive for the currencies and economies of countries that are commodity exporters, such as Australia and Canada.

The same can be said for emerging market equities. A stronger US dollar is regarded as detrimental for emerging market economies while a weaker US dollar is supportive for emerging markets. This is partly because a majority of debt held by emerging market countries is denominated in US dollars, so if the US dollar strengthens, the cost of servicing that debt increases. Equity markets, commodity-linked currencies, and emerging markets are collectively referred to as risk assets, meaning they perform well when investors are willing to accept more risk. Bonds and safe haven currencies, on the other hand, tend to act well when investors want to avoid risk. Broadly speaking, when economic growth is strong, risk assets perform well, and when economic growth weakens, risk assets perform poorly.

Fluctuations in currency exchange rates are beneficial for investors eventually, but they can have a negative impact on your investment returns in the short term. I recall managing a US equity fund denominated in Canadian dollars and generating a 16% rate of return in US dollar terms for the year but then losing it all to a 16% appreciation in the Canadian dollar. Canadian investors in the fund earned a net return of zero percent that year. It is a difficult conversation to have when investors see the US stock market up 16% and yet they earned a zero percent return for the year after the effect of currency. However, it is important to remember that exposure to foreign currencies can also boost your investment returns and should help make the value of your portfolio fluctuate less over time. Figure 6.2 shows some of the world's major currencies and how they performed over time against a base currency, in this case the US dollar.

The shaded numbers show a period when the currency appreciated against the base currency (the US dollar in this case) and therefore exposure to the foreign currency would have enhanced the portfolio's investment return. Conversely, the unshaded numbers are periods when the foreign currency depreciated and would have reduced the portfolio's investment return. Of the currencies listed here, investors would have been best served owning Chinese renminbi (CNY) in 2021 and the Swedish krona (SEK) in 2020. Owning any currency other than the US dollar was detrimental in 2015, however, since the US dollar appreciated against all other currencies listed.

RISKS OF INVESTING GLOBALLY

YEAR	AUD	BRL	CAD	CHF	CNY	EUR	GBP	INR	JPY	KRW	MXN	RUB	SEK	SGD
2000	-15%	-7%	-3%	-1%	0%	-6%	-7%	-6%	-10%	-10%	-1%	-2%	-10%	-4%
2001	-7%	-15%	-5%	-2%	0%	-5%	-2%	-3%	-12%	-3%	4%	-7%	-9%	-5%
2002	7%	-42%	1%	13%	0%	12%	8%	0%	8%	8%	-10%	-4%	13%	5%
2003	34%	24%	23%	13%	0%	21%	13%	6%	12%	-1%	-11%	11%	22%	3%
2004	4%	9%	8%	9%	0%	8%	8%	5%	5%	15%	1%	6%	9%	4%
2005	-7%	13%	4%	-16%	3%	-16%	-12%	-4%	-16%	3%	5%	-4%	-21%	-2%
2006	-8%	10%	0%	9%	4%	12%	14%	2%	-1%	9%	-2%	10%	16%	9%
2007	11%	18%	16%	7%	7%	10%	1%	12%	7%	-1%	-1%	7%	6%	7%
2008	-14%	-17%	-13%	3%	4%	-3%	-21%	-14%	11%	-20%	-16%	-11%	-12%	0%
2009	27%	31%	17%	4%	0%	3%	12%	6%	-3%	10%	7%	-3%	11%	3%
2010	13%	5%	6%	11%	4%	-8%	-4%	4%	14%	3%	6%	-2%	7%	9%
2011	0%	-11%	-2%	0%	4%	-3%	0%	-17%	5%	-3%	-12%	-5%	-2%	-1%
2012	1%	-11%	2%	3%	1%	2%	5%	-4%	-14%	9%	8%	6%	6%	7%
2013	-20%	-19%	-8%	4%	4%	5%	2%	-16%	-27%	1%	-2%	-9%	1%	-4%
2014	-10%	-12%	-10%	-12%	-3%	-14%	-7%	-2%	-14%	-4%	-13%	-79%	-22%	-5%
2015	-12%	-48%	-19%	-1%	-4%	-11%	-6%	-5%	0%	-7%	-16%	-25%	-8%	-7%
2016	-1%	19%	3%	-2%	-7%	-3%	-20%	-3%	3%	-3%	-21%	17%	-8%	-2%
2017	9%	-2%	8%	5%	7%	15%	10%	7%	4%	14%	6%	7%	12%	9%
2018	-10%	-15%	-8%	-1%	-5%	-4%	-5%	-8%	2%	-4%	0%	-18%	-8%	-2%
2019	0%	-4%	6%	2%	-2%	-2%	5%	-3%	1%	-5%	5%	13%	-7%	2%
2020	10%	-33%	2%	10%	7%	9%	3%	-3%	6%	7%	-6%	-22%	14%	2%
2021	-7%	-9%	1%	-4%	3%	-9%	-1%	-2%	-14%	-11%	-3%	-1%	-12%	-2%

FIGURE 6.2 **Major Currency Returns versus the US Dollar**
Data source: Bloomberg, as of January 16, 2022.

You should note that the table in Figure 6.2 can also be used to estimate the relative performance between different currencies in any given year by subtracting the returns shown. The currency with the higher return is the currency that appreciated, or increased, in relative value. For example, in 2021 the Australian dollar (AUD) appreciated against the Brazilian real (BRL) by approximately −7% minus − 9% = 2%, although both fell versus the US dollar. The importance of this table is to highlight the fact that in any given year, currency fluctuations can have a substantial impact on returns and that the best-performing currency changes each year. A few of the currencies shown here have depreciated significantly over the past 20 years, suggesting that investors residing in those countries would have benefited greatly from exposure to the US dollar as well as other currencies that appreciated over the period. Figure 6.3 demonstrates a simplified method for approximating the effect that changes in exchange rates have on investment returns.

An investor purchases 1,000 shares of two businesses, Company H, which is located in their home country, and Company F, which is located in a foreign country.

After owning the shares for one year, both share prices go up in value by 10% in their home or local currency. Assuming the currency of the foreign country in which Company F is located appreciates in value by 5% compared to the home currency, the investor's return would be increased by 5%, as shown in the "Total Return" column in the following table:

	Price Return	Currency Return	Total Return
Company H	10%	0%	10%
Company F	10%	5%	15%

Conversely, if the foreign currency fell 3% in value compared to the investor's home currency, the return to the investor would be decreased by 3%.

	Price Return	Currency Return	Total Return
Company H	10%	0%	10%
Company F	10%	−3%	7%

FIGURE 6.3 Impact of Foreign Exchange Fluctuations on Investment Returns

This extremely basic example highlights the fact that exposure to foreign currencies can greatly enhance or reduce investment returns, especially over the short term. We noted in Chapter 4 that having exposure to a basket of currencies is beneficial over a long time period due to the positive impact of diversifying currency returns. Conversely, having excessive exposure to a single currency (foreign or domestic) could add significant risk to your portfolio and materially impact your investment return (positively or negatively). It is critical for investors to avoid investing in currencies that are likely to depreciate significantly, which leads us to discuss currency crises.

■ Currency Debasement and Crashes

Government and central bank policy usually strives to create exchange rate stability, but there are times when a deliberate effort is made to cause a currency to appreciate or depreciate compared to foreign currencies. Countries that wish to help their exporters, for example, may choose to weaken their currency so the goods they produce become less expensive for foreign buyers. Currency debasements like this may be modest and temporary in nature, in which case they would not be cause for concern. However, a continuous or severe debasement of a currency will erode investment gains and is a concern. As an investor, you must watch these situations closely and assess their significance.

The most important currency-related risk for the global investor is a currency crash, where the value of a currency falls significantly versus that of other currencies in a brief period of time. We noted earlier that even without direct exposure to the falling currency, a currency crash can eventually affect markets globally and therefore changes in currency exchange rates must be monitored on an ongoing basis. The most severe currency crashes may prompt investors to shun all risk assets, causing equity markets around the world to fall. Figure 6.4 lists some of the more notable currency crashes that have occurred in the recent past.

One of the examples listed in Figure 6.4 is referred to as the Russian financial crisis, in which declining productivity and rampant inflation led Russia's central bank to devalue the ruble. As a result, the ruble fell against the US dollar by close to 70% in less than a month, from August 14 to September 8, 1998. Stock market investors foresaw the challenges facing Russia at the time and drove stock valuations down almost 90% between late April and early October 1998. By the time the ruble was devalued, the

Currency	Time Period	Change vs. USD (%)
Turkish lira (TRY)	November 2020 – December 2020	−54.8%
Zimbabwean dollar (ZWL)	May 2019 – August 2020	−93.7%
Russian ruble (RUB)	September 1993 – March 1999	−96.3%
Thai baht (THB)	June 1997 – January 1998	−58.3%
Philippine peso (PHP)	July 1997 – January 1998	−41.6%
Mexican peso (MXN)	December 1994 – March 1995	−53.6%
Argentinian peso (ARS)	January 2002 – June 2002	−74.7%

FIGURE 6.4 Examples of Modern-Day Currency Crashes
Data source: Bloomberg, as of January 16, 2022.

stock market had already fallen by almost 70%. Through the actions of the central bank and aided by a strong recovery in world oil prices, Russia was able to recover from this financial crisis quickly. Domestic businesses also received help from the rapid devaluation of the currency, which made imported goods expensive for domestic consumers.

In our earlier discussion of the Asian financial crisis, we noted that some countries peg their currency to a major currency, such as the US dollar or euro. The purpose of doing this is to create exchange rate stability. However, if the country experiences severe economic woes, having a pegged currency can cause the country's economic problems to worsen. In some instances, especially where a currency has been pegged to a foreign currency or basket of foreign currencies, rapid currency depreciation may be deliberate. In other situations, currency depreciation may be the result of a large and sudden increase in inflation, fiscal mismanagement, or a particularly weak economic environment. Either way, if you hold investments in countries that experience a large drop in the value of their currency, your investment returns will be negatively affected.

■ Managing Currency Risk

As noted previously, most currency exchange rate fluctuations are modest and will reverse over time as they have a built-in self-correction mechanism. The primary concern for investors is avoiding exposure to currencies that are vulnerable to significant depreciation. Fortunately, for investors who are aware of and watching for them, there are warning signs that often precede a currency crisis.

A banking crisis is one event that can lead to currency depreciation. Since banking crises are often preceded by a significant increase in home prices, monitoring changes in house prices and housing affordability around the world is one easy step you can take to protect your portfolio. Of course, not all housing booms lead to a banking crisis. As an investor you must decide whether home price increases are based on sound and sustainable lending standards and what effect a deteriorating economic environment might have on the ability of homeowners to continue to meet their mortgage payments. Low housing affordability combined with elevated levels of consumer debt and rising mortgage rates stands out as a high-risk scenario. It should be noted that house price changes can affect the loan-to-value (LTV) ratio of underlying mortgages. If house prices are declining, the LTV will increase, resulting in the lender having less collateral to guard against a default. This makes the loan riskier and increases the probability that losses will be incurred when loans become delinquent.

Inflation also often precedes currency crashes, especially in countries that have experienced frequent bouts of inflation in the past. According to Reinhart and Rogoff ". . . by and large, inflation crises and exchange rate crises have traveled hand in hand in the overwhelming majority of episodes across time and countries (with a markedly tighter link in countries subject to chronic inflation, where the pass-through from prices to exchange rates is greatest."[1] As mentioned earlier, countries with high levels of external or domestic debt have a history of stimulating inflation in order to "inflate away" their debt burden and should be avoided. In situations where a country is having trouble repaying debt owed to foreigners or its citizens, it has four options: (1) reduce spending and increase taxes, (2) renegotiate the terms of the debt, (3) default, or (4) devalue the debt through inflation. The first option is the most difficult politically as the impact will be felt most by its citizens. The second option of renegotiating the terms of existing debt is attractive for the borrower but requires the cooperation of those who are owed the money. These lenders may be unwilling to agree to a reduced payment or longer repayment period. The third option of default has been used from time to time, but most countries will use this only as a last resort, as it impacts the country's status on the world stage and may hinder its ability to borrow in the debt markets well into the future. This leaves inflation as a common solution used by countries that have borrowed too heavily to reduce their debt load.

Defaulting on debt through inflation may sound complicated, but the process is quite simple. Assume you are owed a sum of money and while you are waiting to be repaid, the prices of all goods and services double. The money you are owed is now effectively worth one-half of what it was worth when you loaned it out. In earlier times, when currency was based on coinage, monarchs sometimes created money by reducing the amount of gold or silver content in their coins to mint more coins (an old-school version of currency debasement). Today, a country's central bank can simply print money and use it to repay the country's debt. The debt has been repaid but with currency now worth less than before the central bank's actions. This invariably leads to inflation.

Consistently elevated levels of inflation or a sudden and rapid rise in expected inflation indicate an elevated risk of a currency crash. In these circumstances there is no sense in waiting around for this to happen. Government policies that appear to promote price inflation and currency debasement should be taken seriously. If you begin to have significant doubts about where a certain situation is headed, sell the shares of the companies you hold in that country and move on. The world's equity markets are vast, allowing you to exit a country that appears to be heading down the wrong path and find a better opportunity to invest in a great business where a currency debasement or crash is unlikely.

Currency hedging provides another means to mitigate currency risk. However, Jeremy Siegel noted that "[a]lthough hedging seems like an attractive way to offset exchange rate risk, in the long run it is often unnecessary and even detrimental."[2] The best approach to manage currency risk is to diversify your portfolio by currency, watch for the warning signs listed previously, and act if needed. However, if currency risk poses a serious concern and exiting the position is not an option, using currency forwards to hedge (offset) the risk may be possible. A currency forward is a contract that allows you to exchange a set amount of two currencies on a specified date in the future and at a predetermined exchange rate. This can be a very cost-effective method for hedging currency risk but is limited to investors with a sizeable amount of assets, typically with a minimum of several million dollars. Since currency forwards are restricted to institutional and high-net-worth investors, and because exposure to a basket of currencies will help investors over the long term, I will leave the discussion on currency forwards for another day.

Currencies as we know them today are termed *fiat* currencies since their value is based on government decree. The currency market is the largest and most liquid financial market in the world, with daily trading volumes estimated to be the equivalent of US$6.6 trillion, far surpassing the combined dollar value of all stock and bond trades each day. Some currencies like the US dollar, Japanese yen, and Swiss franc are considered safe havens, and investors will often flock to them at times of crisis. Safe haven currencies tend to strengthen as global equity markets fall, thereby acting as a natural hedge or shock absorber for a portfolio. Although currency fluctuations can have a negative impact on portfolio returns temporarily, investors are better served by holding a basket of currencies in the long run. The greatest concern for investors is to avoid investing in countries where currency devaluation is probable. Countries at the greatest risk of a currency devaluation are those that frequently experience elevated levels of inflation and that have large amounts of external and internal debt.

Geopolitical Risk

The last major category of risk that we consider is that of geopolitical risk. Geopolitical risks arise from the actions and interactions of countries. Globalization has served to increase the frequency of contact between countries as well as increase competition for scarce goods, raising the possibility of disagreements and conflict. On the other hand, globalization has also led to greater integration and alignment of economic interests, which incentivizes countries to favor diplomacy as a tool of foreign policy. Although greater economic integration between the world's economies is likely to lead to fewer military confrontations, Russia's attack on Ukraine in 2022 reminded us that a peaceful solution to disputes is not always guaranteed.

While most disagreements between countries are resolved peacefully through diplomatic channels, the threat of a disagreement escalating to economic or military conflict must be continuously monitored by global investors. This chapter considers how competing national agendas and resulting geopolitical events can affect equity markets, and how investors can monitor and respond to them effectively. The severity of any given situation is dependent on the importance placed by each party on a particular issue, and the level of urgency for an outcome. Shared interests must also be considered. Issues where the desired outcomes are incompatible and deemed vital to both parties have a greater probability of escalating than those not considered vital to national interests, or where some common ground exists.

■ Types of Geopolitical Risk

In this chapter we separate geopolitical risk into two broad types: internal risks and external risks. Internal geopolitical risks originate from an individual country while external geopolitical risks emanate from the interactions of two or more countries. Internal risks include regulation, changes to restrictions on foreign ownership, and changes to tax regimes or other laws that can impact the profitability of a given business or industry. External risks include diplomatic and economic sanctions, trade wars, and, in extreme situations, military conflicts. As discussed in Chapter 3, the global supply chain also poses risks for businesses, especially in cases where companies rely heavily on outsourcing. As businesses have sought to lower costs by moving production to (or sourcing components from) lower-cost regions of the world, they expose their business operations to foreign jurisdictions and possibly to risks associated with shipping bottlenecks. Supply chain relationships can be extremely complex and may not be fully disclosed by the company, meaning that most investors will not fully comprehend the underlying risks. For example, you may invest in a company that has outsourced the production of a critical component from a firm in another country. Problems in that foreign jurisdiction could cause the firm you invested in to struggle. Similarly, if you invest in a company that has outsourced its client service functions to a foreign country, civil strife or labor disruptions in that country could cause significant difficulties for the companies you own.

To stay abreast of internal risks, investors must continuously scrutinize social and political developments in countries in which they are invested. Government policy can change quickly, and so there is a need to be aware of statements made by government authorities that could foreshadow upcoming tax or regulatory changes. Perhaps the most dramatic events result from an outright change in political leadership, where a political party comes to power with a radically different policy agenda. Social unrest is another potential precursor to significant political change. While such events often have only a modest impact on businesses, it is imperative that the global investor watch these developments closely.

Perhaps more challenging is effectively protecting your portfolio from external geopolitical risks. With an increasingly interconnected world economy comes a heightened potential for disagreements and conflicts to arise. This is primarily because countries around the world often have national interests that clash with those of other countries. In some instances, these disagreements are of small enough concern that the parties involved might be willing to overlook them. When this is not the case, there are several ways that disagreements between countries can be resolved peacefully, including through various mechanisms provided by trade agreements and the intergovernmental organizations discussed earlier. If these mechanisms fail, or if the issue exists outside of the scope of those entities, countries may have other options available to help them achieve their goals, depending largely on their comparative economic and military strength. I refer to these as the tools of international politics. When countries find themselves in a dispute, there are three main categories of tools that can be employed to achieve their goals: diplomacy, economic influence, and military coercion.

Diplomacy

The first tool usually employed by a country seeking to achieve a certain outcome while resolving a dispute with another country is diplomacy. Diplomacy is often conducted by direct contact between state officials, such as ambassadors or trade negotiators. However, as global telecommunications have evolved and made people more politically aware, influencing the citizens of other countries has become an increasingly important aspect of international relations. Convincing foreign citizens that your policies are the most desirable path for them to follow is not a new concept, but modern technology has certainly made it easier for governments to disseminate propaganda. The art of diplomacy therefore includes the use of propaganda as a key policy tool. Propaganda is often benign, where a country tries to promote a particular political cause. In its more sinister form, however, propaganda can be used to undermine the policy and political structure of a rival country, even to the point of destabilizing foreign political regimes. A former professor of mine, political scientist K. J. Holsti, noted that "[t]he officials making propaganda hope that these foreign groups or the entire population will in turn influence the attitudes and actions of their own government."[1] Propaganda can therefore be aimed at an entire population, or a specific subsegment of the population, both with the desired objective of influencing a foreign government's policy decisions. Propaganda can take many forms, including persistent and repeated advertisements of ideas and slogans.

As well, diplomatic relations are more than simply symbolic. They are a valuable commodity, providing structure and assurance of a willingness to resolve disputes peacefully, and, where possible, to the general advantage of both parties. Having an immediate presence on foreign soil in the form of an embassy or consulate therefore shows a desire from both countries to maintain good relations. When relations break down, the withdrawal of embassy or consular staff is often one of the first actions taken by governments to try and coerce the other country into a desired course of action. Breaking diplomatic relations should therefore be viewed as an extreme measure and cause investors to reassess the businesses they own in those countries. Depending on the parties involved and the reason for severing diplomatic relations, investors should consider looking for a safer investment opportunity elsewhere.

Economic Incentives

Countries that are unable to resolve conflicts through diplomacy may pursue their goals using economic incentives. Concessions on trade or other economic matters, as well as supplying economic aid, may entice the opposing country to agree with the desired settlement. Naturally, not every country is able to use economic incentives as a policy tool effectively. Wealthy countries, especially those with exceptionally large economies like China and the United States, are in the enviable position of being able to use their economic power to achieve their economic and political goals. Reducing trade tariffs, aiding the foreign country in developing its infrastructure, supplying goods or loans, and loan forgiveness are examples of economic incentives that may be used to achieve foreign policy goals.

Trade Wars and Sanctions

If economic incentives prove to be ineffective, countries may resort to economic coercion. These measures include trade wars and sanctions. A trade war involves "tit-for-tat" tariff increases which makes the exports of the target country more expensive to domestic buyers, thus reducing demand and hurting the foreign country economically. In extreme cases, this can have a dramatic effect on the economy of both countries involved. In most instances, however, tariffs are used in a tactical manner, focusing on specific industries in a move designed to force concessions from the opposing country. Tariffs are often used to cause the greatest amount of economic pain to a specific industry, with the goal of either appeasing one's domestic voting base or weakening political support for the opponent.

Escalating the use of economic coercion further would involve imposing sanctions. Economic sanctions are usually employed to achieve specific political aims, such as preventing another country from developing nuclear weapons, engaging in a military conflict, or supporting terrorist organizations. Sanctions may be reactionary and used to punish another state for an action already taken, or they may be preventive and meant to deter a specific action. There are numerous examples of sanctions being employed, often meeting with mixed results. Sanctions can target an entire country or specific individuals within a country's political regime. Freezing assets of politically influential individuals, for example, makes it difficult for them to travel or conduct financial transactions. Another form of economic sanction prevents the target state from importing certain goods, such as weapons, sensitive technology, or machine parts. Sanctions could also be designed to prevent the target country from exporting certain goods (such as oil) that it relies on to earn revenue and support the economy. The purpose of economic sanctions is to starve the targeted individuals or country of the access to critical goods or financial capital. The use of economic tools to achieve political goals is also referred to as geoeconomics.

Military Coercion

The final tool available to countries for resolving disputes is military coercion, which is the threat or use of force. In situations where one country has a clear military advantage over another, the simple threat of force may be sufficient to convince the weaker country to concede. However, the threat or use of force may have unexpected consequences, including more powerful countries coming to the defense of the weaker country, drawing ridicule on the world stage, or causing other countries to employ economic or diplomatic sanctions against the aggressor.

Figure 7.1 shows the relative military power of select countries. These rankings are based on conventional (nonnuclear) military capability, but include all countries known to possess nuclear weapons.

It is not coincidence that the world's top military powers have large economies since wealth is needed to supply and support a military establishment. Economic and military strength enable a country to exert its influence throughout a region, or even around the world. This is referred to as the country's sphere of influence, and in world politics, a country that has considerable influence or control over a large geographic region is commonly referred to as a hegemon. Hegemons have great power and are capable of using all of the tools of international relations to protect their interests and project their influence. A country that is able to exert its influence over a significant portion of the world is referred to as a superpower.

Rank	Country	Military Personnel (Thousands)	Annual Defense Budget (Billions USD)	Nuclear Warheads
1	United States	1,832	770.0	5,600
2	Russia	1,350	154.0	6,257
3	China	3,134	250.2	350
4	India	5,132	49.6	160
5	Japan	309	47.5	–
6	South Korea	1,130	46.3	–
7	France	415	40.9	290
8	United Kingdom	231	68.0	225
9	Pakistan	1,640	7.7	165
10	Brazil	2,100	18.8	–
14	Iran	1,015	5.0	–
18	Israel	646	17.8	90
30	North Korea	2,000	4.5	45

FIGURE 7.1   Countries Ranked by Military Power

Source: Adapted from Global Firepower, "2022 Military Strength Ranking," https://www.globalfirepower.com/countries-listing.php, and The Federation of American Scientists, "Status of World Nuclear Forces," https://fas.org/issues/-nuclear-weapons/status-world-nuclear-forces/, both accessed February 5, 2022.

War is one of the most terrible afflictions faced by humanity. The amount of human suffering and the destruction of property caused by conventional warfare is unimaginable for most people. All-out nuclear war would be far worse and could bring about the end of our species. For this reason, it is extremely unlikely that any country would intentionally use nuclear weapons, whose main purpose should be to deter others from attacking. Any reference to warfare in this book therefore relates to conventional (nonnuclear) warfare, and any notion of the financial markets being able to recover from a war assumes that nuclear weapons are not used. The devastation caused by nuclear weapons is so vast that the global economy and even the existence of humanity would be threatened in the event of their use.

It may come as a surprise that humanity's ability to adapt to even the most difficult circumstances means that conventional war usually has a minimal, or at least short-lived, impact on one's investments. Figure 7.2 shows the impact that wars have had on the US capital markets. The wars considered in this figure include World War II, the Korean War, the Vietnam War, and the Gulf War.

While large-cap stocks returned an average of 10.0% annually from 1926 to 2013, the return during wartime was actually slightly higher, at 11.4%. Small-cap stocks also performed slightly better than average during

	Large-Cap Stocks	Small-Cap Stocks	Long-Term Bonds	Long-Term Credit	Inflation
1926 – 2013					
Return	10.0%	11.6%	5.6%	5.9%	3.0%
Risk	19.0%	27.2%	8.4%	7.6%	
Wartime					
Return	11.4%	13.8%	2.2%	2.8%	4.4%
Risk	12.8%	20.1%	6.4%	5.5%	

FIGURE 7.2 Capital Market Performance During Wartime

Source: Adapted from Mark Armbruster, "What Happens If America Goes to War?" CFA Institute, 2013.

wartime. Not only were stock returns higher during wartime, but their level of risk (measured by the volatility of their returns) actually fell. Curiously, long-term government bonds and long-term credit (corporate bonds) generated lower returns during times of war. This may be because historically inflation has been higher during wartimes and bonds react negatively to rising inflation (bond returns are negatively correlated with inflation). Another possible explanation is that governments borrow more during wars, thus driving bond yields up and bond prices down.[2]

While the higher returns and lower risk shown by stocks during wartime may seem counterintuitive, it is often the period leading up to war and the early days of a war that uncertainty and risk are highest. Once a conflict breaks out and investors become familiar with the scope and size of the conflict, the stock market tends to recover fairly quickly. In addition, corporate earnings may actually get a boost from warfare, as governments increase spending to pay for the goods and services consumed while conducting the war.

Figure 7.3 shows how the US stock market reacted to the outbreak of the Korean War in 1950, and it illustrates how brief stock market reactions can be to war. In this case, the US stock market fell by 20.5%, technically entering into a bear market. However, the effect was short-lived, and the US stock market fully recovered to its prewar level by September 14 that same year, a mere 56 days after the war began.

The US stock market's reaction to the outbreak of the Gulf War is another example of a muted response to military conflict. The S&P 500 began to fall in July, just two weeks before Iraq's invasion of Kuwait on August 2, 1990. Once again, the market fell by slightly more than 20%, bottoming in mid-October but then fully recovering to prewar levels by February of the following year.

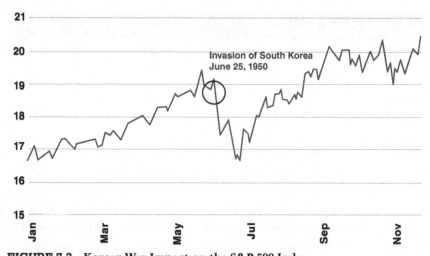

FIGURE 7.3 Korean War Impact on the S&P 500 Index
Data source: Standard & Poor's Financial Services, LLC, accessed via Bloomberg.

It is important to note that the data shown here relates to the US capital markets. Since the United States enjoys a significant economic and military advantage compared to most other countries and because the wars were fought in other parts of the world, any assessment made based on these examples may understate the effects of war on the capital markets. These wars would have had a more dramatic and enduring impact on the economies and financial markets of those countries where the war was actually being waged. The impact of war on individual stock markets will therefore depend greatly on the nature and location of the conflict and the countries involved.

■ Geopolitical Hotspots

> The geopolitical landscape is in a constant state of change and marked by areas where conflict is more likely. These areas are commonly referred to as geopolitical "hotspots"—regions where a significant disagreement between two or more countries exists and where tensions are already high. These areas deserve special attention since an accident or misstep by one country could readily escalate into a military confrontation. We supply a brief summary of each of these regions as they exist today, highlighting the countries involved.

Eastern Europe

Eastern Europe (Figure 7.4) is a focal point in the rivalry between Russia and members of the North Atlantic Treaty Organization (NATO). NATO is a military alliance that was formed in 1949 between 12 countries, including the United States, Canada, France, Italy, the United Kingdom, and several other European countries. Since that time, NATO has grown to 30 member states with numerous other countries aspiring to join the alliance, some of which are former members of the Soviet Union. As new members have joined the alliance, Russia has expressed concern over NATO's expansion eastward and tensions between the two military powers have escalated. Russia is a key supplier of energy to several NATO member countries, making the economies of both parties vulnerable to a potential conflict in the region.

While drafting the manuscript for this book, this situation deteriorated to the point that the largest conflict since World War II broke out in Europe. Russia's invasion of Ukraine on the pretense of self-defense in 2022 threatened to destabilize the entire region. Although the probability of the conflict widening to engulf more of Europe is low, there is still a risk of it escalating into a direct conflict between Russia and NATO, and thereby the United States. Both the United States and Russia know that a war between the two countries would be devastating and would increase the risk of nuclear warfare. The

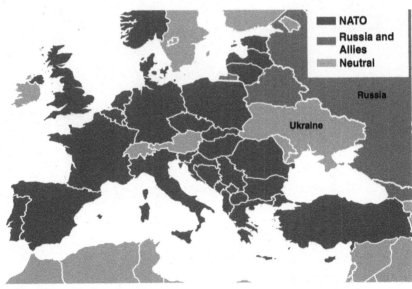

FIGURE 7.4 Eastern Europe

sanctions imposed on Russia by NATO members in response to the invasion are unprecedented and intended to apply pressure on Russian leaders to withdraw their forces from Ukraine. Russia retaliated with threats to cut off the supply of energy to Europe, which would have a significant negative impact on European and global economic growth. While higher levels of interdependence can help reduce the risk of disagreements becoming violent, it can also lead countries to underestimate how their opponents will react to the actions they take. It is clear that this is what has occurred between Russia and Western powers in 2022. Can it happen again in other regions and between different countries? Absolutely, especially when ambiguity exists and where countries do not fully understand one another's political agenda.

Iran and the Middle East

Iran (Figure 7.5) is a regional military power in the Middle East that is trying to develop nuclear weapon capability. Some Western countries see Iran as a threat to regional stability and have used economic and political sanctions, diplomacy, and propaganda in an attempt to pressure Iran into giving up on its nuclear aspirations. Iran has a strong conventional military, and some countries believe it may pose a threat to several US allies in the region, including Israel, Saudi Arabia, and the United Arab Emirates.

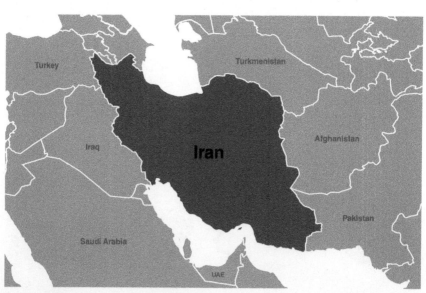

FIGURE 7.5 Iran and the Middle East

The Korean Peninsula

Like Iran, North Korea is viewed by most Western powers as a potential threat to regional stability. Although North Korea does not have the same conventional military power as Iran, it already possesses nuclear weapons. North Korea's proximity to US allies Japan and South Korea (Figure 7.6) also adds to the importance of this region on the world stage.

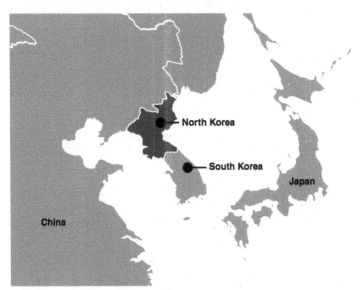

FIGURE 7.6   The Korean Peninsula

India and Pakistan

Another geopolitical hotspot is the disputed Kashmir region of India and Pakistan (Figure 7.7). Kashmir is split into two segments, one administered by each country. Skirmishes have broken out along the line of control between the two countries, resulting in some military and civilian casualties. Any one of these clashes had the potential of causing a broader military conflict. It is important to note that both Pakistan and India have strong conventional military capabilities and that they each possess nuclear weapons. Not far from Kashmir along the border between China and India, there have also been instances where Indian and Chinese forces have exchanged fire. Fortunately, none of these armed clashes has led to a major conflict.

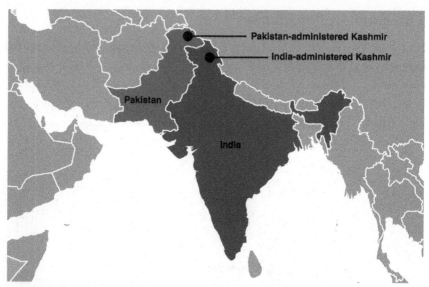

FIGURE 7.7   India and Pakistan

The South China Sea

One of the most important geopolitical regions today is centered around the South China Sea. This is where the interests of the world's first truly global superpower, the United States, come into close contact with the interests of the world's emerging superpower, China. As the evolutionary cycle evolves, the probability of conflict between the current leading power (the United States) and an emerging world power (China) become elevated. This is especially true when the emerging power increases defense spending to match its economic growth. Rapid improvements in military capability by an emerging power are often perceived as a threat to the world's current leading power. This is precisely what we see happening today, with China's emerging strength seen as a potential threat to the current world order and the leading role played in it by the United States.

For millennia, China was the dominant economic and cultural center of Asia. In fact, China's role in Asia could be equated to that of the Roman Empire in Europe. The two empires coexisted, unaware of the other's existence, but each ruling their known world at the time. China's dominance ended in the first half of the nineteenth century when it collided with the more industrialized and militarily advanced countries of Western Europe. Today, China has recovered much of its economic, political, and military power and views most of the East and South China Seas as its sovereign territory, including the Taiwan region, shown in Figure 7.8 by what is known as

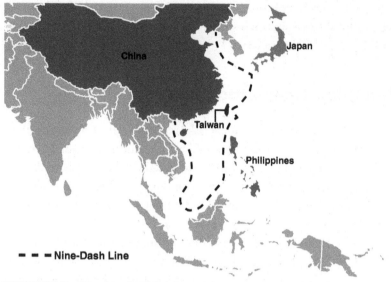

- - - Nine-Dash Line

FIGURE 7.8 The South China Sea

the "nine-dash line." This area includes smaller islands as well, some of which are claimed by competing countries, such as Japan. As we noted earlier, the South China Sea is strategically important to the global economy, with significant amounts of trade flowing through its waters. This fact, combined with defense alliances between the United States and several Asian countries, including Japan and the Philippines, places Chinese and United States' interests at odds in the region.

China views the United States as an interloper in the region, while the United States wants China to accept and adhere to the current world order that the US established out of the ashes of World War II. The United States has therefore resisted China's attempts to expand its political sphere of influence in the region. The United States often sends navy convoys to the South China Sea to ensure the freedom of navigation for foreign vessels, while China responds by sending its own naval vessels to the region to deter what it views as interference in its internal affairs. There have been several near-misses between the warships of the two countries, and there is a risk that an accident could quickly escalate and lead to a military conflict. Although the odds of a conflict between the United States and China are increasing over time, war between the two countries is not inevitable. In the words of Graham Allison, "[h]istory shows that major ruling powers can manage relations with rivals, even those that threaten to overtake them, without triggering a war."[3]

Geopolitical hotspots deserve special attention, but they do not preclude investing in businesses of the countries involved. While close calls and skirmishes will surely continue, and have the potential to develop into broader conflicts, there are some simple ways investors can limit the potential damage caused by these events.

■ Managing Geopolitical Risk

The first step to managing geopolitical risk is to stay vigilant. Investing globally requires you to stay abreast of world affairs, noting potential areas of concern as they arise and monitoring them. Based on the various tools used by countries in managing their foreign relations described previously, you must learn to recognize when a disagreement between two or more countries is likely to escalate to a point where economic or military coercion is used. Economic coercion could be as mild as symbolic trade tariffs on non-critical goods, or it could lead to all-out economic warfare, including broad-based tariffs as well as the complete suspension of trade or the imposing of economic sanctions. It is also important for investors to be aware of the geopolitical hotspots noted earlier.

How do we recognize when a situation is likely to deteriorate enough to negatively affect our investments? One simple approach to managing internal geopolitical risk is to set a minimum credit rating for each country you plan to invest in as an investment constraint. This is referred to as the country's sovereign credit rating, and it reflects the safety of investing in the country. Sovereign credit ratings are issued by a number of leading credit rating agencies and are generally available on their websites (some of which are provided at the end of the book). The major rating agencies include Fitch, Moody's, and S&P Global. Monitoring sovereign credit ratings can be a helpful tool in ensuring that the countries you have invested in remain attractive and are shareholder friendly. These credit ratings can also protect you to an extent from external geopolitical risk, although credit-rating agencies may not adjust their ratings quickly enough to account for a confrontation that is rapidly escalating. For that reason, it is important to watch propaganda and political statements issued by countries whose actions could affect the businesses in which you have invested. Where disputes between countries arise, it is vital that you keep an eye on those issues and, if a military conflict is likely, avoid investing in companies that are domiciled in the countries involved. This is especially true when a military confrontation is likely to inflict considerable damage to a country's economy. In situations where a conflict is possible but the expected impact to your portfolio is minor your best bet is to stay the course and continue to focus on the fundamentals of the businesses you own.

Geopolitical risk may also be mitigated by ensuring that your portfolio is properly diversified and that you own businesses that are not overly exposed or reliant on a region or country whose economy is at risk of wars or other geopolitical events. Proper portfolio construction (discussed in Chapter 20) is a critical part of risk mitigation and successful investing, and we continue advancing toward that goal now by looking more closely at how to identify and analyze good businesses from around the world.

Chapter 7 Highlights

Internal geopolitical risks originate from an individual country while external geopolitical risks emanate from the interactions of two or more countries. Internal risks include regulation, changes to restrictions on foreign ownership, and changes to tax regimes or other laws that may affect business fundamentals. External risks include diplomatic and economic sanctions, trade wars, and, in extreme situations, military conflicts. With an increasingly interconnected world economy comes a heightened potential for disagreements and conflicts to arise. Disagreements between countries are often resolved through trade agreements and intergovernmental organizations. If these mechanisms fail, countries may employ the tools of international politics: diplomacy, economic influence, and military coercion. Investors must monitor geopolitical hotspots—regions where a significant disagreement between two or more countries exists and where the possibility of economic or military conflict is high. While war is perhaps the greatest affliction facing humanity, people's ability to adapt to even the most difficult circumstances means that conventional war usually has a minimal, or at least short-lived, impact on one's investments. Setting a minimum sovereign credit rating and diversifying your portfolio by country and region is the most effective way of mitigating geopolitical risk.

PART IV

Buying Global Businesses

CHAPTER 8

Company Analysis

In Chapter 1 we discussed the characteristics of a good business. Good businesses operate in growing industries with relatively predictable pricing, hold a dominant and defensible position within that industry, and have a strong balance sheet, an astute management team, and a positive image in society. The characteristics of a good business can be further broken down into profitability, earnings sustainability, balance sheet strength, growth prospects, investment risks, and valuation. We now take a deeper look at each of these in detail.

■ Profitability

Profitability can vary significantly between distinct types of businesses. The amount of money needed to operate a business (its capital intensity), the required level of technical expertise, economies of scale in manufacturing or distribution, and brand recognition, product differentiation, and degree of competition in the industry all help determine a company's profitability. Differentiated products are those that have specific features that distinguish them from competing products and make them more desirable. The perception of scarcity or superiority typically allows businesses to earn higher profits on those goods. Often this is achieved through better functionality or quality, but differentiation can also be derived from brand name recognition.

Luxury goods retailers are an excellent example of businesses that generate higher profits due to the perception of scarcity. Consumers who believe that these goods are of higher quality or that they are proof of one's success are often willing to pay higher prices for them. Businesses that produce goods that are not differentiated in some way and that face intense competition tend to generate lower profits. Businesses that offer common products that are easily substituted or replicated (often referred to as commoditized products) typically compensate for the lower profitability of each unit sold by selling large quantities of them.

There are exceptions to these rules, where some combination of the above factors results in high levels of profitability. For instance, industries that require low levels of capital investment but require advanced technological knowledge often produce remarkably high profit margins. Software developers, for example, tend to generate high profit margins due to a mix of lower capital requirements and unique product features that often deliver productivity gains for customers. While a competitor may not need significant financial capital to enter the software market, producing a software platform that is superior to others in the market requires advanced knowledge. Industries that are less competitive or whose products require advanced manufacturing ability also tend to generate higher levels of profitability.

Good businesses distinguish themselves through superior profitability. Profitability can be measured in several ways, but two of the most common measures are net income margin (also referred to here as profit margin) and return on equity (ROE). Net income margin is the company's final income (after all accounting adjustments) as a percentage of revenue. ROE is also based on a company's final (net) income but expressed as a percentage of shareholder equity. Unfortunately, these measures are heavily influenced by a company's capital structure (how much debt it has versus how much equity shareholders have accumulated in the firm), as well as by the accounting methods used by the company. Although simple to calculate, these measures may be misleading and prevent them from being truly representative of a company's profitability.

Alternative measures for assessing profitability include return on invested capital (ROIC) and EBITDA margin. ROIC is calculated by dividing net operating profit after tax by invested capital, while EBITDA margin is equal to earnings before interest, taxes, depreciation, and amortization (EBITDA) as a percentage of revenue. In certain respects, both ROIC and EBITDA margin may be cleaner measures of profitability because they are less susceptible to accounting manipulation. The general idea for ROIC is that if a company's rate of return on the capital it invests is higher than the cost of obtaining that capital (known as the weighted average cost of capital, or WACC), value is being created for shareholders. The difficulty in relying on these measures is that they ignore taxes and interest charges, which have an exceptionally large impact on profitability for most publicly traded businesses. A thorough analysis would also include intermediate measures of profitability, such as operating margins, as these can provide helpful insights into the company's financial and operational position.

It is important to remember that levels of profitability can differ significantly between industries. Businesses that require a lower level of assets (referred to as being asset-light), such as software companies, will often have higher profit margins than those requiring a higher level of assets, such as a utility company. For some industries, the standard measures of profitability may not be suitable. We noted earlier that when analyzing banks, for example, the most common indicator of profitability is net interest margin, which measures net interest received divided by the bank's interest-generating assets.

One way to overcome the shortfalls inherent in the measures of profitability just discussed is to conduct a DuPont analysis. DuPont analysis works by breaking down ROE into its five individual components, namely the tax burden, interest burden, EBIT margin, total asset turnover, and leverage as shown in the following formula:

DuPont Analysis

$$\text{ROE} = \frac{\text{Net income}}{\text{Average shareholder equity}} = \underbrace{\frac{\text{Net income}}{\text{EBT}}}_{(\text{tax burden})} \times \underbrace{\frac{\text{EBT}}{\text{EBIT}}}_{(\text{interest burden})}$$

$$\times \underbrace{\frac{\text{EBIT}}{\text{Revenue}}}_{(\text{EBIT margin})} \times \underbrace{\frac{\text{Revenue}}{\text{Average total assets}}}_{(\text{asset turnover})} \times \underbrace{\frac{\text{Average total assets}}{\text{Average shareholder equity}}}_{(\text{leverage})}$$

Note that EBT means earnings before tax and EBIT means earnings before interest and tax. By breaking out these individual components of ROE, we can develop a better understanding of what is driving a company's profitability. Collectively, these ratios measure profitability while accounting for the company's operational efficiency and financial structure. It is also helpful to compare a company's profitability to the industry average or its closest competitors. All of the data needed to conduct a DuPont analysis can typically be found in the company's financial statements.

Finally, it is necessary to look at the trend in a company's profitability. Falling profit margins could be a sign that a company is being run inefficiently, experiencing cost pressures, or facing increased competition. A good example of this is the emergence of the internet and the impact it had on the printed newspaper industry. With consumers increasingly able to gather news from the internet, newspaper publishers faced a serious threat to their long-term viability. As print subscriber numbers began to fall, profitability across the industry declined. Figure 8.1 shows the declining trend in profitability and subsequent effect on share price for the New York Times Company.

The company's profitability, measured by ROIC, fell from a high of nearly 27% in December 2004 to a low of –20% in September 2007. Combined with the global financial crisis, this drop in profitability caused the company's share price to fall by 93.5%, plummeting from a high of $53 in mid-2002 until it finally bottomed in February 2009 at a price of $3.44. You will also notice that the share price began to drop before the company's profitability declined meaningfully, suggesting that investors were able to predict the reduction in the newspaper industry's near-term profitability and began selling the shares before it happened. Fortunately, the management team at the *New York Times* was able to transform the company over time, enabling it to compete effectively in the digital age, after which the share price fully recovered. You will also note that as the company recovered, profitability led the share price higher, suggesting that investors incorrectly believed that management could not reposition the company and restore profitability.

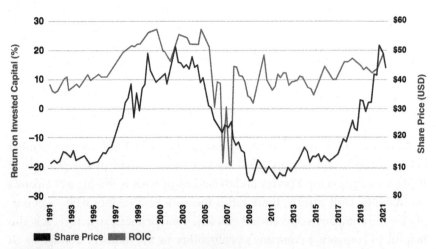

FIGURE 8.1   The New York Times Company
Data source: Bloomberg and Yahoo Finance, as of September 30, 2021.

■ Earnings Sustainability

Finding companies that can generate above-average levels of profitability in their industry is a good starting point, but you should also be confident that the company can continue to sustain an elevated level of earnings power into the future. An investor must have a thorough understanding of industry dynamics to estimate the future earnings growth of an industry and the companies that operate in it. This includes the likelihood of new technologies being developed and whether those advances are achieved by the business you own or by a competitor. New entrants can disrupt industries and make the competitive advantages of the current industry leaders obsolete. This is especially true where margins are abnormally high and barriers to entry comparatively low, as these industries will attract greater competition. Less competitive industries, where companies generate moderate but reliable earnings streams, may make a better long-term investment than companies in industries that produce high margins but are extremely competitive.

The trend in profit margins for a company can supply valuable insights into earnings sustainability. Reviewing the past few years of ROE, operating and EBITDA margins, for example, can show how strong the company's business is and may reveal problems as they emerge, allowing you to sell the stock early and avoid a significant loss. If margins are trending downward, it is particularly important to understand why. Increasing competition or other factors may be affecting the industry's profitability, or the company in question could be losing operational efficiency. If the share price already reflects this bad news, there may be an opportunity to invest if management has a plan to address the reduction in margins and improve profitability. The only way to gauge a company's earnings sustainability is through due diligence, including potentially speaking to management or the company's investor relations department to learn whether they are aware of the problem and how they plan to address it. If the management team is not aware of the issue or does not seem concerned, you should reevaluate your investment in the business.

■ Balance Sheet Strength

When investors say a company has a strong balance sheet, they are referring to the company's capital structure, specifically the amount of debt the company owes versus the amount of equity that has been accumulated by shareholders in the firm. The capital structure of a company can have a significant impact on earnings in different economic environments, and affect its share price at different stages of the market cycle. There can be certain tax advantages for companies to have some debt, and debt may be required periodically to fund and grow the business. However, relying on a high level of debt can spell trouble for companies during tough economic times because lenders begin to charge a higher interest rate to compensate for the increased level of risk. This can make it difficult for companies to refinance their debt, potentially causing them to default on their loan obligations. This risk is heightened in the event of a liquidity crisis.

A liquidity crisis occurs when the supply of money in the economy (liquidity) dries up and there is insufficient capital available to allow the financial system to operate effectively. If steps are not taken to provide adequate liquidity to the financial system, a liquidity crisis can quickly evolve into a credit crisis when banks and other lenders collectively stop lending money for fear of not being repaid. Liquidity crises developed in 2008 and again in the early days of the 2020 global pandemic. In the case of the 2020 pandemic, central banks were able to avert a credit crisis by pumping tremendous amounts of liquidity into the global financial system. In 2008 a slower response by central banks to the drop in liquidity gave way to a credit crisis where firms with higher levels of debt were not able to borrow money or refinance their debt and many of these businesses went bankrupt as a result. These factors led to the global financial crisis.

A commonly used measure for balance sheet health is the net debt-to-shareholder equity ratio. This is calculated by adding short-term debt plus long-term debt, subtracting liquid assets (such as cash and investments that can be sold quickly), and then dividing this number by shareholder equity. A strong balance sheet is characterized by low levels of debt compared to shareholder's equity. A quick review of a company's financial statements will reveal how much short-term and long-term debt the company holds, as well as cash and other short-term investments and shareholder equity. Comparing these figures to a company's peers is an effective way to quickly assess whether a company deserves closer analysis, and if so, the investor must delve further into the balance sheet and consider off-balance-sheet items. Off-balance-sheet items (OBSIs) include assets and liabilities attributed to the company but that are not shown on the balance sheet. Examples may include operating leases, certain accounts receivable, contingent liabilities, joint ventures, financial guarantees, or letters of credit.

Other useful measures include the interest coverage ratio, which compares the interest paid on debt by the company as a percentage of net income.

The higher the interest coverage ratio, the better. The more debt a company has and the higher the rate of interest paid on that debt, the more problematic it becomes. Low net debt-to-equity and high interest coverage ratios are preferred, but they must be viewed in the context of the industry in which the company operates. Higher-growth firms in the technology sector, for example, will often have little or no debt, while providers of electric or water utilities may have substantial amounts of debt. Both types of businesses can be beneficial to investors at different points in the market cycle and may complement one another in a well-diversified portfolio.

Mature companies can often increase their after-tax return to shareholders by issuing debt and so there may be instances when it makes financial sense for a company to carry more debt on its balance sheet. As well, a company may wish to finance a strategic acquisition that improves its long-term profitability by issuing debt. Assessing a company's debt structure is best accomplished by comparing its balance sheet to those of other companies in the same industry and looking through notes to the financial statements in order to identify OBSIs. As an investor, you must decide whether these items should be included in the net debt-to-shareholder equity calculation.

■ Growth Prospects

Most businesses constantly strive to grow, whether through increased sales, profits, or both. Future expected growth is an important determinant of a company's current value. The most common approach to analyzing growth is to estimate the future cash flows of the company and then to discount (reduce) those cash flows to arrive at an estimate of the value for the shares in today's terms. The reason for discounting future cash flows is simple: $1.00 of earnings generated 10 years from now is worth less than $1.00 of earnings today. Inflation erodes the value of money since goods will cost more in the future, and there is an opportunity cost for delaying the receipt of earnings, because money received today could be invested and used to generate additional returns.

For some companies, expected earnings growth represents most of the value reflected in its current share price, even though that future growth is not guaranteed. In fact, of all the aspects of a business we need to assess as investors, the prospects for future earnings growth are the most difficult to accurately forecast. Many variables affect a company's ability to grow that are outside management's control. A factor that will affect a company's earnings power in the future may not even exist at the time an investment is made. For example, a company may launch an innovative new product that disrupts the industry, rapidly taking market share from competitors. This competitive advantage could last for decades, or it could be displaced by a competing product shortly thereafter. Regulations are another potential change that occurs outside of management's control. An industry that is very profitable could suddenly become less appealing if the government changed the rules in a way that reduces its after-tax profitability.

■ Investment Risk

Investment risk is an important consideration when making any investment decision. Most people view investment risk as the possibility of losing money. There are countless ways you can lose money on an investment, even if your logic for making the investment is sound. Investment risk can be broken down into two broad categories. The first relates to factors that fundamentally affect the operations of the business, while the second results from the behavior of the company's share price. If the stock market were efficient, a company's share price would always reflect the fundamentals of the business, trading at a price that equals the fair or intrinsic (true) value of the company. However, a company's share price frequently differs from its business fundamentals.

Fundamental business risk refers to events that may adversely impact the operations of the business, thereby lowering the long-term earnings power and value of the company. All businesses face risks to their fundamentals, and these vary significantly by industry and region. Anything affecting a company's balance sheet, growth prospects, sales, or profitability could be considered a risk to business fundamentals. Summarized in Figure 8.2 are important fundamental factors that are relevant to all companies that investors should monitor. In cases where a meaningful change occurs or the company's fundamentals are deteriorating, it is important for investors to understand what caused the change and how it may affect the company going forward.

For investors, risk is most often measured in terms of how much a company's stock price fluctuates (known as its standard deviation or volatility), or how much the share price changes compared to a relevant index or benchmark (referred to as the stock's beta). For example, a stock with a beta of 1.2 means that for every 1% change in the index (up or down), the stock would likely move 1.2% in the same direction. Stocks with a beta of 1.0

What to Watch For	Potential Problem
Rising expense ratios	Costs are not being controlled
Rising debt levels	Debt is being used to pay dividends or fund liabilities due to a lack of cash flow, or used to make subpar investments
Rising accounts receivable	May indicate financial deterioration of customer base as they take longer to pay for goods/services delivered by the company
Rising inventory levels	Demand may be falling, sales are being lost to a competitor, or near-term customer demand has been fully met
Insider selling	Could indicate near-term problems that will hurt earnings, or that the shares are overpriced
Change of auditor	Auditors may resign if they detect any wrongdoings or flaws in accounting controls
Executive changes	Loss of key management can hinder or impair a business

FIGURE 8.2   Potential Signs of Weakening Business Fundamentals

generally move in line with the index, while stocks with a beta below 1.0 move less and are therefore considered to be defensive in nature. Examples of stocks with (typically) low betas are the shares of utilities or companies that produce consumer goods, like soap and toothpaste. Stocks with high betas tend to be higher-growth companies such as technology companies, as well as those whose businesses are more cyclical in nature, like energy and mining companies. There are times in the business cycle when owning high-beta companies is beneficial, and times when owning them can cause large losses. I refer to stock beta and standard deviation collectively hereafter as share price volatility.

Another consideration is how the share prices of the businesses you own move in relation to one another. This is known as correlation. Stocks whose prices move in a similar manner are said to be positively correlated, while those that move in the opposite direction are said to be negatively correlated. When two or more share prices move in a purely random fashion relative to one another, they are said to be uncorrelated. Owning several companies that are positively correlated (their share prices tend to move together in the same direction) does not provide the same diversification benefits as investing in several companies that operate in different industries and that do not move in tandem during market cycles. Correlation and the benefits of diversification are particularly important considerations when constructing an investment portfolio, as discussed in Chapter 20.

The importance of owning stocks that are uncorrelated or negatively correlated is illustrated in the example shown in Figure 8.3. Here, we compare owning a portfolio consisting only of banks and energy stocks to owning a broad stock market index. Figure 8.3 shows how one dollar invested equally

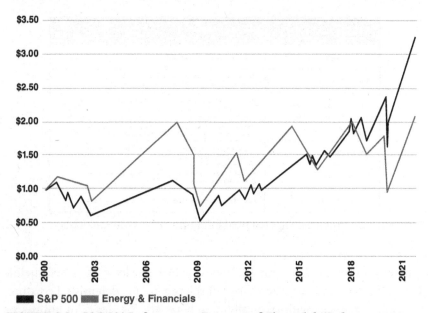

FIGURE 8.3   S&P 500 Index versus Energy and Financials Only
Data sources: Yahoo Finance and Standard & Poor's Financial Services LLC, sourced via Bloomberg.

in only energy and financial stocks would have performed compared to investing the same dollar in the S&P 500 Index.

As you can see from the figure, there were periods (2000–2007 in particular) when holding the more concentrated portfolio consisting only of energy and financials would have been rewarding. However, over the full time period investors were better off holding the more diversified portfolio, which would have also included holdings in technology, healthcare, and industrials (among others) since it fluctuated less in value. Compared to the concentrated portfolio, share prices for the S&P 500 Index fell less in 2007–2009 and 2018, reflecting the fact that the S&P 500 Index consists partially of stocks whose share prices are uncorrelated. Keep in mind that for long-term investors, short-term fluctuations in share prices should be less concerning and in fact provide opportunities for patient investors to add to their holdings. Patience and the ability to withstand short-term price drops, buying when share prices fall and selling when share prices become expensive, are perhaps the most requisite skills for achieving long-term investment success. In addition to the investment risks outlined earlier, companies that operate globally are also subject to risks related to market cycles, currency fluctuations, and geopolitics, which we discussed in detail in Chapters 5, 6, and 7.

■ Valuation

How much you pay for a company, regardless of whether you are buying only a few shares or the entire business, is critical to a successful investment. Throughout history, investors are repeatedly fooled into thinking that price does not matter and that someone else will come along and pay more for their shares at an even higher price. History has proven repeatedly that this so-called "greater fool theory" is unsustainable in the long term. Betting that someone will eventually pay more for an asset you own, regardless of price, is one of the greatest mistakes an investor can make. Intrinsic value matters and in the end, prices will reflect economic reality and business fundamentals. Figure 8.4 shows that the price you pay for a business today will affect your future investment returns. This chart shows the 10-year future return for the S&P 500 Index for each quarter from 1954 through 2011 based on the price-to-earnings ratio of the Index.

The downward-sloping line shows the relationship between stock market valuation and forward 10-year returns. It demonstrates that the best investment returns are generated by buying companies when they are inexpensive. Paying too much for a business today may make it difficult or impossible to generate a reasonable return on your investment, even over many years. In fact, when valuations are expensive, there is a significant probability the next 10 years could result in a loss on your investment.

Valuation can be measured several ways. The most widely used metric is the price-to-earnings (P/E) ratio, which is appealing because of its simplicity. Unfortunately, this ratio uses as the denominator the company's reported

FIGURE 8.4 S&P Valuation versus Future 10-Year Return, 1954–2011
Data source: Standard & Poor's Financial Services LLC, sourced via Bloomberg, as of November 2021.

earnings, which can be manipulated by unscrupulous management teams and may also be distorted by a firm's capital structure or accounting methods. Another, perhaps cleaner, measure of valuation is the price-to-sales (P/S) ratio. This ratio is easy to calculate like the P/E ratio, but it is less prone to manipulation because a company's sales or revenues are less subject to accounting manipulation. However, while it is usually more difficult for a company to manipulate its sales numbers, it is not impossible. Nevertheless, comparing the current price-to-sales ratio of a company's shares to historical values can be a useful exercise when assessing a company's valuation. Unfortunately, some companies may choose to grow revenue at the expense of profitability, for example, by cutting prices in order to gain market share from competitors. The P/S ratio therefore does not provide any insights into the quality of revenue growth. Investors should always understand why a company appears to be expensive or inexpensive before deciding to invest.

Enterprise value (which is equal to stock market capitalization plus total debt minus cash and equivalents) to EBITDA is another potentially useful measure of a company's valuation. This ratio approximates the total value of the company to how much cash flow it generates. It is therefore less subject to manipulation than the P/E ratio and, unlike the P/S ratio, considers the operational efficiency of the business. As with all valuation metrics, it helps to look at how current EV/EBITDA values compare to historical levels, the firm's competitors, and the broader stock market.

The price-to–cash flow (P/CF) ratio is another widely accepted measure of valuation. The benefits of using P/CF over P/E or P/S to value a company are similar to that of EV/EBITDA. The key difference between EV/EBITDA and P/CF is that P/CF considers interest payments, taxes, and investment income in its analysis. This is especially important when analyzing companies with different levels of debt or that require large amounts of fixed capital investment. High levels of debt result in higher interest expense, while higher fixed costs (plant and equipment) increase amortization expense. A variation of P/CF is price to free cash flow (P/FCF), which subtracts capital expenditures from cash flow to arrive at an estimate of the amount of cash available to pay dividends and repurchase shares. Free cash flow is therefore the cash flows available to shareholders of the company after all working capital and capital expenditure requirements have been met. The calculation of a company's price-to–cash flow ratio can be done by dividing its share price by its cash flow per share, which is generally found in the statement of cash flows from the company's most recent financial report. Where a per-share amount is not readily available, the investor must divide total cash flow by the number of shares outstanding to arrive at a per-share cash flow amount. These financial reports can generally be obtained from regulatory filings or the company's website. For these reasons, using P/CF or P/FCF for valuing companies is often preferable to P/E or P/S; however, assessing valuation using all of these ratios can provide helpful insights into the inner workings and health of the business.

Valuation should always be considered in the context of market conditions and company fundamentals. Dramatic changes in the P/E or P/CF ratios could be the result of a temporary drop or spike in earnings or cash flow. A sudden drop in earnings due to one-time events, for example, could cause the P/E ratio to increase significantly because the price of the security may not have changed, while the earnings have temporarily vanished. Looking at a specific point in time, especially at a single measure of valuation, may lead investors to an incorrect assessment of the company's valuation. For this reason, valuation should always be considered in relation to the stock's historical averages as well as the company's closest competitors and to the overall market. It also pays to read the Manager Discussion and Analysis (MD&A) section within the company's annual report as well as the notes to the financial statements. While some companies publish reports only annually, many companies publish quarterly reports as well, so it is best to obtain all reports issued by the company over the past few years.

Whether a stock trades below or above the market average (the average valuation for all publicly traded companies in their respective market) depends on a few key factors, shown in the following relative valuation matrix in Figure 8.5. The relative placement of a company for each factor should indicate whether its shares are likely to trade above or below the average valuation for the market.

Low Valuation —————————————————————————— High Valuation

Low	Growth rate versus its industry and the market	High
Low	Profitability versus its industry and the market	High
Low	Predictability of earnings versus the market	High
High	Debt levels versus its industry and the market	Low
High	Degree of geopolitical risk	Low

FIGURE 8.5 Relative Valuation Matrix

Companies that operate in stable political and economic environments, are growing faster, generate above-average levels of profitability, have a history of producing consistent earnings, pay attractive dividends, and do not have excessive debt tend to trade at valuation multiples above that of the average stock in the market. Conversely, companies that are growing slower and operating in unstable environments, generate below-average profitability and unpredictable earnings, and have a high level of debt tend to trade at below-average valuations.

One challenge to thinking about valuation lies in the fact that when most investors buy shares in a company, it is for a relatively small amount of money, or at least a small ownership stake in the business. There is also a tendency to equate price with value, but in reality, a stock trading at a price of $5 could be vastly more expensive than a stock trading at a price of $200. Price does not equal value when it comes to equity investing. It also becomes easier to downplay the importance of valuation when only investing a few hundred or a few thousand dollars, and it is also a natural human tendency to want to own a larger number of shares, so getting 200 shares versus five shares for a $1,000 investment sounds more appealing. To avoid making these mistakes, evaluate every investment you make as if you were buying the entire business, regardless of share price.

A fitting example of the importance of valuation is former Canadian technology firm Nortel Networks. From the time it began trading as a public company in 1983 to the peak of the technology bubble in 2000, Nortel's share price rose from 18 CAD to a high of 1,220 CAD, as shown in Figure 8.6. In 10 short years, the company went from being valued at $6.5 billion to $363.8 billion in August 2000. The company's share price benefited from the technology boom of the late 1990s, when investors ignored business fundamentals and anything technology-related rose in value. A lack of innovation and mismanagement caused Nortel's business fundamentals to deteriorate. Reality eventually set in and the tech bubble burst, causing Nortel's share price to collapse and reach a low of 0.185 CAD before the shares were finally delisted from the stock exchange.

For several years, Nortel was a stock market darling. Investment managers who did not own the company's shares had a tough time explaining to clients why they missed such a great opportunity. After the technology bubble burst, the tables turned and investment managers who had invested heavily in Nortel at sky-high valuations were the ones having to explain their decisions to clients.

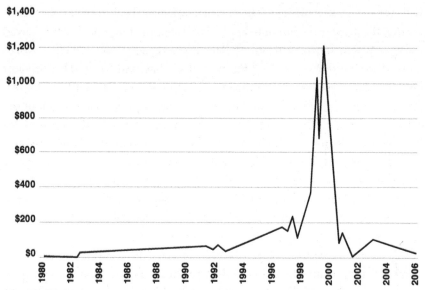

FIGURE 8.6 Nortel Networks Share Price, in CAD (Canadian dollars)
Data source: Bloomberg, as of November 13, 2021.

■ Estimating Share Value

Analysts most often estimate the fair (intrinsic) value of a company's common shares using either an absolute or a relative approach. Estimating share price in relative terms involves calculating financial ratios and comparing the results to historical values, close competitors, and the overall stock market. Valuation methods aimed at deriving an absolute (target) share price are based on a company's ability to generate cash flows for shareholders.

Absolute Valuation

There are several different methods used by investors to estimate the absolute value of a company's shares, each with its own pros and cons. One common approach is to estimate the future unlevered free cash flows (UFCFs) generated by the business, and then discount them to arrive at a current value. A company's UFCF is equal to:

UFCF = EBITDA – Capital expenditures – Change in net working capital

Expected UFCFs are discounted (divided by an appropriate interest rate) to account for the time value of money and for the risk that these cash flows will not occur as expected. The further out into the future the cash flow occurs, the greater the discount applied to it. Simply put, one dollar received today is worth more than one dollar received next year, which is worth more than one dollar received the year after that, and so on. The discount rate should consider the company's weighted average cost of capital (WACC), but also any other factors that increase or decrease the risk of the company realizing those cash flows. The more uncertain the future cash flows of a company are, the higher the discount rate used. Higher discount rates are therefore often used for smaller companies, businesses in emerging industries, companies with a lot of debt, and sometimes in cases where a single entity, family, or individual controls a majority of the voting rights. Not only are the company's future cash flows uncertain, but the resulting target price is extremely sensitive to the discount rate.

Figure 8.7 provides a basic example of how to discount the free cash flows for a company, assuming end-of-year cash flows. Readers will note that the current year's UFCF is not discounted in this example, which indicates that it is the end of the current year. A 10% discount rate (r) is used in this example to simplify the calculation, but investors should carefully consider the risks and uncertainties of the company's cash flows before deciding on the discount rate to use. Importantly, the final year's cash flow also includes the terminal value of the shares, which is the cash flow the investor expects to receive upon the sale of the shares. To arrive at the discounted UFCF per share, we divide the annual UFCF per share by the discount factor for that year.

Adding these together we calculate the current value of the company's future free cash flows to be €5.00 + €5.23 + €5.37 + €5.07 + €4.78 + €35.70 = €61.15. From this amount we must subtract net debt to arrive at a fair value estimate of the company's shares. Net debt is equal to the value of non-operating assets (such as an investment in another company) minus debt and other non-equity claims. In this example, if we assume the company has non-operating assets per share of €5.00 and debt of €2.00 per

	Current Year (CY)	CY+1	CY+2	CY+3	CY+4	CY+5
UFCF per Share (€)	5.00	5.75	6.50	6.75	7.00	57.00
Earnings per Share (€)	2.25	2.85	3.10	3.25	3.50	3.90
Discount Factor	–	1.10	$(1.10)^2$	$(1.10)^3$	$(1.10)^4$	$(1.10)^5$
Discounted FCF (€)	5.00	5.23	5.37	5.07	4.78	35.70

FIGURE 8.7 Discounted Cash Flow Example

share, the estimated fair value for the shares would be €61.15 + €5.00 − €2.00 = €64.15. In theory, if the shares are trading below the €64.15 fair value estimate, the investor could buy the shares and generate a positive return. If per-share data is not available, investors must make this calculation using data for the entire company and then divide the end result by the total number of shares outstanding to arrive at a per-share price. For companies that consistently pay dividends, investors may instead employ a dividend discount model. The formulas used to calculate discounted cash flows or dividends are readily available on financial and investing websites.

Relative Valuation

Relative valuation methods estimate the fair value of a company's shares by applying a multiple to one of its financial metrics, including current or expected earnings, sales, or cash flow. These ratios are often based on the average multiple of competitors, the broad stock market, or historical values for the company. These approaches are commonly known as multiplier models. Using the data from the earlier example, if we apply a 10 times P/FCF multiple to the expected free cash flows, we arrive at a fair value estimate next year (CY+1) of €5.75 × 10 = €57.50, and €6.50 × 10 = €65.00 in two years (CY+2). Similarly, we could apply a price-to-earnings multiple to our estimated earnings per share to arrive at a future estimate of the share price. If we employ a P/E ratio of 20 times, the target price for one year from now would be €2.85 × 20 = €57.00 and for two years out the target price would be €3.10 × 20 = €62. The variability of results achieved using different approaches means that it is most helpful to use a combination of methods to estimate fair value, including discount models as well as multiplier models based on different metrics, such as earnings, sales, or cash flow.

Assessing whether a company is inexpensive enough to buy is often difficult. At market extremes, the answer may be obvious for the seasoned investor, but when sentiment is not at an extreme, estimating the fair value of a company is highly subjective. It is therefore best to consider valuation both in absolute and relative terms, comparing where the stock's current valuation metrics stand compared to your fair value estimate, the market, and to where it has traded in the past. Comparing the company's valuation to its closest competitors is also critical. Finally, companies in different industries are often assessed using different valuation metrics to better account for the operational realities of the business. In fact, for conglomerates and other large companies that operate in multiple industries, a sum-of-the-parts analysis may be the best approach to assessing valuation. A sum-of-the-parts analysis involves valuing each major business segment individually using the appropriate valuation metric for that industry, and then adding them to arrive at a total valuation for the company. We address these unique situations when we discuss global industries in Part Five.

Social Factors

Another area of growing importance to investors is a company's environmental, social, and governance (ESG) characteristics. The exponential growth of the internet has allowed the global exchange of information to flourish. It is common now to see environmental calamities and political upheaval as they occur in distant parts of the world in real time. Younger generations of investors are becoming increasingly aware of how businesses from around the world behave and may avoid doing business with or investing in companies that are socially or environmentally irresponsible. Good governance, which is also becoming increasingly important, requires that the board of directors controlling the company have their interests aligned with shareholders and that the composition of the board is diverse in terms of gender, race, and ethnicity. The growing expectation that businesses must act in a socially responsible manner has therefore made ESG considerations critically important to company boards. Being perceived as uncaring on environmental issues such as climate change or social issues can cost a business its customers and affect a company's long-term business fundamentals. Medium- to long-term impacts of climate change could also affect the viability of a company due to the effects of severe weather, flooding, and fires in locations in which the company operates, causing the value of the company's assets to decline. Therefore, it is essential to consider the impact of ESG factors on the company's viability. Even if you are not concerned about environmental, social, or governance issues personally, having a poor ESG rating could negatively impact a company's business prospects and share price.

Companies are increasing disclosures of their ESG policies and initiatives, but it is incumbent upon investors to discern whether these claims are legitimate. Fortunately, there are an increasing number of presumably independent businesses that assess the ESG policies of public companies and provide ratings for each business they analyze. Unfortunately, ESG ratings are not yet standardized, and in fact some areas of the field continue to evolve. For example, standards for climate change are still being developed. In addition, the impact of diversity on returns is not understood. Current diversity reporting focuses on outward signs of diversity so there is a risk of an actual lack of diversity in ideas. The major providers of ESG ratings for companies include S&P Global, Sustainalytics, Bloomberg, Thompson Reuters, ISS, MSCI, Dow Jones, and RepRisk. Most of these require a paid subscription to access, but your broker or trading platform may be able to provide ESG data to you at little or no cost. If not, a little extra research may be needed for you to decide whether a company has acceptable ESG policies in place.

Returning Capital to Shareholders

As noted earlier, perhaps the most important factor to consider when analyzing a business is the management team. The best companies have strong management teams whose compensation is structured in a way that promotes shareholder interests. This also means that the best management teams are effective stewards of investor capital. Periodically, management teams will find themselves with no attractive reinvestment opportunities and it is therefore critical that they make good choices about the use of cash being generated by the business. As industries mature, they become saturated and eventually consolidate until they are dominated by only a few large companies. Once these businesses have captured the addressable market entirely and can no longer buy competitors, they must find new sources of revenue in order to continue growing faster than the economy. Investors should be wary of management teams that buy other businesses purely for the sake of growth. Dedicating enormous amounts of capital to new endeavors and acquisitions must make sense for current shareholders. Astute management teams will recognize when there is a lack of prudent investment opportunities available and will instead choose to return excess cash to shareholders, either by issuing dividends or buying back stock. The latter is also known as a share repurchase and benefits shareholders in a comparable way to a dividend. Since repurchased shares are no longer a claim of ownership of the company's earnings, each remaining shareholder receives a slightly bigger piece of the pie as the total number of shares outstanding falls, causing earnings per share to rise. In addition to being visionaries in their industry, great management teams therefore have the ability to navigate a company through tough economic times and recognize when they should return capital to shareholders.

Assessing Acquisitions

Businesses can grow either organically (by investing in themselves) or through mergers and acquisitions. As an active investor, you will no doubt find yourself in a position where a business you own acquires, or is acquired by, another company. If the business you own is the company being acquired (the target), the thought process is relatively simple. If you believe the terms and price being paid is fair, you can simply agree to surrender your shares to the acquiring company in exchange for the offered price. Although acquisitions are often made entirely with cash, the price paid may be comprised of both cash and shares of the acquirer. In cases where shares of the acquiring company are being offered as compensation, investors must assess whether they want to continue to be an owner of the new business entity.

When an acquisition is announced, the share price of the target company usually jumps to a level close to the stated purchase price. If there is some doubt that the transaction will proceed, the share price may remain at a discount to the announced purchase price and slowly climb as it becomes clear the acquisition will be approved by regulators and shareholders. As an investor, you will have to decide whether it makes sense to continue holding shares of the target company, or to simply sell them in the open market and invest the proceeds in another business. This decision will depend on the current discount to the purchase price, the expected time needed to close the acquisition, as well as the availability of other investment opportunities. Keep in mind that acquisitions may require approval from more than one regulatory body, especially when they involve companies that operate in multiple countries.

If you own the acquiring business, the process of assessing the acquisition is more complex. You must determine whether the management team you have entrusted with your money is making a sound investment and whether the price they are paying is reasonable. As an owner of the company making the acquisition, investors should determine whether the acquisition is accretive and causes earnings per share (EPS) to rise, or dilutive and causes EPS to fall, if there are strategic benefits for the acquiring firm (such as giving it access to new customers or essential new technology), whether cost savings will be realized from merging the companies, and if the price paid for the business was reasonable. If a company you own announces an acquisition that does not make strategic sense to you, or you believe the price being paid is too high, you should consider selling your shares and looking for another investment opportunity.

■ Summary

To summarize, there are a few common characteristics present in all good businesses from around the world. They have defensible, leading market positions in growing industries, astute management teams, strong balance sheets, and a strong social conscience. The checklist in Figure 8.8 highlights some of the questions you should be able to answer with confidence prior to making an investment in any business.

It is not enough to answer these questions once and then forget about them. Things can change quickly in the business world and so it is crucial to revisit these questions regularly with respect to each of your holdings and their primary competitors. Unless you are vigilant and take a moment to contemplate these issues on a recurring basis you may miss an opportunity to exit a business that is on the brink of declining or buying into a business showing emerging strength. This chapter has provided a brief overview of how to identify a great business, but for a detailed discussion on company analysis I strongly suggest you read *Security Analysis* by Benjamin Graham and David Dodd.

We now switch gears and review the sectors and industries in which these global businesses operate.

Does the company generate similar or higher profits than its competitors?	
What is the competitive advantage that is driving higher growth and profitability?	
Is the company's competitive advantage sustainable?	
Is the company's revenue stream sustainable? Will it grow or shrink?	
Is the company an industry leader or a laggard in research and development?	
Can the company successfully expand into new regions or closely related markets?	
Does the company have sound economic, social, and governance policies?	
Is the management team experienced and focused, or are they untested or distracted?	
Will the company be able to service its debt if the economy weakens?	
Will management grow by acquiring? If so, how good is their acquisition track record?	
Does the compensation structure of management align with shareholder interests?	
Is the management team committed to returning excess cash to shareholders?	
Is the company attractively priced versus competitors and in relation to its earnings power?	

FIGURE 8.8 Company Checklist

Identifying good businesses involves a detailed analysis of a company's profitability, earnings sustainability, balance sheet strength, growth prospects, investment risks, and valuation. Paying too much for a business may make it difficult to generate a reasonable return on your investment, even over many years. Companies that operate in stable political and economic environments, are growing faster, generate above-average levels of profitability, have a history of producing consistent earnings, pay attractive dividends, and do not have excessive debt tend to trade at valuation multiples above that of the average stock in the market. The fair (intrinsic) value of a company can be estimated using either an absolute or a relative approach. Estimating share price in relative terms involves calculating financial ratios and comparing the results to historical values, close competitors, and the overall stock market. Valuation methods aimed at deriving an absolute (target) share price are based on a company's ability to generate cash flows for shareholders. Another area of growing importance to investors is a company's environmental, social, and governance (ESG) characteristics. The best management teams are effective stewards of investor capital that make sound acquisitions and return capital to shareholders when opportunities to reinvest for profitable growth are lacking.

PART V

GLOBAL SECTORS AND INDUSTRIES

A s discussed in Parts Two and Three, all businesses operate in a global environment, albeit to varying degrees. This section of the book provides
a brief primer on the world economy's major sectors and the industries
that comprise them (see the following table). We review 11 sectors and 91
global industries based on 10 of the largest publicly traded companies in
each industry. The primers cover key variables that affect sales growth and
profitability for the industry, how the companies in the industry are commonly valued by analysts, and the principal factors that should be considered
by investors when evaluating those businesses.

I have restricted the companies listed to those located in countries with
investment-grade credit ratings on their government-issued (sovereign)
debt. As a result, you will note that there are no companies listed from certain countries such as Brazil, Greece, Russia, Turkey, or Vietnam, among
others. Since sovereign credit ratings are subject to change, the list of countries that meet this criteria will change over time.

The industry categories are my own variation of the standard industry
classification systems you will find elsewhere and are not exhaustive since
some small subindustries have been omitted or combined into a larger

Communications Services	Consumer Discretionary	Consumer Staples	Energy	Financials	Healthcare	Industrials	Technology	Materials	Real Estate	Utilities
Advertising	Auto Manufacturing	Beverages	Coal	Asset Management	Biotechnology	Aerospace & Defense	Communications Equipment	Agriculture Products	Diversified REITs	Electric Utilities
Broadband Services	Auto Components	Grocery & Convenience Stores	Energy Equipment & Services	Banks	Healthcare Equipment & Supplies	Air Freight & Courier Services	Electronic Components	Chemicals	Industrial REITs	Gas Utilities
Interactive Entertainment	Auto Parts & Service	Household Products	Exploration & Production	Capital Markets	Healthcare Facilities	Air Travel	Fintech & Payment Processing	Construction Materials	Office REITs	Multi-Utilities
Interactive Media	Auto Retail	Hypermarkets	Integrated Oil & Gas	Consumer Finance	Healthcare Services	Building Products	IT Services	Containers & Packaging	Residential REITs	Renewable Energy
Media Content & Broadcasting	Casinos & Gaming	Packaged Foods	Refining & Marketing	Financial Conglomerates	Life Science Tools & Services	Commercial Services	Semiconductors	Industrial Metals	Retail REITs	Water Utilities
Telecommunications	General Merchandise Stores	Tobacco	Storage & Transportation	Financial Data & Analytics	Pharmaceuticals	Construction & Engineering	Semiconductor Equipment	Mining	Real Estate Development	
	Homebuilding			Life & Health Insurance		Electrical Equipment	Software	Paper & Forest Products	Real Estate Services	
	Hotels, Resorts & Cruise Lines			P&C Insurance		Environmental & Facility Services	Technology Hardware		Specialty REITs	
	Household Durables			Securities Exchanges		Heavy Equipment				
	Internet Retail					Industrial Conglomerates				
	Leisure Products					Industrial Machinery				
	Luxury Goods					Infrastructure Management				
	Restaurants					Marine Shipping				
	Textiles & Apparel Retail					Railroads				
						Trading & Distribution				
						Trucking & Logistics				

group. I have tried to group companies together based on common factors that affect their business operations as well as their behavior in a typical market cycle. Some companies may fit into more than one category, and two businesses within any given industry group could have vastly different business models. Investors should also expect new industries to appear as innovative technologies are developed and as market conditions evolve.

The 10 companies chosen for each industry were selected based primarily on their most recently reported revenue and EBITDA for the preceding 12-month period (both measured in US dollars). I then chose representative publicly traded businesses for each industry from around the world. Each list would be made up of different companies if the criteria for ranking them were to change, so the reader should therefore not construe the companies in these lists as the best or the largest in each industry. Readers should also be aware that government regulations in your home country may prohibit you from owning one or more of the companies listed in these industry primers. Be sure to check before you invest in any foreign company to ensure that it is not classified as a restricted investment by your local authorities.

Investors must also consider risks and opportunities in the equity markets that have only recently appeared but were not explicitly factored into the company selection process. These include blockchain technology and cryptocurrencies, cybersecurity, ESG factors, including climate risks, digital banking, woke culture movements, cancel culture, fake news, deep fakes, and meme stocks. While many of these can be attributed to market noise, it is more important than ever to focus on the intrinsic value and earnings power of a business. As part of your due diligence, you would want to consider how a company is affected by these risks. As noted earlier, the companies in these chapters were selected from among the largest publicly traded companies in each industry. Small and mid-sized companies are also worth considering as an investor, but keep in mind that size has its advantages in the business world, and that added due diligence may be needed for smaller companies, especially those that are relatively young and for which less historical financial data is available.

In addition to providing a list of 10 representative companies operating in each industry, the tables in Chapters 9 to 19 show how characteristics for each industry compare to the average for the sector, and the (implied) market. For our purposes, each industry is comprised only of the 10 companies listed, and each sector is made up of all of the businesses included in each underlying industry. The market characteristics are based on the average of all 900 or so businesses listed in Part Five. Companies denoted with an asterisk have been listed more than once because they have leading positions in more than one industry. One such company is Microsoft, which has dominant positions in both the software industry and the interactive entertainment (video game) industry. Given their relative complexity, I do not break down conglomerates in this fashion. While the 10 companies listed for each industry are among the largest in the industry, one should not assume that they are the best-run companies in the industry or that they are good investments.

The reader should note that the relative sector and industry characteristic ratings provided in the forthcoming tables reflect a single point in time and are based on the average for only the 10 companies listed. Furthermore, these ratings are based on data from only the past few years and therefore the relative valuation, profitability, and growth ratings should not be interpreted as being a target or that they will persist in the future. These tables are simply meant to aid the reader by providing a consistent framework for analyzing and comparing sectors, industries, and companies. These relative characteristics may change meaningfully over time.

In these tables we focus on the following key characteristics: valuation, profitability, sales growth, profit growth, debt levels, dividend yield, dividend payout ratio, dividend growth, earnings predictability, and share price volatility. The valuation comparison is based on the average P/E ratio for each company in the group over the past 10 years. Keep in mind that for industries that are growing quickly and require considerable amounts of reinvestment, a simple P/E multiple may make them appear to be egregiously expensive and so other metrics that employ cash flow or EBITDA should also be considered. Sales growth refers to the average annual growth rate in net sales over the prior five-year period, while profit growth refers to the five-year geometric growth rate in profit margin. Debt levels are measured by net debt-to–shareholder's equity. We use net debt on the assumption that any cash held by the firm could be used to pay down debt if needed. Dividend yield is calculated using the company's expected dividend payments over the next 12 months divided by the current share price. The dividend payout ratio is calculated by dividing the company's total dividend payment by its net income, while dividend growth is measured by the annualized percentage increase in dividends per share over the past five years. Earnings predictability is assessed based on the standard deviation of annual earnings estimates over the next two years. Share price variability is measured by taking the average monthly change in share price over the past 10 years.

As a reference point, valuations for stock markets in developed countries over the past 25 years or so have averaged 21–22× for price to earnings (P/E), 10–11× for price to cash flow (P/CF), and 23–24× for price to free cash flow (P/FCF). This compares to 15–16× P/E, 8× P/CF, and 34× P/FCF for developing markets. In aggregate, the long-term average valuation for all stocks currently sits at 20–21× P/E, 10× P/CF, and 22× P/FCF. Over the past 20 years or so, return on equity (ROE) has averaged 11.2% for developed markets and 12.7% for developing markets, while profit margins have averaged 6.4% for developed markets and 8.8% for developing markets. The dividend payout ratio has averaged 50% for developed market companies and 36% for developing market companies. Historically, the higher payout ratio for developed market companies makes sense since, broadly speaking, they tend to be more mature businesses with comparatively few opportunities to reinvest and grow. Similarly, the higher growth rates and profitability metrics of developing markets intuitively make sense given the comparably higher underlying economic growth rates of the countries in which they operate.

The goal of these sector and industry primers is to provide the reader with a basic framework to build on, enabling them to improve their understanding and make more informed investment decisions. These primers should therefore simply be viewed as a starting point for investors as they begin their journey into global investing. Please refer to the tools and resources section near the end of this book for more sources of information used to analyze companies in the industries listed in Chapters 9 through 19.

Communication Services

The global communication services sector includes companies providing wired and wireless phone services, interactive media (such as social media platforms), media content, home entertainment, gaming, and advertising. At one time the communications sector was regarded as defensive, generating consistent profits regardless of fluctuations in economic growth. However, the composition of the sector has undergone significant transformation in recent years. Traditional advertising and wired telecommunications have been surpassed by internet-based media and services as well as wireless communications as the primary forms of communication. Newer industries within this sector, such as interactive media, offer higher growth rates than were available historically, but companies in these industries typically come with a higher degree of earnings variability when compared to the sector's legacy businesses.

Sector Characteristics versus Market

	Lower	≈	Higher
Valuation		●	
Profitability	●		
Sales Growth		●	
Profit Growth			●
Debt Levels	●		

	Lower	≈	Higher
Dividend Yield		●	
Payout Ratio			●
Dividend Growth	●		
Earnings Predictability			●
Share Price Volatility		●	

Data source: Bloomberg, as of March 18, 2022.

When compared to the market (previously defined in the beginning of Part Five), the average communication services companies mentioned in this chapter have traded at similar valuations over the past few years while generating above-average growth in profits. As a group, they also had lower debt levels and paid competitive dividend yields compared to the market. Relative share price performance for companies in the communication services sector varies significantly during the market cycle because of their sensitivity to the economic cycle. In general terms, however, the communication services sector overall tends to perform well in bull market corrections and the late stage of a bull market. They can be particularly weak in bear markets, suffering losses greater than that of the broader stock market. In this chapter we take a closer look at the six main industry groups within the communication services sector: (1) advertising, (2) broadband services, (3) interactive entertainment, (4) interactive media, (5) media content and broadcasting, and (6) telecommunications.

Advertising

Businesses			Relative Characteristics						
Company	**Country**			**Sector**			**Market**		
				Lower	≈	Higher	Lower	≈	Higher
Cheil Worldwide Inc.	South Korea		Valuation	●			●		
Dentsu Group Inc.	Japan		Profitability	●			●		
Hakuhodo DY	Japan		Sales Growth	●			●		
Interpublic Group of Cos	United States		Profit Growth	●					●
JCDecaux Co. Ltd.	France		Debt Levels		●		●		
Leo Group Co. Ltd.	China		Dividend Yield		●				●
Omnicom Group Inc.	United States		Payout Ratio	●			●		
Publicis Groupe SA	France		Dividend Growth	●			●		
Stroeer SE & Co. KGaA	Germany		Earnings Predictability		●				●
WPP PLC	United Kingdom		Share Price Volatility		●			●	

Data source: Bloomberg, as of March 18, 2022.

Traditional advertising agencies and public relations firms help businesses, government agencies, and even individuals build and protect their brands. They accomplish this by designing advertising campaigns aimed at convincing consumers to purchase a specific good or service. In times past advertising campaigns primarily employed newspaper, television, radio, and billboards. Today, much of advertising has shifted to the digital world, adding social media and other online platforms to the mix. This has resulted in some agency businesses losing market share to newer businesses that focus on digital ad platforms, which I have included in the interactive media industry. In addition to their direct advertising peers, these businesses also compete with in-house marketing teams as well as advertising and public relations consultants. Advertising companies are more dependent on prevailing economic conditions than some of the other industries in the communication services sector. As the economy weakens and consumer spending falls, companies often reduce advertising spending to conserve cash. Economic factors that affect the advertising industry include personal consumption, GDP growth, consumer confidence, and the unemployment rate. Compared to the communication services sector as well as the broader market, advertising companies have tended to trade at lower valuations over recent years as a result of lower profitability and lower sales growth. As a group these businesses have carried more debt than other industries within the communication services sector, but less than the market. Important metrics to track for this industry include revenue growth, operating and profit margins by business segment, SG&A expense ratios, and debt levels. When comparing valuations between companies in this group, P/E or EV/EBITDA ratios are commonly used.

■ Broadband Services

Businesses		Relative Characteristics	Sector Lower	≈	Higher	Market Lower	≈	Higher
Company	**Country**							
BT Group PLC	United Kingdom	Valuation	●			●		
Charter Communications	United States	Profitability		●		●		
Comcast Corp.	United States	Sales Growth	●			●		
Cyfrowy Polsat SA	Poland	Profit Growth	●			●		
Grupo Televisa SAB	Mexico	Debt Levels		●				●
Kabel Deutschland Holding AG	Germany	Dividend Yield		●				●
Liberty Latin America	United States	Payout Ratio	●			●		
Oriental Pearl Group Co. Ltd.	China	Dividend Growth	●			●		
Shaw Communications	Canada	Earnings Predictability		●				●
Telenet Group Holding NV	Belgium	Share Price Volatility	●				●	

Data source: Bloomberg, as of March 18, 2022.

Broadband service companies provide customers with cable television and internet connectivity as well as media content. Some businesses in this industry also create the content delivered through their cable and broadband networks, allowing them to capture profits in multiple segments of the value chain. There is a trend within the broadband industry away from video (cable television) to broadband (internet) subscriptions because services such as Netflix and Disney+ sell media content directly to consumers at prices that are generally lower than traditional paid cable subscriptions. The importance for most consumers of maintaining internet connectivity reduces the sensitivity of these businesses to economic growth. Economic factors that have the greatest impact on broadband service providers include population and GDP growth, housing starts, broadband penetration rates, and the unemployment rate. Building out a competitive broadband network requires significant capital investments and therefore these businesses tend to carry higher levels of debt compared to other industries within the sector. Despite the elevated level of competition in their industry, broadband providers generate strong and stable cash flow and earnings which allows them to pay out a significant amount of earnings to shareholders in the form of dividends. Furthermore, once the network is built, economies of scale allow for high relative profitability within the sector as well as good earnings predictability. While the broadband service industry is mature in some regions of the world like North America and Western Europe, other regions still have lower levels of broadband connectivity and offer the possibility of higher growth. Key metrics to track include net changes to video and broadband subscriber numbers as well as ARPU (average revenue per user), which shows how much revenue is generated per customer. Steady declines in either of these could signal problems with service quality or a lack of competitiveness either in terms of cost or content. Investors should also monitor changes in operating and profit margins. Both P/E and EV/EBITDA are commonly used to assess valuations for broadband service providers.

■ Interactive Entertainment

Businesses		Relative Characteristics	Sector			Market		
Company	Country		Lower	≈	Higher	Lower	≈	Higher
Activision Blizzard Inc.	United States	Valuation		●				●
Electronic Arts Inc.	United States	Profitability		●				●
Microsoft Corp.*	United States	Sales Growth		●				●
NetEase Inc.	China	Profit Growth		●				●
Nintendo Co. Ltd.	Japan	Debt Levels	●			●		
Sony Group Corp.*	Japan	Dividend Yield	●			●		
Square Enix Holdings Co.	Japan	Payout Ratio	●			●		
Take-Two Interactive	United States	Dividend Growth		●				●
Tencent Holdings Ltd.*	China	Earnings Predictability	●					●
Ubisoft Entertainment	France	Share Price Volatility	●				●	

Data source: Bloomberg, as of March 18, 2022.

The interactive entertainment industry is focused on video gaming and is made up of both hardware and software providers. Leading hardware platforms include Nintendo's Switch, Microsoft's Xbox, and Sony's PlayStation. While these companies develop their own games, there are numerous external developers that create video games for these platforms as well as for personal computers. Once considered the pastime of a handful of lazy teenagers, video gaming has become big business. Successful gaming franchises can sell hundreds of millions of copies and bring in billions of dollars in revenue. In addition, eSports (where spectators watch gamers play as they compete for prize money) have taken off in popularity. Rather than sell games in physical packages, game developers are able to sell games directly to consumers at higher profit margins via online stores and through gaming hardware. Game developers are also providing enhanced features and digital content, which are helping to increase margins even further. Software developers are also trying to shift consumers to subscription-based models, where the consumer pays a monthly fee that allows them to play whatever game they like. The subscription model creates a more stable earnings stream, making game developers less dependent on new game launches. New and improved hardware platforms are released every few years, leading developers to create new games. When multiple new hardware platforms are released at the same time, a gaming super-cycle can result as industry-wide game sales grow quickly across all of the newly updated platforms. As an investor, you want to own these businesses at the start of a gaming super-cycle, but not as it is ending. From an economic perspective, consumer sentiment and consumer spending are the most important drivers of revenue and sales growth for the industry.

High growth rates and intense competition in the industry means that dividend yields have been below average as cash is needed for reinvestment. Important metrics for investors to follow include number of units sold (for hardware producers), physical store game sales and revenue, digital game downloads and revenue, extra content revenue, subscription and mobile revenues, research and development costs, license and royalty revenue, goodwill and intangible assets, leverage (net debt/EBITDA), operating income, and EPS. It is best to track revenue numbers and margins by franchise (game title) whenever possible. Analysis of valuation can be made using P/E, EV/revenue, EV/FCF, or EV/adjusted EBITDA. Valuations for these businesses tend to be higher due to their higher growth rates and the appeal of owning companies in this industry.

Interactive Media

Businesses		Relative Characteristics						
Company	**Country**		Sector			Market		
			Lower	≈	Higher	Lower	≈	Higher
Alphabet Inc.	United States	Valuation			●			●
Baidu Inc.	China	Profitability	●			●		
Kakao Corp.	South Korea	Sales Growth			●			●
Kuaishou Technology	China	Profit Growth			●			●
Meta Platforms Inc.	United States	Debt Levels	●			●		
NAVER Corp.	South Korea	Dividend Yield	●			●		
Snap Inc.	United States	Payout Ratio	●			●		
Tencent Holdings Ltd.*	China	Dividend Growth			●			●
Twitter Inc.	United States	Earnings Predictability	●			●		
Z Holdings Corp.	Japan	Share Price Volatility		●			●	

Data source: Bloomberg, as of March 18, 2022.

Companies in the interactive media industry produce and publish news and entertainment content online, in addition to operating social media platforms. A substantial portion of revenue for these companies is generated from advertising and therefore online traffic and the number of users on platforms such as YouTube, TikTok, WeChat, Instagram, Twitter, Pinterest, and Snapchat are important drivers for the industry. The industry benefits from the fact that much of the content is generated by the users themselves, which helps reduce costs. Companies in the interactive media and services industry are integrating artificial intelligence and machine learning into their platforms to make advertisements unique to each individual user. Rapid growth in e-commerce over the past several years has driven extraordinarily strong online ad spending, but since ad spending is tied to the general level of economic activity, revenue and earnings for the industry are sensitive to changes in economic growth. The rapid growth of this industry requires these companies to reinvest most of the cash flow they generate back into the business. As a result, interactive media companies tend to have lower dividend yields and lower dividend payout ratios. On the other hand, the multitude of growth opportunities lend themselves to higher rates of growth in sales and profits. These businesses also tend to trade at higher valuations because of their high growth rates, while earnings tend to be less predictable. Important metrics to track include the number of users or subscribers by platform, the total number of daily or monthly active users, average revenue per user, and operating and profit margins. Investors should also monitor regulatory risks closely, as these businesses continue to expand their reach and influence within society and may be subject to increased regulatory scrutiny as a result. For many businesses in this industry P/CF or P/FCF may be more appropriate than P/E or EV/EBITDA for valuation purposes since most capital is reinvested in the business and is therefore not counted as part of earnings.

■ Media Content and Broadcasting

Businesses	
Company	Country
ITV PLC	United Kingdom
Lagardere SA	France
Netflix Inc.	United States
News Corp.	United States
Paramount Global	United States
RTL Group SA	Luxembourg
Spotify Technology SA	Sweden
Universal Music Group NV	Netherlands
Vivendi SE	France
Walt Disney Co.	United States

Relative Characteristics	Sector			Market		
	Lower	≈	Higher	Lower	≈	Higher
Valuation		●				●
Profitability			●			●
Sales Growth		●				●
Profit Growth			●			●
Debt Levels			●	●		
Dividend Yield	●			●		
Payout Ratio	●			●		
Dividend Growth	●			●		
Earnings Predictability			●			●
Share Price Volatility			●			●

Data source: Bloomberg, as of March 18, 2022.

Media businesses produce, broadcast, and publish news and entertainment content for consumers. This industry has undergone tremendous change in recent years as widespread internet access and improved download speeds are enabling content developers to sell directly to consumers, rather than being limited to cable television networks and movie theaters for distribution. Consumers now only need an internet connection to buy media content directly from any provider. Content ownership is becoming increasingly important in the media industry because of the trend toward streaming content. Disney+ is a splendid example of a traditional media company shifting its business model to sell content directly to consumers, increasing profit margins and giving it greater control over pricing, not to mention capturing a greater share of advertising spending in the process. For these business segments, changes in subscriber numbers are an important indicator for how companies in the industry are performing. There are significant differences in valuation levels within the industry, with younger companies that are focused solely on the online world growing faster and trading at significantly higher multiples than those businesses that still have exposure to traditional media. It is likely that this large valuation gap will fall over time. Some of these companies are more mature businesses and therefore offer only average growth in sales and profits. Important metrics to track include broadband net adds, video net adds, mobile net adds, residential average revenue per user, number of streaming subscriber or monthly active accounts, and streaming average revenue per user. For companies that are active in developing countries, broadband penetration rates (the percentage of homes with internet connectivity) can also provide insights into future profitability. For companies with a long history of generating earnings, media companies can be valued effectively using P/E multiples; otherwise a discounted cash flow analysis may be more appropriate.

■ Telecommunications

Businesses		Relative Characteristics						
Company	Country		Sector Lower ≈ Higher			Market Lower ≈ Higher		
America Movil SAB de CV	Mexico	Valuation	●			●		
AT&T Inc.	United States	Profitability		●		●		
China Mobile Ltd.	Hong Kong	Sales Growth	●			●		
Deutsche Telekom AG	Germany	Profit Growth	●			●		
Nippon Telegraph & Telephone	Japan	Debt Levels		●			●	
Orange SA	France	Dividend Yield		●				●
SK Telecom Co. Ltd.	South Korea	Payout Ratio		●				●
Telefonica SA	Spain	Dividend Growth		●			●	
Verizon Communications Inc.	United States	Earnings Predictability	●					●
Vodafone Group PLC	United Kingdom	Share Price Volatility	●			●		

Data source: Bloomberg, as of March 18, 2022.

Businesses in the telecommunications industry supply the networks used for voice communications globally. In addition to wired and wireless communications, many of these companies also provide broadband services. The industry is very capital intensive, meaning that enormous amounts of capital are required to compete effectively in this market. The high degree of capital intensity means that the industry is well-suited for an oligopolistic or monopolistic structure, where incumbents can thwart new entrants and exert significant pricing power. For this reason, the industry has become increasingly regulated in most countries, with the goal of stimulating competition and thus lowering costs for consumers. As the costs associated with switching between providers have fallen, the level of competition has become increasingly intense to the point where slight differences in service quality can lead to significant shifts in market share. Despite the highly competitive nature of the industry, consumer reliance on communication services allows telecom providers to generate strong and stable earnings, and to pay out a significant amount of profit to shareholders in the form of dividends. There has been a prevailing trend away from landlines (wired telecommunications) to wireless communications and this is expected to continue as telecom companies roll out 5G networks that will further improve functionality for wireless devices. Key metrics to monitor include wireless service revenue growth, operating expense ratio, pre- and postpaid net subscriber adds, and ARPU, as well as churn, which shows how many existing subscribers were lost in the period. Spikes in churn could signal problems with service quality or a lack of cost competitiveness. P/E and EV/EBITDA are usually suitable metrics for assessing company valuation.

CHAPTER 10

Consumer Discretionary

T he global consumer discretionary sector is comprised of businesses that provide goods and services to consumers that are "discretionary" in nature, meaning that the purchases of these goods and services are nonessential and may be delayed by consumers. As a result, the consumer discretionary sector consists of businesses that are more affected by the economic cycle. When economic times are good, consumer discretionary businesses will earn significantly greater profits, but when economic conditions weaken, this effect works against them, and they will generate below-average profits. The importance of scale and brand power vary by industry within the consumer discretionary sector, depending on a number of factors, including the capital intensity of the business and the importance and perception of product quality and exclusivity.

Sector Characteristics versus Market

Characteristic	Lower	≈	Higher		Characteristic	Lower	≈	Higher
Valuation			●		Dividend Yield		●	
Profitability	●				Payout Ratio	●		
Sales Growth	●				Dividend Growth	●		
Profit Growth	●				Earnings Predictability		●	
Debt Levels		●			Share Price Volatility		●	

Data source: Bloomberg, as of March 18, 2022.

When compared to the market, the companies mentioned in this chapter have traded at above-average valuations over the past few years despite delivering below-average profitability and lower growth in sales, profits, and dividends. Below-average profitability and lower sales and profit growth are partially a result of the substantial effect the 2020 global pandemic had on the travel-related industries within the consumer discretionary sector.

Higher sensitivity to the economic cycle causes investors to invest more heavily in consumer discretionary companies when economic conditions are expected to improve. Conversely, when the economy weakens, earnings for discretionary stocks fall more than the average company and so investors often sell them in favor of businesses whose earnings are more stable. For these reasons, consumer discretionary companies tend to exhibit improving relative share price performance as the bull market evolves, up until the late cycle when inflation begins to pick up and the central bank starts to raise interest rates. Especially in cases where consumer debt levels are high, rising interest rates force consumers to shift money away from spending on things that are "nice to have" to those that are necessities, such as buying food, paying utility bills, and making mortgage and loan payments. The opposite happens near the end of recessions as central banks lower interest rates to help spur economic growth, enabling consumers to spend more on discretionary goods and services.

In this chapter we take a closer look at the 14 main industry groups within the consumer discretionary sector: (1) auto manufacturing, (2) auto components, (3) auto parts and service, (4) auto retail, (5) casinos and gaming, (6) general merchandise stores, (7) homebuilding, (8) hotels, resorts, and cruise lines, (9) household durables, (10) internet retail, (11) leisure products, (12) luxury goods, (13) restaurants, and (14) textiles and apparel retail.

■ Auto Manufacturing

Businesses		Relative Characteristics						
Company	**Country**		**Sector**			**Market**		
			Lower	≈	Higher	Lower	≈	Higher
Bayerische Motoren Werke AG	Germany	Valuation	●			●		
Ford Motor Co.	United States	Profitability		●		●		
General Motors Co.	United States	Sales Growth	●			●		
Honda Motor Co. Ltd.	Japan	Profit Growth			●		●	
Hyundai Motor Co.	South Korea	Debt Levels	●			●		
Mercedes-Benz Group AG	Germany	Dividend Yield			●			●
SAIC Motor Corp. Ltd.	China	Payout Ratio	●			●		
Stellantis NV	Netherlands	Dividend Growth	●			●		
Toyota Motor Corp.	Japan	Earnings Predictability	●			●		
Volkswagen AG	Germany	Share Price Volatility			●			●

Data source: Bloomberg, as of March 18, 2022.

Auto manufacturing, also referred to as original equipment manufacturing (OEM), is a capital-intensive business. Input costs are a relatively high portion of the company's total costs, and purchasing a car is a large financial decision for most consumers. While most OEMs rely on high sales volumes of relatively lower-cost, lower-margin models, some OEMs like Ferrari produce fewer higher-cost, higher-margin automobiles. In both cases production efficiency and scale are critical. Action on climate change is causing many auto OEMs to develop new electric vehicle or hybrid models, or in some cases switch all of their automobile production to electric vehicles (EVs). In addition to electrification, another emerging trend in the auto OEM industry has been the shift toward autonomous (self-driving) vehicles, which has been enabled by new hardware and software technologies. It is worth noting that consumer preferences vary by region. For example, US consumers prefer larger trucks and SUVs while European consumers prefer smaller cars. As a result of shorter driving distances, battery sizes in electric vehicles tend to be smaller in Europe than in North America. Interest rate changes can influence auto sales because most new car purchases are financed based on prevailing interest rates and dealer incentives. Since cars have a limited useful life, investors should track the average age of cars on the road whenever possible (IHS Markit tracks this data in some markets). As the average age of cars on the road rises, the need for consumers to buy new replacement vehicles increases. Other economic factors that influence firm profitability include commodity costs (such as steel, rubber, and aluminum) and labor costs. Lower profitability has caused the shares of auto manufacturers to trade at valuations below the market over the past few years. Auto manufacturers that have been around for a long time may also have inflated costs related to funding pension liabilities, which should be considered when making an investment. Important metrics to monitor for auto OEMs include gross margin, operating margin, free cash flow, and car sale reservations (especially for newer companies in the EV marketplace). Despite remaining a relatively small part of the cost of building a new car, semiconductors are now critical components of cars, and their availability is therefore essential to an OEM's operations. Commonly used valuation measures for auto manufacturers include P/E and EV/EBITDA.

■ Auto Components

Businesses		Relative Characteristics						
Company	Country		Sector			Market		
			Lower	≈	Higher	Lower	≈	Higher
Aisin Corp.	Japan	Valuation	●			●		
Bridgestone Corp.	Japan	Profitability		●		●		
Cie Generale (Michelin)	France	Sales Growth	●			●		
Continental AG	Germany	Profit Growth	●			●		
Denso Corp.	Japan	Debt Levels	●			●		
Huayu Automotive	China	Dividend Yield			●			●
Hyundai Mobis Co.	South Korea	Payout Ratio	●			●		
Magna International Inc.	Canada	Dividend Growth			●	●		
Schaeffer AG	Germany	Earnings Predictability	●			●		
Valeo	France	Share Price Volatility			●			●

Data source: Bloomberg, as of March 18, 2022.

Auto component companies sell directly to OEMs and are also capital-intensive businesses. Input costs are relatively high as a portion of the company's total costs, and since component manufacturers sell directly to OEMs, they are impacted by many of the same economic factors, including interest rates. Like OEMs, commodities such as steel, plastic, and rubber can represent a major part of the cost structure for component manufacturers. Some component manufacturers sell into multiple OEMs, which serves to diversify their earnings stream. As well, some component manufacturers, such as tire producers, sell into both the new and used car markets and so a delay in new car purchases may not impact earnings as much as businesses that sell only to OEMs. Aside from tracking average fleet age, investors should also watch for changes in interest rates and dealer incentives. As the average age of cars on the road increases, the need for consumers to buy new replacement vehicles grows. The companies in this industry have been trading at below-average valuations in recent years but have generated attractive dividends and grown their dividends at an above-average rate. Important metrics for component suppliers include EBIT and EBITDA margins, and growth rates compared to the OEM industry are also important to monitor as higher growth rates can signal market share gains and vice versa. Conversely, share gains and losses by each OEM may also provide insights into the component manufacturers that are most closely tied to them as suppliers. Profit and operating margins are also important variables to monitor as changes in market share may be driven by price concessions that would reduce margins. While market share gains are positive, any gains made through cost alone are not usually sustainable and so share gains that coincide with falling margins should be viewed as temporary. For battery manufacturers, output (measured in GWh) and margins are key factors to watch. Commonly used valuation measures for auto manufacturers include P/E and EV/EBITDA.

■ Auto Parts and Service

Businesses			Relative Characteristics						
Company	Country			Sector			Market		
				Lower	≈	Higher	Lower	≈	Higher
Advance Auto Parts Inc.	United States		Valuation	●			●		
AutoZone Inc.	United States		Profitability			●	●		
Bapcor Ltd.	Australia		Sales Growth			●		●	
Boyd Group Services Inc.	Canada		Profit Growth			●	●		
Genuine Parts Co.	United States		Debt Levels	●			●		
Inchcape PLC	United Kingdom		Dividend Yield			●			●
LKQ Corp.	United States		Payout Ratio	●			●		
MEKO AB	Sweden		Dividend Growth			●			●
Super Retail Group Ltd.	Australia		Earnings Predictability			●			●
Yellow Hat Ltd.	Japan		Share Price Volatility		●			●	

Data source: Bloomberg, as of March 18, 2022.

Auto parts and service companies provide after-market goods and services needed to maintain vehicles and extend their useful life. The same factors that can affect the new car market can impact the parts and service industry since a slowdown in the sale of new cars means that consumers must keep their old cars on the road longer, resulting in higher levels of maintenance. As automobiles age, the costs of maintaining them increase until finally they become inoperable or it becomes more cost effective to buy a new, or at least newer, used vehicle. Investors should also track miles driven whenever this information is available because higher amounts of driving also lead to greater need for repairs and maintenance. Gasoline prices can impact this industry as higher gas prices cause consumers to drive less, thereby requiring less maintenance and repairs. Other economic factors that can affect the industry include population and GDP growth, and the unemployment rate. Since new cars do not typically need major repairs or maintenance, higher new car sales could be negative for the after-market industry, at least on a short-term basis. Strong balance sheets and above-average profit and sales growth versus the market have allowed these businesses to pay attractive dividends and grow them at an above-average rate. Important metrics to track include new vehicle sales, same-store sales, gross margin, operating margin, EBIT margin, selling, general, and administrative (SG&A) expense ratios, and market share in both the do-it-yourself (DIY) and do-it-for-me (DIFM) end markets. Valuation comparisons can usually be made using P/E or EV/EBITDA multiples.

■ Auto Retail

Businesses		Relative Characteristics						
Company	Country		Sector			Market		
			Lower	≈	Higher	Lower	≈	Higher
ALD SA	France	Valuation	●					●
Astra International Tbk	Indonesia	Profitability		●		●		
AutoNation Inc.	United States	Sales Growth			●			●
CarMax Inc.	United States	Profit Growth			●			●
China Grand Automotive	China	Debt Levels			●			●
Eagers Automotive Ltd.	Australia	Dividend Yield			●			●
Hotai Motors Co. Ltd.	Taiwan	Payout Ratio	●			●		
Jardine Cycle & Carriage Ltd.	Singapore	Dividend Growth			●			●
Penske Automotive Group	United States	Earnings Predictability			●			●
Zhongsheng Group	China	Share Price Volatility		●			●	

Data source: Bloomberg, as of March 18, 2022.

In addition to selling new and used cars, many auto retailers also supply finance, insurance, maintenance, and repair services, which serve to further enhance their profitability and diversify their sources of revenue. Auto dealerships pay for their inventory using floor plan financing, which is essentially a revolving credit line secured by the vehicles themselves. The auto retail industry has undergone meaningful change in recent years as vehicle sales have shifted to online marketplaces. Online retailers allow consumers to search for a car, buy it (with financing if necessary), and have it delivered directly to their home without ever setting foot on a dealership floor. In addition, advancements in software helped to transform the auto retail industry by automating much of the car purchase and customer care functions conducted by dealerships. Changes in interest rates and the availability of credit can have a material impact on car sales. Rising costs for cars (either through higher prices or financing rates) can have a negative impact on earnings and profit margins, as can rising levels of unemployment or other factors that cause consumer buying power to weaken. The businesses listed above have paid above-average dividend yields and have been able to grow those dividends at an above-average rate. Despite carrying above-average levels of debt, these businesses have generated above-average profit and sales growth versus the market, allowing them to pay attractive dividends and grow them at an above-average rate. Investors should track new and used car sales data, same-store sales growth for new and used cars, as well as parts and service, gross profit per unit (GPU), and SG&A expense as a percentage of gross revenue. Standard valuation measures such as P/E and EV/EBITDA can usually be used to assess valuations in this industry.

Casinos and Gaming

Businesses		Relative Characteristics						
Company	**Country**		**Sector**			**Market**		
			Lower	≈	Higher	Lower	≈	Higher
Aristocrat Leisure Ltd.	Australia	Valuation		●				●
Caesars Entertainment Inc.	United States	Profitability		●		●		
Entain PLC	United Kingdom	Sales Growth		●				●
Evolution AB	Sweden	Profit Growth		●				●
Flutter Entertainment PLC	Ireland	Debt Levels		●				●
Galaxy Entertainment Group Ltd.	Hong Kong	Dividend Yield	●			●		
MGM Resorts International	United States	Payout Ratio	●			●		
Penn National Gaming Inc.	United States	Dividend Growth	●			●		
Sands China Ltd.	China	Earnings Predictability		●				●
Tabcorp Holdings Ltd.	Australia	Share Price Volatility		●				●

Data source: Bloomberg, as of March 18, 2022.

As with many other industries, the Digital Revolution has had a major impact on the casino and gaming industry. The industry has emerged from a period of stagnation and is now experiencing strong growth, as governments around the world have come to view the industry as a potential new source of tax revenue. This has led governments to increasingly legalize sports betting and internet-based gaming (iGaming). Casinos face regulatory risk, including the potential loss of their gaming licenses in certain jurisdictions. Regulation can therefore have a major impact on the industry, as seen in China's crackdown on junket (VIP) business due to concerns over tax evasion and other criminal activity. While the iGaming market in the United States has experienced lower margins than other areas such as Europe and Australia, these are expected to improve over time as companies reduce advertising and promotion costs related to acquiring new customers. From an economic perspective, growth in GDP and personal consumption expenditures (PCEs) as well as labor costs are important drivers of earnings and revenue growth for the industry. In some geographic areas, weather can also have a significant short-term impact on profitability. Dividend yields, payout ratios, and dividend growth rates were all heavily affected by the 2020 global pandemic, as the precipitous drop in foot traffic caused casino operators to cut their dividends in order to preserve cash. As global leisure travel resumes, casino and gaming companies will likely reinstate their dividends, bringing these metrics back to a more normalized level. Valuations appear elevated due to the large drop in earnings caused by the global pandemic over the past couple of years. Important metrics to track include casino gross gaming revenue (GGR), hotel room revenue, online gaming market share, EBITDA, and EBITDAR (earnings before interest, taxes, depreciation, amortization, and restructuring or rent costs). Since iGaming and sports betting are responsible for the industry's recent growth spurt, it is also important to monitor revenue, EBITDA, and market share trends in those business segments specifically. Commonly used valuation measures for casino and gaming companies include P/E and EV/EBITDAR.

◼ General Merchandise Stores

Businesses in the general merchandise industry sell a variety of goods that are at least somewhat discretionary, such as clothing. As a result, sales for most of these businesses are highly correlated to economic conditions and

Businesses		Relative Characteristics						
Company	**Country**		**Sector**			**Market**		
			Lower	≈	Higher	Lower	≈	Higher
Canadian Tire Corp.	Canada	Valuation	●			●		
Central Retail Corporation PCL	Thailand	Profitability	●			●		
Dollar Tree Inc.	United States	Sales Growth	●			●		
El Puerto de Liverpool SAB de CV	Mexico	Profit Growth	●			●		
Falabella SA	Chile	Debt Levels	●			●		
Kohl's Corp.	United States	Dividend Yield	●			●		
Lotte Shopping Co. Ltd.	South Korea	Payout Ratio		●				●
Macy's Inc.	United States	Dividend Growth	●			●		
Marks & Spencer Group	United Kingdom	Earnings Predictability	●			●		
Takashimaya Co Ltd.	Japan	Share Price Volatility		●			●	

Data source: Bloomberg, as of March 18, 2022.

experience lower sales as economic conditions weaken. The exceptions are discount and dollar stores, which may actually benefit from deteriorating economic conditions, at least on a relative basis. This is the result of consumers shifting down the value chain in order to reduce their spending. This industry continues to be challenged by the shift to online shopping, although some companies have managed to develop successful online platforms. The ability to drive sales by generating traffic in stores and online via product and brand launches, store remodels, and compelling fulfillment options have been important determinants of success in this industry. Inflation can negatively impact these businesses as higher prices for essential goods leaves less money for consumers to spend on discretionary items. Lower relative valuations for the industry over recent years have been driven by below-average profitability, sales, profit, and dividend growth. Investors should monitor same-store sales statistics, including how much growth comes from traffic volumes versus average ticket (purchase) size, new-store openings and closures, new-store productivity including unit/store growth, SG&A per store, and SG&A per square foot. Other key metrics include total revenue, EBIT and EPS growth, gross margin and EBIT margin, leverage (net debt/EBITDA), and lease-adjusted leverage (net debt including operating leases/EBITDAR). Also, analyzing SG&A per store or SG&A per square foot growth can be used to normalize for changes in store count. Standard valuation measures such as P/E and EV/EBITDA can be used to assess valuations in this industry.

■ Homebuilding

Businesses		Relative Characteristics						
Company	**Country**		Sector			Market		
			Lower	≈	Higher	Lower	≈	Higher
Barratt Developments PLC	United Kingdom	Valuation	●			●		
DR Horton Inc.	United States	Profitability			●	●		
Kaufman & Broad SA	France	Sales Growth		●			●	
Iida Group Holdings	Japan	Profit Growth			●			●
JM AB	Sweden	Debt Levels	●			●		
Lennar Corp.	United States	Dividend Yield			●			●
Persimmon plc	United Kingdom	Payout Ratio	●			●		
PulteGroup Inc.	United States	Dividend Growth			●			●
Sekisui House Ltd.	Japan	Earnings Predictability			●			●
Sumitomo Forestry	Japan	Share Price Volatility			●			●

Data source: Bloomberg, as of March 18, 2022.

Homebuilder earnings are heavily influenced by mortgage rates, which of course are derived from the prevailing interest rates. Changes in interest rates can therefore have a significant impact on home sales. Lumber prices also impact home sales due to the fact that lumber typically represents a relatively large portion of the cost of building a new home. Higher input costs can both reduce profit margins for builders and make homes less affordable for consumers and reduce demand. Important economic factors include mortgage rates, job growth, building costs, labor costs, labor availability, the existing supply of homes, household debt, and income levels (to gauge the ability of consumers to service their debt). In the United States, investors should also track new building permits, housing starts, new and existing home sales, and home prices, since rising home prices suggest more homes need to be built. These metrics may not be available in all countries, but investors should keep track of similar data wherever it is available. For example, investors can track mortgage approvals and the nationwide house price index in the United Kingdom, and they can monitor housing starts in Japan. The global housing market has been strong in recent years due to a limited supply of homes and strong demand, which has been boosted by the low interest rate environment, allowing these businesses to generate above-average profits and profit growth, dividends, and dividend growth. Despite this they have tended to trade at below-average valuations in recent years. Homebuilders have increasingly shifted toward an asset-light land contracting model, where they hold options to build on land rather than hold the land itself. This has served to improve capital efficiency and reduce debt levels. Company-specific metrics that investors should track include absorption rates in each market (how quickly homes are sold), net order growth, and gross margins. Both P/E and EV/EBITDA ratios are commonly used to assess valuations across companies in the homebuilding industry.

■ Hotels, Resorts, and Cruise Lines

Businesses		Relative Characteristics						
Company	**Country**		Sector			Market		
			Lower	≈	Higher	Lower	≈	Higher
Accor SA	France	Valuation	●					●
Airbnb Inc.	United States	Profitability	●			●		
Amadeus IT Group SA	Spain	Sales Growth	●			●		
Hilton Worldwide Holdings Inc.	United States	Profit Growth	●			●		
InterContinental Hotels Group PLC	United Kingdom	Debt Levels		●				●
Marriott International	United States	Dividend Yield	●			●		
Royal Caribbean Cruises Ltd.	United States	Payout Ratio	●			●		
Scandic Hotels Group AB	Sweden	Dividend Growth	●			●		
Shanghai Jin Jiang Capital Co.	China	Earnings Predictability		●				●
TUI AG	Germany	Share Price Volatility		●			●	

Data source: Bloomberg, as of March 18, 2022.

Hotels and resorts can be split into asset-heavy and asset-light business models. An asset-heavy model is where the company owns properties directly, while an asset-light model is where the company owns the brand and is paid a royalty from the property owner. Economic factors that affect the hotel, resort, and cruise line industry (especially for asset-heavy companies) include personal consumption expenditures (PCE), discretionary spending, GDP growth, fixed business investment, unemployment rates, and labor costs. For cruise line operators, fuel prices, labor costs, and availability of labor are important drivers of revenue growth and profitability. Labor shortages pose a concern for the industry as companies often struggle to attract and retain talent amid tight labor markets. The outbreak of Covid-19 in 2020 revealed how susceptible the industry is to global pandemics. As demand recovered, the need to restaff hotels became more pronounced, particularly for hotel operators who are facing pressures from brands to maintain brand standards and reintroduce services (such as food and beverage and housekeeping). The global pandemic caused a transition to remote work for many businesses across numerous industries. Should this trend continue. the hotel industry could face significant loss of revenue, as corporate customers account for approximately two-thirds of total hotel room demand. The global pandemic also caused the industry to suffer significant losses, depressing longer-term profitability and growth averages compared to the overall market, while adding significantly to the debt levels of most operators. As travel continues to recover, these metrics should improve on an absolute and relative basis. Key metrics to track include corporate travel, total room count, occupancy, average daily room rate (ADR), revenue per available room (RevPAR), bookings, and the number of rooms under development. Capacity additions (in the form of either hotel rooms or new ship builds), whether organic or through acquisition, are a means to grow the businesses and enhance economies of scale. Commonly used valuation measures for hotel and resort companies include P/E and EV/EBITDA.

■ Household Durables

Businesses		Relative Characteristics					
Company	Country		Sector			Market	
			Lower ≈ Higher			Lower ≈ Higher	
Electrolux AB — Sweden		Valuation	●			●	
Haier Smart Home — China		Profitability			●	●	
Home Depot Inc — United States		Sales Growth	●			●	
Kingfisher PLC — United Kingdom		Profit Growth			●		●
Lowe's Cos. Inc. — United States		Debt Levels			●		●
Midea Group Co. — China		Dividend Yield		●			●
SEB SA — France		Payout Ratio	●			●	
Wesfarmers Ltd. — Australia		Dividend Growth			●	●	
Whirlpool Corp. — United States		Earnings Predictability			●		●
Yamada Holdimgs Co. Ltd. — Japan		Share Price Volatility		●			●

Data source: Bloomberg, as of March 18, 2022.

Businesses in the household durable industry help make your house a home, providing furniture, home electronics, and appliances, as well as everything you need for your home renovation project. Key trends in the industry include market consolidation, growing small appliance purchases, and online penetration. Another important industry trend has been the move to the Internet of Things (IoT), which serves to increasingly integrate homes with the internet. Appliances and security systems, for example, can now be checked and adjusted from a smartphone. Successful companies stand out through brand management, innovation, product quality and safety, and customer service. A business's ability to pass on higher costs, whether driven by rising product, wage, or transportation costs, are crucial to success in an inflationary environment. Despite generating above-average profit growth, these businesses have been trading at below-average valuations, most likely due to elevated debt levels and below-average sales growth. Economic factors that affect the industry include house prices and inflation. Rising home prices give homeowners access to more equity (which can be used to buy new appliances or for home renovations, for example), while inflation (especially gas and food prices) will serve to reduce consumer spending on durable goods. Logically, factors that influence homebuilders also impact the household durables industry, such as new and existing home sales, average product age (which determines the replacement cycle), mortgage and interest rates, and home improvement spending (professional and do-it-yourself). Input costs, which can include industrial metals, lumber prices, electrical equipment, and transportation costs all influence profit margins and sales growth for the industry. Investors should track same-store sales growth, the source of growth (i.e., traffic vs. ticket), unit-per-store growth, new-store productivity, total revenue growth, changes in margins and SG&A expense ratios, SG&A per store or SG&A per square foot growth (to normalize for changes in store count), growth in EBIT and EPS, leverage (net debt/EBITDA), and lease-adjusted leverage (net debt, including operating leases/EBITDAR). Standard valuation measures such as P/E and EV/EBITDA are commonly used to assess valuations in this industry.

■ Internet Retail

Internet retailing is the sale of goods and services through the internet, either business-to-business (B2B) or business-to-consumer (B2C). With increasing penetration of mobile devices and internet services,

Businesses		Relative Characteristics					
Company	**Country**		Sector			Market	
			Lower	≈	Higher	Lower	≈ Higher
Alibaba Group	China	Valuation		●			●
Amazon.com Inc.	United States	Profitability		●		●	
ASOS PLC	United Kingdom	Sales Growth		●			●
Cnova NV	Netherlands	Profit Growth		●			●
Coupang Inc.	South Korea	Debt Levels	●			●	
eBay Inc.	United States	Dividend Yield	●			●	
JD.com Inc.	China	Payout Ratio	●			●	
Rakuten Group Inc.	Japan	Dividend Growth		●		●	
Wayfair Inc.	United States	Earnings Predictability		●			●
Zalando SE	Germany	Share Price Volatility		●			●

Data source: Bloomberg, as of March 18, 2022.

e-commerce has emerged as a major global shopping platform. Active user/buyer growth and consumer spending are important numbers to monitor. Economic factors that affect profitability and sales growth include labor costs, the level of unemployment, and consumer sentiment. Consumer spending is directly tied to wealth creation, and we can expect a continuing shift in spend to e-commerce from "brick and mortar" stores. Consumers' propensity to spend and e-commerce penetration are also important variables for investors to track. Businesses in the internet retail industry have the potential to grow their earnings by expanding into new end markets, such as groceries and pharmaceuticals, as well as to offer rush and on-demand delivery options. Strong sales and earnings growth in recent years has caused these businesses to trade at above-average valuation multiples. Important metrics to monitor include gross merchandise value (GMV), GMV (or revenue) per user and by region, frequency of purchases by average user, number of users or active buyers, customer retention, total revenue, ad spending, as well as EBIT and EBITDA margins. For companies that sell third-party merchandise on their platforms, take-rate data (the fee companies earn from third-party sellers) should also be monitored. For most businesses in the internet retail industry, P/E or EV/EBITDA ratios are fine for comparing valuation, but for a more diversified company like Amazon, which operates multiple business lines, a sum of the parts valuation analysis is recommended.

■ Leisure Products

Businesses		Relative Characteristics	Sector			Market		
Company	**Country**		Lower	≈	Higher	Lower	≈	Higher
BRP Inc.	Canada	Valuation	●			●		
Brunswick Corp.	United States	Profitability		●		●		
Callaway Golf Co.	United States	Sales Growth		●				●
Giant Manufacturing Co. Ltd.	Taiwan	Profit Growth		●			●	
Hasbro Inc.	United States	Debt Levels	●			●		
Polaris Inc.	United States	Dividend Yield	●			●		
Shimano Inc.	Japan	Payout Ratio	●			●		
Thor Industries Inc.	United States	Dividend Growth		●				●
Trigano SA	France	Earnings Predictability		●				●
Yamaha Corp.	Japan	Share Price Volatility		●				●

Data source: Bloomberg, as of March 18, 2022.

Companies in the leisure products industry manufacture a wide range of goods, including bicycles, boats, fishing rods, golf clubs, jet skis, all-terrain vehicles (ATVs), snowmobiles, motorcycles, pool tables, toys, and recreational vehicles (RVs). Brand recognition plays a significant role in this industry. Economic factors that can impact sales and profit growth for leisure product companies include consumer confidence, input (raw material) costs, employment levels, and interest rates (more so for large-ticket items that require purchase financing, such as RVs). These products are discretionary in nature, which means that earnings for these businesses are heavily influenced by economic growth. If the economy is strong, consumers will have a larger amount of discretionary income that they can spend on items they want but do not need. As a rule of thumb, goods that are expensive and unnecessary are more sensitive to economic conditions, which means that sales of leisure products are among the most vulnerable of all consumer goods to periods of economic weakness. Fitness- and sports-related goods, such as bicycles and golf clubs, are currently benefiting from a trend toward healthier lifestyles. Key trends for powersports and RV manufacturers include electrification, expansion into new regions around the world, and internet-connected vehicles (which may provide manufacturers with recurring subscription-based revenue streams as additional services are created). Strong economic growth over the past several years has helped support strong sales and profit growth for the industry and enabled businesses to increase their dividends at an above-average rate. Principal factors to track include dealer inventory levels, capital expenditures, gross margins, and EBIT and EBITDA profit margins. Valuation comparisons can be made using P/E and EV/EBITDA multiples.

■ Luxury Goods

Businesses		Relative Characteristics	Sector Lower	Sector ≈	Sector Higher	Market Lower	Market ≈	Market Higher
Company	Country							
Burberry Group PLC	United Kingdom	Valuation	●			●		
Capri Holdings Ltd.	United Kingdom	Profitability			●	●		
Cie Financiere Richemont SA	Switzerland	Sales Growth	●			●		
Hermes International	France	Profit Growth	●			●		
Hugo Boss AG	Germany	Debt Levels	●			●		
Kering SA	France	Dividend Yield	●			●		
LVMH Moet Hennessy Louis Vuitton SE	France	Payout Ratio	●			●		
Moncler SpA	Italy	Dividend Growth			●			●
Prada SpA	Italy	Earnings Predictability			●			●
Salvatore Ferragamo SpA	Italy	Share Price Volatility	●			●		

Data source: Bloomberg, as of March 18, 2022.

The luxury goods industry has been a prime beneficiary of the growth in wealth around the world. Economic growth generates wealth, which is not distributed evenly in a country's population, and so those who are able to accumulate greater amounts of wealth often look to purchase goods that demonstrate their financial success. For this reason, brand recognition is extremely important to luxury goods consumers, while price is often secondary. Companies with global exposure can sell through company-owned stores, sell as wholesalers through other stores, or enter joint ventures with local firms in foreign countries. Some of the world's most famous luxury brands, including Chanel and Gucci, are privately held companies and therefore do not appear on this list, while many other globally recognized brands are owned by the companies shown. Economic factors that have the greatest impact on firm earnings and sales include labor costs, commodity prices, freight costs, supply chain disruption, consumer sentiment, total consumer expenditure, and retail foot traffic. Higher rates of economic growth in developing economies, such as in Asia, are quickly increasing the number of wealthy people globally and have become a major growth driver for the luxury goods industry in recent years. Online sales have been rising as a percentage of total sales (partially due to the global pandemic) and are generally detrimental for profit margins. Whether the online sales trend will persist remains to be seen. Rising input costs and wage inflation also tend to put downward pressure on margins. Investors should monitor sales by product type and by channel (physical stores, online, and wholesale), same-store sales, gross margin, rent costs, SG&A expenses, shipping costs, and store openings and closings, as well as inventory and debt levels. Valuation comparisons can be made using P/E and EV/EBITDA multiples.

■ Restaurants

Businesses		Relative Characteristics			
Company	**Country**			**Sector**	**Market**
				Lower ≈ Higher	Lower ≈ Higher
Alsea SAB de CV	Mexico	Valuation		●	●
AmRest Holdings S.E	Spain	Profitability		●	●
Compass Group PLC	United Kingdom	Sales Growth		●	●
Darden Restaurants	United States	Profit Growth		●	●
Haidilao International Holding Ltd.	China	Debt Levels		●	●
McDonald's Corp.	United States	Dividend Yield		●	●
Restaurant Brands International	Canada	Payout Ratio		●	●
Skylark Holdings Co. Ltd.	Japan	Dividend Growth		●	●
Starbucks Corp.	United States	Earnings Predictability		●	●
Yum China Holdings	China	Share Price Volatility		●	●

Data source: Bloomberg, as of March 18, 2022.

Restaurant business models have been transformed in recent years through increased digitization and expanded delivery options. International expansion is still a huge driver for the industry with accelerating unit growth and advantages for larger chains in digital, marketing, and store investment. Economic factors that have the biggest influence on firm profit and sales growth include labor costs, commodity costs, freight and fuel costs, the level of unemployment, disposable personal income, and consumer sentiment. There are significant differences between regions in margin structure and labor costs, as well as the acceptance of restaurant chains generally and for specific categories. International markets for fast food tend to be master franchised, whereas the United States and some developed markets are owned by independent franchisees (which provide higher revenue to the parent company). Key industry trends include a shift to digital ordering, delivery and off-premises consumption, digital and automation tools to reduce labor costs, and the need to adapt to new ordering channels, as well as new formats like ghost kitchens (restaurants without dining space). Another challenge the industry faces is the emergence of semi-prepared meal delivery, and grocery delivery offerings. Also, the shift to restaurant meal delivery apps, like UberEats or DoorDash, has added to operating costs and eroded profit margins. Key metrics investors should monitor include same-store sales, success of loyalty programs, menu innovations and digital innovations, and restaurant count and new restaurant growth, as well as the percentage of the business that is franchised versus company-owned and -operated. Same-store sales growth, unit growth, system sales growth, restaurant margins, consolidated operating margins, and labor and food costs as a percentage of sales are also important metrics to track. Commonly used valuation measures for the restaurant industry include P/E and EV/EBITDA.

■ Textiles and Apparel Retail

Businesses		Relative Characteristics						
Company	Country		Sector			Market		
			Lower	≈	Higher	Lower	≈	Higher
Adidas AG	Germany	Valuation	●			●		
Fast Retailing Co.	Japan	Profitability			●	●		
H&M Hennes & Mauritz AB	Sweden	Sales Growth	●			●		
Industria de Diseno Textil SA	Spain	Profit Growth	●			●		
NIKE Inc.	United States	Debt Levels	●			●		
Nordstrom Inc.	United States	Dividend Yield	●			●		
Pou Chen Corporation	Taiwan	Payout Ratio		●		●		
Puma SE	Germany	Dividend Growth			●		●	
TJX Companies	United States	Earnings Predictability			●			●
VF Corp.	United States	Share Price Volatility	●			●		

Data source: Bloomberg, as of March 18, 2022.

The textile and apparel industry continues to experience a shift to online sales from physical stores, a trend that was accelerated by the 2020 global pandemic. Increasing competition from pure internet-based retailers will likely continue to take market share from brick-and-mortar retailers. Economic factors that have the greatest impact on restaurants include labor costs, commodity prices, freight costs, supply chain disruption, consumer sentiment, total consumer expenditure, and retail foot traffic. Rising input costs and wage inflation would negatively affect margins. The unemployment rate can also have a significant impact on industry profitability and sales growth, as can global consumer trends. Companies with global exposure have different distribution models, including operating their own stores, employing distributors, or engaging in joint ventures with local firms. Low inventory levels and low promotional activity have allowed profit margins to stay elevated versus the sector in recent years but are likely to decline as promotional activity normalizes. As with other industries, rising e-commerce penetration is generally detrimental for retailers' margins due to additional shipping and return costs. It is important for investors to track sales by channel (stores, e-commerce, and wholesale), region, and product, monitor the success of a company's digital platforms (mobile apps and member engagement), and assess the company's innovation and speed to market (the ability of a company to capitalize on a trend). Investors should also monitor changes in store count, SG&A expense ratios, inventory levels, debt levels, raw material costs, rent costs, transportation costs, and wages. Standard valuation measures such as P/E and EV/EBITDA are often used to assess valuations in this industry.

CHAPTER 11

Consumer Staples

Businesses in the global consumer staples sector provide goods and services to consumers that are nondiscretionary in nature, meaning they are essential. These are items that consumers purchase regardless of economic conditions. Sales and profits for companies in the sector traditionally grow at the same rate as the underlying economy. The reason for this is that the main driver of growth is through increasing sales volumes, which is primarily driven by economic and population growth. Most of the goods and services these businesses supply are similar with close substitutes, and therefore the scale of production and brand recognition are particularly important factors for separating the winners from the losers. In fact, consumers often base their purchase decision on brand and are often reluctant to change their preferences. Industries within the consumer staple sector therefore do not usually experience sudden changes in market share between key competitors. In the beverage industry, for example, consumers usually prefer either Coca-Cola or Pepsi products and rarely switch between the two. Despite this, companies do emerge with products having unique characteristics that enable them to grow quickly for an extended period of time. Eventually, however, competitors will begin to offer comparable products at lower prices and thereby eliminate any short-term advantages.

	Lower	≈	Higher		Lower	≈	Higher
Valuation	●			Dividend Yield		●	
Profitability	●			Payout Ratio	●		
Sales Growth	●			Dividend Growth		●	
Profit Growth	●			Earnings Predictability			●
Debt Levels			●	Share Price Volatility	●		

Data source: Bloomberg, as of March 18, 2022.

In general, consumer staple companies are less sensitive to the economic cycle because they sell everyday items such as groceries as well as certain household products like cleaning supplies and toothpaste. Whether economic conditions are good or bad, these businesses earn relatively stable profits. The relatively predictable nature of earnings for consumer staple companies means that most investors view them as being defensive, and investors often shift capital into the sector when economic conditions are expected to worsen as a means of preserving capital. It is therefore during bear markets that consumer staple stocks show the best relative performance. The lower relative growth rates for most consumer staple companies leads investors to move money out of them once economic conditions improve and we enter a bull market, instead favoring businesses in industries that will benefit more during periods of strong economic growth.

In this chapter we take a closer look at the six main industry groups within the sector: (1) beverages, (2) grocery and convenience stores, (3) household products, (4) hypermarkets, (5) packaged foods, and (6) tobacco.

■ Beverages

The beverage industry includes producers of both alcoholic and nonalcoholic drinks. Some of the companies noted here, such as Pepsi, also produce

Businesses		Relative Characteristics						
Company	Country		Sector			Market		
			Lower	≈	Higher	Lower	≈	Higher
Anheuser-Busch InBev SA/NV	Belgium	Valuation		●		●		
Asahi Group Holdings	Japan	Profitability			●			●
Coca-Cola Co.	United States	Sales Growth			●	●		
Diageo PLC	United Kingdom	Profit Growth		●		●		
Heineken Holding NV	Netherlands	Debt Levels	●				●	
Keurig Dr Pepper Inc.	United States	Dividend Yield	●			●		
Kirin Holdings Co.	Japan	Payout Ratio		●		●		
Kweichow Moutai Co.	China	Dividend Growth		●			●	
PepsiCo Inc.	United States	Earnings Predictability		●				●
Pernod Ricard SA	France	Share Price Volatility		●		●		

Data source: Bloomberg, as of March 18, 2022.

a wide variety of snack foods. Beverage producers can grow through acquisition by buying other product lines, and organically by investing in research and development in the hope of developing a successful new product. Either approach allows the company to leverage their strong supply chains and distribution networks. After years of slow growth, the importation of energy drinks into the United States gave a boost to industry growth rates and launched a variety of competitors. Segments of the beverage industry have received negative press at times due to possible health issues arising from consuming excessive amounts of soft drinks and energy drinks. Economic factors that have the greatest impact on profit and revenue growth for the beverage industry include GDP growth, food prices, packaging costs, wages, freight costs, and supply chain disruptions. Availability of containers and packaging can also impact industry profitability. These businesses sell goods that are relatively inexpensive and that many people find difficult to live without. This means that they generate consistent profits regardless of the economic environment and their earnings tend to hold up relatively well during recessions. Most beverage producers earn above-average profit margins, but growth is usually limited to the broader rate of economic growth in the regions in which they operate. Investors should track SG&A expense ratios, ad spending, volume, sales, and profit (EBIT) growth in total and by region. Both P/E and EV/EBITDA ratios are often used to compare valuations between companies in this industry.

■ Grocery and Convenience Stores

Businesses		Relative Characteristics						
Company	**Country**		**Sector**			**Market**		
			Lower	≈	Higher	Lower	≈	Higher
Albertsons Cos.	United States	Valuation		●		●		
Alimentation Couche-Tarde Inc.	Canada	Profitability	●			●		
Fomento Economico Mexicano SAB de CV	Mexico	Sales Growth	●			●		
Koninklijke Ahold Delhaize NV	Netherlands	Profit Growth			●			●
Kroger Co.	United States	Debt Levels	●					●
Loblaw Companies Ltd.	Canada	Dividend Yield	●			●		
Rallye SA	France	Payout Ratio	●			●		
Seven & I Holdings Co. Ltd.	Japan	Dividend Growth			●			●
Tesco PLC	United Kingdom	Earnings Predictability			●			●
Woolworth's Group Ltd.	Australia	Share Price Volatility	●			●		

Data source: Bloomberg, as of March 18, 2022.

Grocery and convenience stores sell food and nonfood staples, sometimes including gasoline. Current trends in the industry include growing demand for food, semi-prepared and prepared meal delivery, as well as a shift toward healthier eating habits. Food is a necessity of life, making the industry perhaps the least sensitive to the economic cycle. However, these businesses do compete with restaurants and other forms of food delivery, such as semi-prepared meals, and consumers are sensitive to rising food costs, which may cause them to buy lower-cost items that typically generate lower profit margins for the business. Economic factors that have the greatest impact on profit and revenue growth for the industry include GDP growth, food prices, packaging costs, wages, freight costs, and supply chain disruptions. Supply chain management is a critical component of success for these businesses, especially to the degree they sell perishable goods. Accordingly, these businesses require operational scale, which gives them buying power (the ability to purchase larger quantities of inventory at lower prices). The grocery industry generates relatively low profit margins in most developed countries and therefore relies heavily on selling large volumes of products to generate earnings in those regions. For companies that cover large geographic areas, higher fuel costs could drive up transportation costs and negatively impact profits. Investors should monitor same-store sales growth, foot traffic, ticket size, new-store growth, new-store productivity, total revenue growth, change in gross margin, SG&A rate (and SG&A leverage),

SG&A per store or SG&A per square foot growth (to normalize for changes in store count), EBIT margin (and change in EBIT margin), EBIT and EPS growth, leverage (net debt/EBITDA), and lease-adjusted leverage (net debt, including operating leases/EBITDAR). Commonly used valuation measures for the industry include P/E and EV/EBITDA.

■ Household Products

Businesses		Relative Characteristics						
Company	Country		Sector			Market		
			Lower	≈	Higher	Lower	≈	Higher
Colgate-Palmolive Co. ———— United States		Valuation	●			●		
Essity AB ———————— Sweden		Profitability			●			●
Estee Lauder Companies Ltd. ——— United States		Sales Growth	●			●		
Henkel AG & Co ————— Germany		Profit Growth	●			●		
Kao Corp. ———————— Japan		Debt Levels			●			●
Kimberly-Clark Corp. ———— United States		Dividend Yield		●				●
L'Oréal SA ———————— France		Payout Ratio		●			●	
Procter & Gamble Co. ———— United States		Dividend Growth			●			●
Reckitt Benckiser Group PLC ——— United Kingdom		Earnings Predictability			●			●
Unilever PLC ———————— United Kingdom		Share Price Volatility	●			●		

Data source: Bloomberg, as of March 18, 2022.

The household products industry produces a wide range of everyday necessities, including toothpaste, shampoo, soap, makeup, and cleaning products. These businesses sell goods that are difficult to live without and therefore they generate relatively consistent profits regardless of the economic environment. Like companies in the beverage industry, household product companies can grow through acquisition by acquiring other product lines or companies, or organically by investing in research and development in the hope of developing a successful new product. Either of these will allow the company to leverage their strong supply chains and vast distribution networks. Companies in this industry are benefiting from continued expansion into developing economies. Although the industry is mature and growth is usually limited to the broader rate of economic growth in the regions in which they operate, their predictable earnings allow them to pay competitive dividends and grow them at an above-average rate. Most household and personal product companies generate attractive profit margins, because of both brand power and manufacturing scale. Availability of containers and packaging, as well as shipping, raw material, and labor costs, can have a significant impact on profitability. Investors should track advertising and promotion spending levels, growth rates in emerging markets (a key area of growth for the industry), organic sales growth, and operating margins. Principal factors for investors to track include gross and EBIT margin, SG&A expenses, and new product innovations. Both P/E and EV/EBITDA ratios are often used to compare valuations between companies in this industry.

■ Hypermarkets

Businesses		Relative Characteristics						
Company	**Country**		**Sector**			**Market**		
			Lower	≈	Higher	Lower	≈	Higher
Aeon Co. Ltd.	Japan	Valuation		●		●		
B&M European Value Retail SA	United Kingdom	Profitability	●			●		
Carrefour SA	France	Sales Growth		●		●		
Casino Guichard Perrachon	France	Profit Growth		●				●
Costco Wholesale	United States	Debt Levels	●				●	
E-MART Inc.	South Korea	Dividend Yield	●			●		
MassMart Holdings Ltd.	South Africa	Payout Ratio	●			●		
Siam Makro Public Company Ltd.	Thailand	Dividend Growth	●			●		
Target Corp.	United States	Earnings Predictability	●			●		
Walmart Inc.	United States	Share Price Volatility		●		●		

Data source: Bloomberg, as of March 18, 2022.

Hypermarkets are large-format stores that sell essential and nonessential products to businesses and consumers, including both food and nonfood items. Customers often visit the store for food or personal products and purchase something they did not intend to buy (there is an element of treasure-hunting at some of these stores). Most retail concepts struggle to expand overseas and are therefore geared to the local market. However, US-based Costco and Walmart are exceptions. Walmart has localized concepts or brands in several Asia-Pacific regions, while Costco has traveled well and successfully expanded internationally. As with other consumer-focused businesses, profitability for hypermarkets can be affected by inflation, whether caused by product, labor, or transportation costs. Similar to the grocery and convenience store industry, hypermarkets often generate comparatively low profit margins and rely heavily on selling large volumes of products. For these companies, operational scale is required to afford them the buying power needed to purchase inventory in volume at lower prices. Pricing power and the ability to offset inflationary pressures is crucial in deciding relative winners and losers in the industry. For companies that cover large geographic areas, transportation costs can meaningfully impact profitability due to higher fuel costs. Important metrics to track include same-store sales growth, the source of growth (traffic volume or ticket size), per-store-unit growth, new-store productivity, revenue growth, gross and EBIT margins, SG&A/square foot growth, EBIT and EPS growth, as well as leverage (net debt/EBITDA) and lease-adjusted leverage (net debt, including operating leases/EBITDAR). Standard valuation measures such as P/E and EV/EBITDA are often used to assess valuations in this industry.

■ Packaged Foods

Businesses		Relative Characteristics						
Company	**Country**		**Sector**			**Market**		
			Lower	≈	Higher	Lower	≈	Higher
Associated British Foods	United Kingdom	Valuation		●		●		
CJ Cheiljedang Corp.	South Korea	Profitability	●			●		
Danone SA	France	Sales Growth	●			●		
Grupo Bimbo SAB	Mexico	Profit Growth	●			●		
Inner Mongolia Yili Industrial Group Co.	China	Debt Levels	●			●		
Kraft Heinz Co.	United States	Dividend Yield	●			●		
Mondelez International Inc.	United States	Payout Ratio		●		●		
Nestlé SA	Switzerland	Dividend Growth			●			●
Uni-President Enterprises Corp.	Taiwan	Earnings Predictability		●				●
WH Group Ltd.	Hong Kong	Share Price Volatility		●		●		

Data source: Bloomberg, as of March 18, 2022.

The packaged food industry prepares food products that are sold through wholesalers, grocery stores, convenience stores, and hypermarkets. Brand strength can be an important consideration in the packaged foods industry. Consumers will often buy a higher-quality brand of food product when economic conditions are good but shift to less expensive products when economic conditions weaken to save money. Economic factors that have the greatest impact on earnings and revenue growth for the packaged foods industry include GDP growth, food prices, packaging costs, wages, interest rates, freight costs, and supply chain disruptions. Inflation can be problematic for the packaged food industry as it can take between six and nine months for companies to pass along higher costs to consumers by increasing prices. Furthermore, as inflation hits consumers in other areas, such as gasoline and rent, it can become difficult for packaged food companies to fully pass along higher costs to consumers and may eventually affect profit margins. As with many other companies in the consumer staple sector, packaged food companies typically sell high volumes of products that generate below-average profit margins. Important metrics for investors to monitor are both segment and geographic organic growth rates, gross profit, gross margin, adjusted profit margin by segment, adjusted operating profit and margin by geographical region, advertising and promotional spending, EBIT, and EBITDA as well as EBIT and EBITDA margins. Both P/E and EV/EBITDA ratios are often used to compare valuations between companies in this industry.

■ Tobacco

Businesses		Relative Characteristics						
Company	**Country**		**Sector**			**Market**		
			Lower	≈	Higher	Lower	≈	Higher
Altria Group Inc.	United States	Valuation	●				●	
British American Tobacco PLC	United Kingdom	Profitability		●				●
Gudang Garam Tbk	Indonesia	Sales Growth		●		●		
Hanjaya Mandala Sampoerna Tbk	Indonesia	Profit Growth	●			●		
Imperial Brands PLC	United Kingdom	Debt Levels	●			●		
ITC Ltd.	India	Dividend Yield		●				●
Japan Tobacco Inc.	Japan	Payout Ratio		●		●		
KT&G Corp.	South Korea	Dividend Growth		●		●		
Philip Morris International Inc.	United States	Earnings Predictability	●			●		
Vector Group Ltd.	United States	Share Price Volatility		●		●		

Data source: Bloomberg, as of March 18, 2022.

Although in long-term secular decline, the use of tobacco products remains at high absolute levels. The World Health Organization estimated that tobacco use had fallen from 1.397 billion people in 2000 to 1.337 billion in 2018, a drop of 60 million people.[1] Despite the slow decline in use of tobacco products, which is expected to continue as a result of increased regulation and growing awareness of the health risks involved with its use, tobacco companies still produce consistent profits and cash flows. For this reason, shares of tobacco companies perform well during times of market uncertainty, as investors often reallocate capital to the industry when the economic cycle is nearing a peak and a recession is likely to occur. Economic considerations include inflation, interest rates, supply chain disruptions, government regulations, and taxation. Investors should track percent change in volume, segment and geographical organic growth, gross revenue, excise taxes, net sales growth, gross profit, gross margin, operating income, operating margin, EBIT, EBITDA, as well as EBIT and EBITDA margins. Since the companies within the tobacco industry are mature and generate consistent earnings, standard valuation metrics such as P/E, P/CF, and EV/EBITDA can be used to compare relative valuations between companies.

CHAPTER 12

Energy

The global energy sector includes companies that discover, produce, and deliver energy products made from fossil fuels to both retail and commercial customers. Since most individuals and businesses around the world require energy on an ongoing basis, one might assume that these products and services are nondiscretionary in nature. However, the energy sector is highly cyclical, primarily because much of the demand for oil comes from industrial companies, and these businesses are cyclical. Manufacturers, for example, expand production during periods of economic growth, thereby increasing their use of energy products. Conversely, as economic growth slows down, manufacturers produce fewer goods and consume less fuel. In the chemical industry, energy products are often a significant component of the goods being manufactured, including paint and plastic. Other industries that would consume less fuel in weak economic environments include transport and shipping companies as well as airlines. Even consumers cut back on their fuel consumption in a weak economy, driving less for vacations or making fewer trips to the shopping center. The result is a strong correlation between oil consumption and economic growth, whereby a 1% increase in global economic growth translates to an approximately 0.5% increase in oil consumption.

Energy derived from fossil fuels has been linked to climate change and has a history of creating environmental calamities, such as oil spills. While the fossil fuel industry is under social and regulatory pressure to change its ways, an immediate end to the use of fossil fuels would be catastrophic for the world economy. Nevertheless, many companies in the energy sector are striving to operate in an environmentally friendly manner in addition to diversifying operations by allocating capital toward the development of renewable energy projects.

Sector Characteristics versus Market

	Lower	≈	Higher		Lower	≈	Higher
Valuation	●			Dividend Yield			●
Profitability	●			Payout Ratio	●		
Sales Growth			●	Dividend Growth	●		
Profit Growth			●	Earnings Predictability		●	
Debt Levels	●			Share Price Volatility			●

Data source: Bloomberg, as of March 18, 2022.

Governments around the world are also investing in renewable energy, further augmenting competition for the energy sector. Renewable energy refers to energy produced through sustainable means such as wind, solar, geothermal, nuclear power, hydroelectricity, and tidal power. Renewable energy is grouped in the utility sector and is discussed in more detail in Chapter 19. The transition from fossil fuels to renewable energy will take considerable time, with the International Energy Agency estimating that oil and gas consumption will continue for another 20–30 years and require significant ongoing investment.

The futures curve for crude oil can be a useful tool for assessing the current state of the energy market. The curve consists of contracted prices for delivery of crude oil today (referred to as the spot price) and at various future points in time (future prices). If the spot price is higher than future prices, the curve is said to be in backwardation. This means that there is strong near-term demand for crude oil, and it is being bid for use. Conversely, if prices are higher in the future, the price curve is said to be in contango. In that case demand for oil today is below what is expected in the future and oil is being bid for storage. In other words, buyers are willing to purchase crude oil today and store it, with the expectation that they can sell it at a higher price sometime in the future. If the futures curve for oil is in backwardation (downward sloping), it is positive for energy companies, boosting near-term demand as well as their profit margins. Examples of both types of futures curve (contango and backwardation) are shown in Figure 12.1.

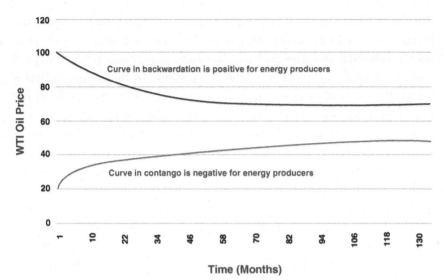

FIGURE 12.1 Sample of Future Price Curves for WTI Oil: Backwardation versus Contango

In this chapter we take a closer look at the six main industry groups within the sector: (1) coal, (2) energy equipment and services, (3) exploration and production, (4) integrated oil and gas, (5) refining and marketing, and (6) storage and transportation.

■ Coal

Businesses		Relative Characteristics						
Company	Country		Sector			Market		
			Lower	≈	Higher	Lower	≈	Higher
Adaro Energy Indonesia Tbk PT — Indonesia		Valuation		●		●		
Arch Resources Inc. — United States		Profitability			●	●		
Banpu PCL — Thailand		Sales Growth			●			●
China Coal Energy Co. Ltd. — China		Profit Growth	●				●	
China Shenhua Energy Co. Ltd. — China		Debt Levels	●			●		
Coal India Ltd. — India		Dividend Yield			●			●
Peabody Energy Co. — United States		Payout Ratio	●			●		
Shaanxi Coal Industry Co. Ltd. — China		Dividend Growth			●			●
Yancoal Australia Limited — Australia		Earnings Predictability			●			●
Yankuang Energy Group Co. Ltd. — China		Share Price Volatility	●			●		

Data source: Bloomberg, as of March 18, 2022.

The use of coal to produce electricity began in the nineteenth century, and it has been used extensively as a source of heat in homes as well as to power industrial and transportation equipment ever since. Metallurgical coal (used to make steel) is included separately in the mining industry within the materials sector. Thermal coal (coal used to produce heat) has been identified as a major cause of climate change, resulting in reduced demand and a shift toward replacing the use of coal with alternative energy sources. Although some companies are trying to develop more environmentally friendly methods for using coal to generate power, investors should expect continued pressure on the industry. While coal is gradually being eliminated as an energy source, it is still used extensively in countries that have not yet been able to replace all of their coal-fired power plants. China, India, and the United States are the largest producers of coal, but they are also leading the world in renewable energy investment. The relative price of thermal coal to oil and gas is a potential indicator of future demand. In many thermal power plants, both oil and gas are readily available substitutes for coal and if the price gap between them grows materially, demand will shift to the lowest-cost fuel. Since coal is a substitute for oil and gas at the margin, increases in oil and gas prices will eventually lead to a corresponding increase in thermal coal prices. Other economic factors that affect sales and profit growth include GDP and population growth, industrial production levels, and fuel costs (diesel and gasoline), especially in situations where coal must be transported to the final customer. The coal producers listed here generated relatively strong, predictable earnings in recent years while maintaining above-average dividend yields. Key factors for investors to monitor include local coal prices, oil and gas prices, coal production and sales volumes, and production cost trends. Valuation comparisons can be made using measures such as P/E and EV/EBITDA multiples.

■ Energy Equipment and Services

Businesses in the energy equipment and service industry supply the products and services necessary for the discovery and extraction of fossil fuels both onshore and offshore. This includes well drilling, geological, engineering, and operational services, as well as supplying derricks, turbines, valves, pumps, drills, and pressure control equipment, among many other items essential to the industry. Oil and gas prices have the biggest

Businesses		Relative Characteristics						
Company	Country		Sector			Market		
			Lower	≈	Higher	Lower	≈	Higher
Baker Hughes Co. — United States		Valuation	●			●		
China Oilfield Services Ltd. — China		Profitability	●			●		
Halliburton Co. — United States		Sales Growth	●			●		
John Wood Group PLC — United Kingdom		Profit Growth		●				●
Saipem SpA — Italy		Debt Levels	●			●		
Schlumberger NV — United States		Dividend Yield	●			●		
Subsea 7 SA — Norway		Payout Ratio	●			●		
Technip Energies NV — France		Dividend Growth	●			●		
TechnipFMC PLC — United Kingdom		Earnings Predictability		●				●
Worley Ltd. — Australia		Share Price Volatility		●				●

Data source: Bloomberg, as of March 18, 2022.

impact on this industry, as higher prices lead to greater investment in exploration and production by energy producers. Due to their reliance on commodity prices, businesses in this industry are highly cyclical and sensitive to changes in economic growth. The same factors that affect oil and gas producers (discussed next) flow through to the equipment and service providers, usually with a delay of several months. Share price volatility for these companies is relatively high, while the depressed valuations, sales growth, and profitability evidenced in this table are the result of weakness in the energy sector in recent years caused in part by overproduction. These characteristics are likely to recover once demand for equipment and services increases and energy producers become profitable again. In addition to oil and gas prices, it is important to monitor the capital expenditure plans of the world's major energy producers. EBITDA is a widely followed metric for the energy service industry, but investors should also monitor discretionary cash flow, which better accounts for the increase in maintenance costs that occurs as EBITDA grows. Other important metrics that investors should monitor include tangible asset turnover as well as net debt/EBITDA ratios. For equipment and services companies, rig counts, day rates (the dollar amount charged by contract drillers), and day costs are also important. For disposal businesses, injection well volumes can also provide useful information. Commonly used valuation measures for the industry include P/E and EV/EBITDA.

■ Exploration and Production

Businesses		Relative Characteristics						
Company	**Country**		**Sector**			**Market**		
			Lower	≈	Higher	Lower	≈	Higher
Aker BP ASA	Norway	Valuation			●	●		
Canadian Natural Resources Ltd.	Canada	Profitability			●	●		
CNOOC Ltd.	China	Sales Growth			●			●
ConocoPhillips	United States	Profit Growth			●			●
EOG Resources Inc.	United States	Debt Levels	●			●		
Inpex Corp.	Japan	Dividend Yield		●			●	
Oxidental Petroleum Corp.	United States	Payout Ratio	●			●		
PTT Exploration & Production	Thailand	Dividend Growth			●			●
Var Energi ASA	Norway	Earnings Predictability			●			●
Woodside Energy Group Ltd.	Australia	Share Price Volatility			●			●

Data source: Bloomberg, as of March 18, 2022.

Exploration and production companies (commonly referred to as E&P companies or energy producers) are engaged in the discovery and extraction of fossil fuels both on land and at sea. The pandemic-driven price collapse in 2020 marked the start of a new era, one defined by pervasive capital discipline, rising free cash flow, and an emphasis on growing shareholder returns instead of production. Given the impact of fossil fuels on the world's climate, investors should expect continued pressure on the industry from an ESG perspective. That said, most large producers are developing climate-friendly technology, including decarbonizing technology that is synergistic with existing operations such as carbon capture, hydrogen, and biofuels. While the price of oil is primarily decided at the global level, demand for natural gas is highly seasonal and prices are very regional. Companies realize different prices based on the spread to major pricing hubs, also known as differentials. Commodity prices are a function of supply and demand and influence company earnings the most. Natural gas prices are also driven by supply (production) and demand (power generation, heating, weather, industrial activity). FCF yield, or FCF/equity, has become a key valuation metric. FCF/EV is another form of FCF yield and it factors in debt on the balance sheet. EV/EBITDA, debt/EBITDA, dividend yield and reinvestment rates (capex as a percentage of cash flow from operations before working capital) are also important metrics since the industry is capital-intensive. Due to the high variability of earnings over the economic cycle, investors should use the price to net asset value (P/NAV) ratio for valuation comparisons, in addition to P/E and EV/EBITDA.

■ Integrated Oil and Gas

Businesses		Relative Characteristics						
Company	**Country**		**Sector**			**Market**		
			Lower	≈	Higher	Lower	≈	Higher
BP PLC	United Kingdom	Valuation			●	●		
Chevron Corp	United States	Profitability		●		●		
China Petroleum & Chemical Co.	China	Sales Growth	●			●		
Eni SpA	Italy	Profit Growth			●			●
Equinor ASA	Norway	Debt Levels	●			●		
Exxon Mobil Corp	United States	Dividend Yield			●			●
PetroChina Co. Ltd.	China	Payout Ratio		●		●		
Saudi Arabian Oil Co.	Saudi Arabia	Dividend Growth	●			●		
Shell PLC	United Kingdom	Earnings Predictability			●			●
TotalEnergies SE	France	Share Price Volatility	●				●	

Data source: Bloomberg, as of March 18, 2022.

Integrated oil and gas companies (also referred to as the majors) are essentially energy conglomerates, whose businesses extend from exploration and production, refining, and transportation all the way to downstream operations in which the end products, such as gasoline, are sold to consumers. As mentioned earlier, concerns over climate change have led to an emerging area of energy production, namely renewable energy. The expected time horizon for the transition to renewables is long, however, and the integrated energy companies may be best positioned to lead the transition. European majors have taken a proactive approach to the energy transition, investing more heavily in renewables compared to North American peers that are still more focused on the traditional oil and gas business. Despite this North American majors have tended to trade at a 1.5–2× multiple premium when compared to European peers. Although sales growth has been below average, profits have grown at an above-average rate, suggesting these businesses have successfully expanded their profit margins relative to the market. All of the factors that impact other energy industry segments will affect integrated energy firms, including global GDP growth, industrial production, trade, and travel, all of which help drive oil and gas prices, which are the most critical determinant of sales and earnings growth for the industry. For the integrated companies, crack spreads (refining margins) and chemicals margins also drive earnings, while input costs such as labor, steel, sand, and chemicals drive capex inflation. Commonly used valuation measures for the integrated oil and gas industry include P/E and EV/EBITDA, but a sum of the parts or discounted cash flow analysis may be most appropriate for these businesses since they often operate in multiple areas of the energy sector.

■ Refining and Marketing

Businesses		Relative Characteristics						
Company	Country		Sector			Market		
			Lower	≈	Higher	Lower	≈	Higher
ENEOS Holdings Inc. — Japan		Valuation		●		●		
Idemitsu Kosan Co. — Japan		Profitability	●			●		
Indian Oil Corp. Ltd. — India		Sales Growth	●			●		
Marathon Petroleum Corp. — United States		Profit Growth	●			●		
Neste Oyj — Finland		Debt Levels	●			●		
Phillips 66 — United States		Dividend Yield	●					●
Polski Koncern Naftowy Orlen SA — Poland		Payout Ratio		●		●		
Reliance Industries Ltd. — India		Dividend Growth		●		●		
SK Innovation Co. Ltd. — South Korea		Earnings Predictability	●			●		
Valero Energy Corp. — United States		Share Price Volatility		●				●

Data source: Bloomberg, as of March 18, 2022.

Companies within the refining and marketing industry are tasked with final processing of the various elements found within raw fossil fuels. During the refining process, impurities such as sand, water, sulfur, and carbon dioxide are removed, and the remaining substances, such as oil, natural gas, and natural gas liquids, are separated and processed into final products such as heating oil, gasoline, jet fuel, and lubricants. The products created through the refining process are also used extensively in the chemical industry and to produce the asphalt used to build roads. According to the US Energy Information Administration, "crack spreads are differences between wholesale petroleum product prices and crude oil prices. These spreads are often used to estimate refining margins. Crack spreads are a simple measure based on one or two products produced in a refinery (usually gasoline and distillate fuel). They do not take into consideration all refinery product revenues and exclude refining costs other than the cost of crude oil."[1] Economic factors that affect the refining industry include GDP growth and the general level of economic activity, industrial production, shipping levels, and travel, which helps drive demand for gasoline and jet fuel. Several refiners listed here also own downstream operations, where they deliver gasoline and other products directly to consumers. Although refiners are influenced by the price of oil and gas, their earnings tend to be more stable than companies engaged in energy exploration and production or that provide energy equipment and services. For refiners, crack spreads (refining margins) and chemical margins also drive earnings. Input costs such as labor, steel, sand, and chemicals impact capital expenditure inflation. Standard valuation measures such as P/E and EV/EBITDA are often used to assess valuations in this industry.

■ Storage and Transportation

Businesses		Relative Characteristics						
Company	**Country**		**Sector**			**Market**		
			Lower	≈	Higher	Lower	≈	Higher
Cheniere Energy Inc.	United States	Valuation	●			●		
Enbridge Inc.	Canada	Profitability			●	●		
Energy Transfer LP	United States	Sales Growth			●			●
Enterprise Product Partners LP	United States	Profit Growth		●				●
Kinder Morgan Inc.	United States	Debt Levels			●			●
Petronet LNG Ltd.	India	Dividend Yield			●			●
Plains All American Pipeline Ltd.	United States	Payout Ratio			●			●
Pembina Pipeline Corp.	Canada	Dividend Growth			●			●
Targa Resources Corp.	United States	Earnings Predictability			●			●
TC Energy Corp.	Canada	Share Price Volatility		●				●

Data source: Bloomberg, as of March 18, 2022.

Energy companies engaged in the storage and transportation of energy products (often referred to as "midstreamers") are comprised primarily of pipeline operators that gather, store, and transport crude oil, natural gas, and fluids between producers and refiners. These businesses also provide a limited amount of treatment and processing where they separate components of the raw commodity through a process called fractionation. Pipelines are used more extensively in large geographic regions where raw fossil fuels must be transported great distances before reaching the refineries needed to convert them into end products. Railroads and trucks compete with pipeline operators to facilitate transportation of energy products. However, these transportation methods tend to be less cost effective and may pose a greater environmental risk. Despite this, it is likely that an increasing amount of fossil fuel will be shipped by rail and road, as it has become exceedingly difficult in many jurisdictions to get approval to upgrade or build new pipelines over environmental concerns and the need to obtain easements through private and public property. Like other industry groups within the energy sector, midstream companies are working toward reducing carbon emissions. Pipeline operators have attractive business models, assuming they can obtain regulatory approval needed for new projects and to effectively maintain their existing networks. Once pipelines are built the cost of maintaining them is low and they are long-lived assets. Pipeline operators are less sensitive to the economic cycle compared to other industries within the energy sector because their contracts are usually take-or-pay, long-term fee for service agreements, or regulatory cost of service, making revenue and earnings stable and predictable regardless of economic conditions. As a result, they generate strong cash flows and can support attractive dividend payouts. Key variables that investors should track include crude production, mainline (pipeline) volumes, refinery throughput, fractionation spreads, prices for oil, gas, and natural gas liquids (NGLs), EBITDA, return on invested capital (ROIC), capital expenditure requirements, leverage (debt/EBITDA), dividend payout ratio, FCF/dividend coverage, and FCF yield. Valuations are most often compared using EV/EBITDA or FCF yield. Contracts are long term and predictable so a discounted cash flow approach (EV/DACF) can also be used for valuation.

CHAPTER 13

Financials

The global financial sector serves as the engine that drives the world economy. From everyday banking transactions to financing the ongoing operations of businesses and world trade, these businesses serve a crucial role in the global economy. While basic financial services like banking and wealth management are a key part of our everyday lives, some of the services these companies provide are dependent on economic conditions, and demand for them can fluctuate significantly. Although relatively predictable, earnings for many businesses in the financial sector are cyclical in nature and vary significantly in different stages of the economic cycle.

191

Sector Characteristics versus Market							
	Lower	≈	Higher		Lower	≈	Higher
Valuation	●			Dividend Yield			●
Profitability			●	Payout Ratio	●		
Sales Growth	●			Dividend Growth			●
Profit Growth		●		Earnings Predictability			●
Debt Levels	●			Share Price Volatility			●

Data source: Bloomberg, as of March 18, 2022.

Despite below-average sales growth over the past several years, the financial sector has generated strong profitability, profit growth, and dividend growth. Many of the companies in the sector are interest rate–sensitive, which means that their business prospects can be heavily affected by changes in the level of interest rates. The relationship between interest rates and financial sector earnings is complex, due to crosscurrents that affect industries differently within the sector. For banks, higher interest rates reduce demand for loans, but serve to disproportionally increase lending rates, thus boosting net interest margin (profitability). Conversely, lower interest rates increase demand for loans, but serve to lower net interest margin. We are primarily concerned with the net (combined) effect of a change in interest rates on these businesses. The performance of the equity markets can also impact the financial sector. Relative performance for the financial sector is usually best during the repair phase of the market cycle and poorest in the mid-cycle phase of a bull market. There are nine main industry groups: (1) asset management, (2) banks, (3) capital markets, (4) consumer finance, (5) financial conglomerates, (6) financial data and analytics, (7) life and health insurance, (8) property and casualty insurance, and (9) securities exchanges.

■ Asset Management

Businesses		Relative Characteristics						
Company	**Country**		Sector			Market		
			Lower	≈	Higher	Lower	≈	Higher
Amundi SA	France	Valuation			●	●		
BlackRock Inc.	United States	Profitability		●				●
Blackstone Inc.	United States	Sales Growth			●			●
Brookfield Asset Management Inc.	Canada	Profit Growth			●			●
Charles Schwab Inc.	United States	Debt Levels	●			●		
China Cinda Asset Management Co.	China	Dividend Yield			●			●
DWS Group GmbH & Co KGaA	Germany	Payout Ratio		●		●		
KKR & Co Inc.	United States	Dividend Growth			●			●
St James Place PLC	United Kingdom	Earnings Predictability			●			●
UBS Group AG	Switzerland	Share Price Volatility		●				●

Data source: Bloomberg, as of March 18, 2022.

Businesses in the asset management industry provide wealth management solutions for individuals, as well as investment management and custody services for institutions. Revenues are principally earned by charging a percentage fee based on the dollar amount of assets under management (AUM) or administration (AUA). Traditional asset managers (those who actively manage stock and bond portfolios) have been losing market share to alternative asset managers, passive index funds, and exchange-traded funds (ETFs) in recent years. However, this trend usually reverses following bear markets during which active managers often outperform passive strategies. Other industry trends include customized investment solutions, lower fees, increasing allocations from high-net-worth clients, and the consolidation of relationships among institutional clients. The asset management industry is heavily regulated, and investors must keep themselves apprised of any upcoming or potential regulatory changes. Any economic or political factors that influence public markets can impact net asset values (NAVs) on which asset managers earn a fee. For private equity firms, any factors that move public markets can influence timing and realized value from exits, as well as the deployment of cash. Growth in sales and profitability is thereby determined largely by general changes in overall wealth. A rising stock market, for example, is good news for these businesses since it grows their AUM or AUA on which they earn a fee. Despite intense competition, the industry has generated strong sales and profit growth combined with strong profit margins and has delivered above-average dividend yields. Important metrics for investors to monitor include AUM by segment or product type, changes in AUM (distinguishing between fund flows and market-driven growth), net interest income, revenue and EPS growth, operating expense ratios, operating margins, and management fee margins. For alternative asset managers, net flows, fee-related earnings margin, and distributable earnings are important metrics to track. Standard valuation metrics such as P/E can be used for comparing valuations, while the slightly modified price to fee-related earnings (P/FRE) may provide additional insights for companies that are heavily dependent on fee income as a source of revenue.

■ Banks

Banks around the world provide people and businesses with a place to keep their savings and borrow funds to invest, buy a home, or fund a new business project. Traditional banks are facing increased competition from online lenders, and there is also a strong trend whereby consumers are conducting more of their banking through online platforms, forcing banks to build out their online presence and improve customer service. Consumer banking tends to be local, while trading and investment banking businesses (considered

Businesses		Relative Characteristics						
Company	Country		Sector			Market		
			Lower	≈	Higher	Lower	≈	Higher
Agricultural Bank of China —— China		Valuation	●			●		
Banco Santander SA —— Spain		Profitability		●				●
Bank central Asia TBK —— Indonesia		Sales Growth	●			●		
BNP Paribas SA —— France		Profit Growth	●			●		
HDFC Bank Limited —— India		Debt Levels	●			●		
HSBC Holdings PLC —— United Kingdom		Dividend Yield		●				●
Industrial & Commercial Bank of China —— China		Payout Ratio	●			●		
JPMorgan Chase & Co. —— United States		Dividend Growth	●				●	
Royal Bank of Canada —— Canada		Earnings Predictability		●				●
Wells Fargo & Co. —— United States		Share Price Volatility	●					●

Data source: Bloomberg, as of March 18, 2022.

separately as part of the capital markets industry, although several of the businesses listed here operate in both industries) tend to be more global in nature. GDP growth, employment levels, and changes in interest rates are among the most important economic factors that affect bank sales and profit growth as well as their profitability. The difference between the rate at which banks pay interest on savings and the rate at which they loan money is referred to as the net interest margin (NIM) and is the primary driver of a bank's earnings. Changes in interest rates (which can be viewed through changes in the yield curve) therefore play a critical role in revenue and earnings growth of banks. As interest rates rise, banks can increase loan rates faster than the rate they pay on savings accounts, generating incremental profits in the process. In recent years, these businesses have traded at attractive valuations despite generating relatively high profit margins and attractive dividends yields, most likely due to below-average sales and profit growth. Return on equity (ROE), return on tangible common equity (ROTCE), net interest margin, total deposits, net interest income, fee growth, total revenue growth, loan growth, loan credit quality, changes in loan loss provisions, actual loan losses, the net charge-off (NCO) ratio, nonperforming loan (NPL) ratios, operating leverage, expense ratio, and net payout ratio are all important metrics for investors to monitor. The common equity tier 1 (CET 1) ratio, which compares the capital a bank holds against its risk-weighted assets, provides investors with a measure of the bank's ability to withstand financial crises. All else being equal, a higher CET 1 ratio is preferable. P/E is usually an appropriate measure of valuation for the banking industry, although a sum of the parts or DCF analysis may be required for large, diversified banks that operate in multiple segments of the financial sector.

■ Capital Markets

Businesses		Relative Characteristics	Sector			Market		
Company	Country		Lower	≈	Higher	Lower	≈	Higher
China Development Financial Holding Corp. — Taiwan		Valuation	●			●		
CITIC Securities Co. Ltd. — China		Profitability	●				●	
Credit Suisse Group AG — Switzerland		Sales Growth		●		●		
Daiwa Securities Group Inc. — Japan		Profit Growth	●			●		
Deutsche Bank AG — Germany		Debt Levels			●			●
Goldman Sachs Group Inc. — United States		Dividend Yield		●			●	
Haitong Securities Co. Ltd. — China		Payout Ratio		●		●		
Jeffries Financial Group Inc. — United States		Dividend Growth		●				●
Morgan Stanley — United States		Earnings Predictability		●				●
Nomura Holdings Inc. — Japan		Share Price Volatility			●			●

Data source: Bloomberg, as of March 18, 2022.

The capital markets industry plays a key role in executing security transactions around the world, including the trading of debt and equity securities, underwriting (facilitating) the sale of debt and equity securities by companies to investors. The performance of recent IPOs can be tracked using an ETF such as the Renaissance IPO ETF. Recent IPO performance provides an indication of current market conditions and has a bearing on whether companies decide to go public or delay until market conditions improve, thus affecting earnings for the industry. Robust performance of newly traded issues (and the stock market as a whole) can therefore be an indicator for new issuances, which drives earnings for underwriting businesses. Business structure can vary by country due to different regulatory environments that may prevent payment for certain services. Any economic factors that affect public equity and bond markets flow through into the capital markets industry by influencing AUM and AUA levels on which most companies earn a management fee. In addition, some economic factors like monetary policy could influence trading volumes, which affect commissions earned on security trades. Industry revenue and earnings are heavily affected by trading volumes of debt, equity, and derivative securities. These businesses have traded at attractive valuations in recent years, most likely due to below-average profitability, above-average debt levels, and below-average sales and profit growth. Important measures for investors to track include AUM, market share gains and losses by business segment, dollar value of interest-earning assets, net interest margin, net payout ratio, return on equity and return on tangible common shareholder equity (ROTCE), operating leverage, expense and compensation ratios, tax rates, trading revenue growth, and investment banking volumes. Standard valuation metrics such as P/E can be used for comparing valuations.

■ Consumer Finance

Businesses

Company	Country
ACOM Co. Ltd.	Japan
American Express Co.	United States
Bajaj Finance Ltd.	India
Capital One Financial Corp.	United States
Credit Saison Co. Ltd.	Japan
Discover Financial Services	United States
Orient Corp.	Japan
Provident Financial PLC	United Kingdom
Samsung Card Co. Ltd.	South Korea
Synchrony Financial	United States

Relative Characteristics

	Sector			Market		
	Lower	≈	Higher	Lower	≈	Higher
Valuation	●			●		
Profitability	●				●	
Sales Growth			●			●
Profit Growth			●			●
Debt Levels		●		●		
Dividend Yield	●				●	
Payout Ratio	●			●		
Dividend Growth	●			●		
Earnings Predictability		●				●
Share Price Volatility	●				●	

Data source: Bloomberg, as of March 18, 2022.

Consumer finance companies are engaged in extending credit to consumers primarily through credit cards and student, auto, and personal loans. Unlike banks, consumer finance companies are not deposit-taking institutions. They earn fees from interest charged on outstanding credit balances and they may also charge a fee on a per-transaction basis, usually a percentage of the transaction value. While most of these companies extend credit and therefore benefit from lower default rates, some businesses are focused on receivables collection and management and therefore benefit from higher default rates. Consumer finance businesses tend to be local and focused on a specific segment of consumer lending. Investors should note that not all credit card companies are the same. The credit card companies listed here (such as

American Express) directly issue credit cards to consumers and, as a result, extend credit to their customers. Visa and Mastercard, in contrast, issue credit cards on behalf of third-party institutions without extending credit to consumers (they simply process transactions). Accordingly, Visa and Mastercard are considered separately in the fintech industry within the technology sector. Economic factors with the biggest influence on firm earnings/sales include GDP growth, interest rates, the level of unemployment, wage growth, and loan default rates. Due to their exposure to consumer spending, they earn higher profits when the economy is strong, and see their profits fall more than the market as economic conditions deteriorate and default rates begin to increase. A substantial portion of revenues are derived from discretionary purchases by consumers, so changes in the health of the economy are an important driver for the industry. These businesses have been trading at attractive valuations despite paying attractive dividends yields and generating above-average sales and profit growth. Important metrics for investors to track include trends in credit losses, loan (or net credit card) growth, consumer spending trends (including travel), and net interest margin. Important financial and operational metrics include ROE/ROTCE, net interest margin, revenue growth, operating leverage, expense ratio, and net payout ratio. Standard valuation metrics such as P/E can be used for valuation purposes.

■ Financial Conglomerates

Businesses		Relative Characteristics	Sector (Lower ≈ Higher)			Market (Lower ≈ Higher)		
Company	Country		Lower	≈	Higher	Lower	≈	Higher
Berkshire Hathaway Inc.	United States	Valuation	●			●		
Brookfield Business Partners LP	Canada	Profitability	●				●	
CITIC Limited	China	Sales Growth			●			●
EXOR NV	Netherlands	Profit Growth			●			●
Groupe Bruxelles Lambert	Belgium	Debt Levels		●		●		
HAL Trust	Curacao	Dividend Yield	●			●		
Investor AB	Sweden	Payout Ratio	●			●		
Legend Holdings Corporation	China	Dividend Growth	●			●		
Power Corp. of Canada	Canada	Earnings Predictability		●				●
Wendel SE	France	Share Price Volatility	●			●		

Data source: Bloomberg, as of March 18, 2022.

Financial conglomerates are essentially holding companies with a significant portion of revenue generated from the financial sector. However, many of these companies also have investments in other sectors of the market. Economic factors that impact businesses in this industry are therefore dependent on the underlying businesses. Since these companies tend to be very broad-based and operate in several industries, revenue and earnings are not only influenced by economic growth but may also be impacted by many other factors, including changes in interest rates, commodity prices, and employment growth. Despite strong sales and profit growth in recent years, ample reinvestment opportunities have prevented these businesses from paying out higher dividends. As a result, dividend yields and dividend growth rates for the industry have been below the market average. P/E may provide an approximate measure of valuation for the industry. However, these businesses are best analyzed by evaluating the individual business divisions and using a sum of the parts approach to valuing the company. This is especially true in cases where the business operates in several, very distinct, end markets. Berkshire Hathaway (listed above) is an example of a financial conglomerate, with direct ownership of both insurance (Geico) and reinsurance (General Re) companies, a railroad (Burlington Northern Santa Fe), a carpet manufacturer (Shaw Industries), specialty chemicals, a battery maker (Duracell), and utility companies, among others. Financial conglomerates may also hold large investments in nonoperating companies that it does not control, such as Apple, American Express, and Coca-Cola. These investments may be valued simply by using the current share price of the underlying company. Financial conglomerates often trade at a discount to what a sum of the parts analysis would suggest.

■ Financial Data and Analytics

Financial data and analytics is big business. These businesses provide data and analytics to the financial sector and include credit ratings for consumers, ratings on debt (issued by both corporations and governmental bodies), risk assessment, and proxy voting services, among others. Data service providers in Europe have historically experienced slower growth rates and traded at lower valuation multiples compared to their North American peers. Notable industry trends include increasing adoption and budgets for data and analytics, embedding solutions and analytics within traditional data to create stickier products, and investing in technology to improve product development cycles. Economic factors that have a significant impact on sales growth and profitability relating to

Businesses		Relative Characteristics			
Company	**Country**			**Sector**	**Market**
			Lower ≈ Higher	Lower ≈ Higher
Allfunds Group PLC	United Kingdom	Valuation	Sector: ≈/Higher	Market: Higher
Broadridge Financial Solutions Inc.	United States	Profitability	Sector: ≈	Market: Higher
Dun & Bradstreet Holdings Inc.	United States	Sales Growth	Sector: Lower	Market: Lower
Experian PLC	Ireland	Profit Growth	Sector: ≈	Market: Higher
Moody's Corp.	United States	Debt Levels	Sector: Higher	Market: Higher
MSCI Inc.	United States	Dividend Yield	Sector: Lower	Market: Lower
RELX PLC	United Kingdom	Payout Ratio	Sector: ≈	Market: Lower
S&P Global Inc.	United States	Dividend Growth	Sector: Higher	Market: Higher
Thomson Reuters Corp.	Canada	Earnings Predictability	Sector: Higher	Market: Higher
Wolters Kluwer NV	Netherlands	Share Price Volatility	Sector: Lower	Market: Higher

Data source: Bloomberg, as of March 18, 2022.

the bond rating segment of these businesses include changes in interest rates, mortgage rates, debt/GDP, and GDP growth. Other business segments would be affected by a variety of factors including GDP growth and business sentiment, along with uptake of ESG ratings. Over the past few years businesses in this industry have traded at above-average valuations, driven by strong relative profitability and strong profit growth. Low payout ratios have allowed these businesses to grow their dividends at an above-average rate. ESG is a new area of growth for the industry, and some of the companies listed are adding ESG analysis services to their businesses. Important metrics for investors to track include organic revenue growth by product line (index subscriptions, analytics, ESG, debt ratings, etc.), customer retention and cancellation rates, and adjusted EBITDA margin. Standard valuation measures such as P/E and EV/EBITDA are often used to assess valuations in this industry.

■ Life and Health Insurance

Life and health insurance companies offer a wide variety of insurance policies and services to support the needs of individuals, groups, and businesses. Product offerings include life insurance, annuities, disability insurance, critical illness, long-term care insurance, health insurance, critical illness, and annuities. The breadth and complexity of product and service offerings can vary significantly by insurer. Premiums are based on the probability of contingent events (such as mortality rates), policyholder behavior, and expected

Businesses		Relative Characteristics						
Company	**Country**		**Sector**			**Market**		
			Lower	≈	Higher	Lower	≈	Higher
AIA Group Ltd.	Hong Kong	Valuation	●			●		
Assicurazioni Generali SpA	Italy	Profitability	●			●		
China Life Insurance	China	Sales Growth	●			●		
Dai-ichi Life Holdings	Japan	Profit Growth	●			●		
Japan Post Insurance	Japan	Debt Levels	●			●		
Legal & General Group	United Kingdom	Dividend Yield			●			●
Manulife Financial Corp.	Canada	Payout Ratio		●		●		
MetLife Inc.	United States	Dividend Growth			●			●
Ping An Insurance Group Co.	China	Earnings Predictability		●				●
Prudential Financial Inc.	United States	Share Price Volatility	●					●

Data source: Bloomberg, as of March 18, 2022.

investment earnings. Individual insurance policies are often long-term in nature with premiums that are set at the time of sale. Group insurance contracts are typically shorter in duration but can include coverages, such as disability insurance, that include long-term obligations. The industry is heavily regulated to ensure that companies retain enough capital to meet their obligations (liabilities) under a variety of adverse scenarios. Fixed income securities comprise the majority of the insurer's asset portfolio supporting its liabilities. These securities provide a steady stream of cash flows to support the liability cash flows. The inability of insurers to match long-term liability cash flows (typically 60 to 80 years into the future) with assets exposes them to reinvestment risk. As interest rates decrease, the insurer may not be able to reinvest at the rates assumed when the premiums were determined. A good time to own life insurance companies is when you think interest rates will rise. Equities are held within the insurer's asset portfolio to support longer-term-liability cash flows and to provide greater yield in both liability and surplus funds, and therefore equity market volatility can significantly impact profitability. Important industry themes include the move to digitization, expense reductions, and improved capital management. Potential changes in accounting standards are important to monitor as they can trigger increased volatility in an insurer's earnings before it can effectively adjust its strategies. Over the past few years, valuations have been below the market, while sales and profit growth have lagged. Important financial and operational metrics to monitor include return on equity, dividend payout ratios, premium growth, net income, accumulated other comprehensive income (AOCI), capital adequacy (solvency ratios), reserve levels and changes, and loss ratios. Given the regulatory pressures on life and health insurers it is important to be aware of potential regulatory changes that could impact the products and services offered. Valuation metrics commonly used include P/E and P/B (AOCI).

■ Property and Casualty Insurance

Businesses		Relative Characteristics						
Company	Country		Sector			Market		
			Lower	≈	Higher	Lower	≈	Higher
Allianz SE	Germany	Valuation	●			●		
Allstate Corp.	United States	Profitability	●			●		
American International Group Inc.	United States	Sales Growth	●			●		
AXA SA	France	Profit Growth	●			●		
MunichRe AG	Germany	Debt Levels	●			●		
People's Insurance Company Group	China	Dividend Yield			●			●
PICC Property & Casualty Co.	China	Payout Ratio			●	●		
Talanx AG	Germany	Dividend Growth			●			●
Tokio Marine Holdings Inc.	Japan	Earnings Predictability		●				●
Zurich Insurance Group AG	Switzerland	Share Price Volatility		●				●

Data source: Bloomberg, as of March 18, 2022.

Property and casualty (P&C) insurers, often referred to as general insurers, provide property and auto insurance coverages to individuals and businesses (including farm). Reinsurance companies, which are used by both P&C and life insurance companies to help manage risk, have also been included in this group since most generate a greater portion of their revenue from the P&C part of their business. To illustrate, if a P&C insurer believes it has too much exposure to one risk factor or geography (such as hurricane insurance in Florida), they can pay a reinsurer to assume some of those liabilities. Natural catastrophes pose the biggest risk to the P&C industry. Hurricane Katrina, for example, is estimated to have cost almost $150 billion, much of which was absorbed by the P&C industry. P&C insurance policies are usually short-term in nature (one year), while life insurance policies could last decades. Solvency ratio calculations (available capital over required capital) differ by geography but, in all cases, indicate the ability of the company to withstand adverse scenarios. A low solvency ratio puts the company in danger of insolvency while a high solvency ratio suggests capital is being underutilized. Both liabilities and investments tend to be shorter in duration for P&C insurers when compared to life and health insurers. The best time to own P&C insurers is when industry pricing is "hard," where the combined ratio is strong (below 100). The combined ratio is a measure of underwriting performance and indicates whether the premiums collected are enough to pay claims. A company's combined ratio should ideally be less than 100 since a higher number means they need to make up for the shortfall through investment income. Expected catastrophe losses are priced into earnings estimates via "reserves." However, an unexpectedly large event or number of events in a condensed period may cause P&C firms to incur losses that exceed reserves, which lowers earnings. Potential changes in accounting standards are important to monitor as they can trigger increased volatility in an insurer's earnings before it can adjust its strategies. Important metrics for investors to follow include operating ROE, growth in gross written premium (GWP) and net premiums earned (NPE), combined ratio, solvency ratios, core loss ratios, and prior year claims development (PYD), representing the change in total claims liabilities net of reinsurance from the prior year. PYD is often expressed as a percentage of NPE. The requirement for rate approvals by regulators (where applicable) can have a significant impact on profitability. Regulatory challenges to increasing premium rates may result in the required premium increases lagging claim cost inflation and lead to an erosion of the combined ratio. Standard valuation measures such as P/E and EV/EBITDA are often used to assess valuations in the industry.

■ Securities Exchanges

Businesses		Relative Characteristics						
Company	Country		Sector			Market		
			Lower	≈	Higher	Lower	≈	Higher
ASX Ltd.	Australia	Valuation		●		●		
CME Group Inc.	United States	Profitability		●				●
Deutsche Boerse AG	Germany	Sales Growth		●				●
Euronext NV	Netherlands	Profit Growth		●				●
Hong Kong Exchanges & Clearing Ltd.	Hong Kong	Debt Levels	●			●		
Intercontinental Exchange Inc.	United States	Dividend Yield	●			●		
Japan Exchange Group	Japan	Payout Ratio		●		●		
London Stock Exchange	United Kingdom	Dividend Growth		●				●
Nasdaq Inc.	United States	Earnings Predictability		●				●
Singapore Exchange Limited	Singapore	Share Price Volatility	●				●	

Data source: Bloomberg, as of March 18, 2022.

Security exchanges provide platforms for the trading of financial securities, including stocks, bonds, options, commodities, futures, and, more recently, cryptocurrency. This once was conducted exclusively in a physical location (exchange floor), but now most trading takes place electronically. Industry earnings are most susceptible to overall trading volumes, which makes them a good indicator for assessing investor sentiment and the overall health of the industry. Investor sentiment is an important economic factor for the exchange industry, as is the pace of new company listings. As with most industries within the financial sector, security exchanges are tightly regulated and have built-in safeguards to protect investors and ensure the integrity of the financial market. A well-functioning exchange is key to the success of a country's long-term economic development. Securities exchanges generate revenue primarily from listing fees, and by selling real-time pricing, trade, and index data generated through the exchange. Sales and profit growth for the industry have also benefited from an abundance of new company listings and new financial products. Companies in this industry have been trading at higher valuations compared to the financial sector largely due to their above-average growth rates and profitability. Although their dividend yields have been below the market, they have grown their dividends at an above-average rate. Important metrics for investors to track include total revenue, trading volumes (dollar value or number of securities/contracts), rates per security/contract, number of new listings, newly listed product types, total expense ratios, adjusted EBITDA, and adjusted EBITDA margin. Standard valuation metrics such as P/E, P/CF, and EV/EBITDA can be used to compare valuations between companies in this industry.

CHAPTER 14

Healthcare

The global healthcare sector provides goods and services that many of us, quite literally, cannot live without. As discussed in Chapter 2, countries tend to increase healthcare spending as their economies grow. This supports the industry's sales growth and provides a long-term secular tailwind for your portfolio should you invest a portion of your assets in healthcare companies that operate in countries whose economies are growing strongly and that are likely to increase healthcare spending.

Sector Characteristics versus Market

	Lower	≈	Higher		Lower	≈	Higher
Valuation	●			Dividend Yield	●		
Profitability		●		Payout Ratio			●
Sales Growth		●		Dividend Growth			●
Profit Growth	●			Earnings Predictability			●
Debt Levels		●		Share Price Volatility	●		

Data source: Bloomberg, as of March 18, 2022.

Businesses in this sector are regarded as defensive in nature, because many of them generate fairly stable revenue and profitability even in weak economic environments. This is not true of all healthcare companies, though. Some healthcare services are more discretionary in nature than others, and some are dependent on the outcome of a single drug or medical device, which can make the earnings of those businesses much more volatile. Despite having similar sales growth to the market, dividend growth has been above average. Over the past few years, valuations have been somewhat below the market.

The defensive nature of the healthcare sector means that it tends to outperform during bear markets but underperform at the beginning of a new bull market. In this chapter we take a closer look at the six main industry groups in the healthcare sector: (1) biotechnology, (2) healthcare equipment and supplies, (3) healthcare facilities, (4) healthcare services, (5) life science tools and services, and (6) pharmaceuticals.

■ Biotechnology

Businesses		Relative Characteristics	Sector Lower	≈	Higher	Market Lower	≈	Higher
Company	Country							
Amgen Inc.	United States	Valuation	●			●		
Biogen Inc.	United States	Profitability			●			●
CSL Ltd.	Australia	Sales Growth		●			●	
Eevia Health Oyj	Finland	Profit Growth	●			●		
Gilead Sciences Inc.	United States	Debt Levels	●			●		
Grifols SA	Spain	Dividend Yield		●		●		
Ipsen SA	France	Payout Ratio	●			●		
Merck KGaA	Germany	Dividend Growth			●			●
Regeneron Pharmaceuticals Inc.	United States	Earnings Predictability		●				●
UCB SA	Belgium	Share Price Volatility		●		●		

Data source: Bloomberg, as of March 18, 2022.

Biotechnology companies develop compounds derived from living organisms for the treatment of illnesses and disease. In general, it is best to avoid investing in businesses that do not generate any revenue and many small biotech firms fall into this category. A small position in a company that has a particularly promising drug in development may be okay for investors willing to put in the time to understand clinical trial data. However, it is important to tread carefully since many of these compounds do not get commercialized. Perhaps more than any other industry, buying a basket of biotech companies may be more appropriate from a risk management perspective than investing in only one or two businesses. Larger biotechnology companies, however, often have multiple commercialized compounds that generate predictable earnings, which help insulate the company from periods of economic weakness. Although earnings and share price volatility have been relatively subdued in recent years, both can be high for biotech companies, especially when a new blockbuster drug is in development. The term "blockbuster" refers to a compound with the potential for $1 billion or more in annual sales. There are key differences by region in terms of the size of addressable patient populations across disease and also in terms of pricing dynamics. Other risks faced by the industry include drug pricing pressures in some markets, as well as the potential for less favorable regulatory environments in the future. When industry valuations are depressed there exists a heightened possibility that merger and acquisition (M&A) activity will increase. For companies that are more mature and generate earnings, investors should track revenue by product, gross margins, SG&A expenses, R&D expenses, operating margins, revenues, revenue growth, EPS, and EPS growth. As previously mentioned, keeping up on clinical trial data is important for biotech investors. Good sites to check in the United States include clinicaltrials.gov and PubMed (pubmed.ncbi.nlm.nih. gov). Valuation analysis for biotech companies can be challenging and may be best accomplished through discounted cash flow analysis. For more mature businesses that generate fairly consistent earnings, standard valuation measures such as P/E and EV/EBITDA may be appropriate.

■ Healthcare Equipment and Supplies

Businesses		Relative Characteristics						
Company	Country		Sector			Market		
			Lower	≈	Higher	Lower	≈	Higher
Abbott Laboratories — United States		Valuation		●				●
Alcon Inc. — Switzerland		Profitability	●			●		
Becton Dickinson and Co. — United States		Sales Growth	●			●		
Koninklijke Philips NV — Netherlands		Profit Growth	●			●		
Medtronic PLC — Ireland		Debt Levels	●			●		
Olympus Corp. — Japan		Dividend Yield	●			●		
Siemens Healthineers AG — Germany		Payout Ratio	●			●		
Smith & Nephew PLC — United Kingdom		Dividend Growth			●			●
Stryker Corp. — United States		Earnings Predictability		●				●
Terumo Corp. — Japan		Share Price Volatility		●		●		

Data source: Bloomberg, as of March 18, 2022.

Healthcare equipment and supply companies manufacture a wide variety of devices and supplies used by hospitals and doctors around the world. These companies make everything from surgical equipment, stents, pacemakers, and endoscopes to orthopedic implants and digital imaging systems. Regulatory approval paths and reimbursement grants vary by both region and device. As a result, indications (approvals) and therefore physician adoption may be different across geographies. For example, certain devices may be indicated for a specific use in the United States, but that use may be contraindicated or off-label (not approved) in Europe. Also, pricing strategies can vary by region due to local players' pricing points and pricing strategies. Healthcare professional shortages (especially nurses) are expected to remain an overhang into the near future. Other economic factors that can impact the industry include supply chain disruptions, raw material costs, labor costs, increasing compensation, healthcare reimbursement changes across hospital inpatients, hospital outpatients, physician payments, and procedure recovery, hospital capital expenditure budgets, R&D reinvestment initiatives (to drive top-line growth), travel (which increases SG&A), tax legislation, and regulatory changes. Important operational metrics that investors should track include sales growth, volume of devices sold, average selling prices, number of sales reps or sales rep adds, sales rep productivity, market share versus other competitors, patient trialing growth versus permanent implant growth, new center adds, per-center cases, and device penetration rates. Important financial metrics include organic revenue growth, gross margin, operating margin, adjusted EBITDA margin, EPS growth, operating leverage, financial leverage, FCF generation, effective tax rates, and net operating losses. Standard valuation measures such as P/E, P/CF, and EV/EBITDA can be used to compare valuations in this industry.

■ Healthcare Facilities

The healthcare facility industry includes hospital and clinic operators, as well as long-term care facilities. Similar to the healthcare sector as a whole, healthcare facility companies are expected to benefit from growing healthcare spending as economies around the world expand. Economic factors that most impact industry earnings and sales growth include inflation, interest rates, tax benefits, rising case intensity, government budgets for healthcare spending, and changes to reimbursements. Important metrics for investors to follow include inpatient (hospital) admissions, revenue per inpatient admission and revenue per equivalent admission, total inpatient

Businesses		Relative Characteristics						
Company	Country		Sector			Market		
			Lower	≈	Higher	Lower	≈	Higher
Community Health System	United States	Valuation	●			●		
HCA Healthcare Inc.	United States	Profitability	●			●		
IHH Healthcare Bhd	Malaysia	Sales Growth	●			●		
Korian SA	France	Profit Growth	●			●		
Mediclinic International PLC	South Africa	Debt Levels		●				●
Orpea SA	France	Dividend Yield	●			●		
Ramsay Generale De Sante SA	France	Payout Ratio	●			●		
Ramsay Health Care Ltd.	Australia	Dividend Growth	●			●		
Tenet Healthcare Corp.	United States	Earnings Predictability		●				●
Universal Health Services Inc.	United States	Share Price Volatility		●		●		

Data source: Bloomberg, as of March 18, 2022.

revenue, total hospital revenue, number of hospitals, number of operational and licensed beds, occupancy rate, number of outpatient surgery centers, same-facility admissions growth, square-foot-adjusted admissions growth, revenue per adjusted admission, salaries and benefits as a percentage of revenue, provision for doubtful accounts, operating and EBITDA margins, and leverage (debt/EBITDA). Investors should also note the sources and mix of revenue for healthcare facility operators, favoring companies with a more diverse source of revenue. In the United States, for example, it may be helpful to compare the amount of revenue generated from private insurance to that derived from public insurance (i.e., Medicare and Medicaid). Typically, private insurance revenue is preferred to public insurance revenue since it is less subject to government-controlled pricing. EBITDA (less non–controlling interest) is used for valuation comparisons between firms. Valuation comparisons can be made using the traditional P/E ratio as well as discounted free cash flow.

■ Healthcare Services

The healthcare services industry includes companies that operate within managed care, retail pharmacy, supply chain and distribution management, and lab services. Telemedicine and internet-based healthcare are emerging opportunities within the industry. Recent entrants into the industry are fueling new innovations aimed at lowering healthcare costs and improving

Businesses		Relative Characteristics						
Company	**Country**		**Sector**			**Market**		
			Lower	≈	Higher	Lower	≈	Higher
Alfresa Holdings Corp.	Japan	Valuation	●			●		
AmerisourceBergen Corp.	United States	Profitability	●			●		
CVS Health Corp.	United States	Sales Growth		●			●	
Fresenius Medical Care AG & Co.	Germany	Profit Growth		●		●		
Jointown Pharmaceutical Group Co.	China	Debt Levels	●			●		
McKesson Corp.	United States	Dividend Yield			●	●		
Medipal Holdings Corp.	Japan	Payout Ratio	●			●		
Sinopharm Group Co.	China	Dividend Growth	●			●		
Sonic Healthcare Limited	Australia	Earnings Predictability		●				●
UnitedHealth Group Inc.	United States	Share Price Volatility	●			●		

Data source: Bloomberg, as of March 18, 2022.

clinical outcomes for patients. There is a trend toward value-based care (VBC), which tries to improve the quality of healthcare and prevent problems before they arise. Most of these improvements are the result of not only better medical tools and devices, but also from enhancements in data management and sharing. Taking a more holistic, data-driven approach and tailoring it to individual patients has allowed companies to make meaningful improvements to patient outcomes. The shift to VBC has been further supported by the adoption of risk-based payment models, where providers are paid a set fee to treat a patient and held accountable for the outcome. This has led to lower hospitalizations, lower medical loss ratios (MLRs), and higher quality scores. Economic factors impacting the industry include GDP growth, inflation, interest rates, government-controlled reimbursement rates (pricing), and healthcare regulation. Potential pricing and regulatory changes are especially important to stay abreast of because the industry is often heavily regulated. For investors focused on the retail pharmacy segment of the industry, store count, generic dispensing rate, revenue per script (generic or branded drug), comparable-store prescription growth, gross profit, and margin (generic or branded drug) and drug price increases are important datapoints to follow. It is important to note that the managed care industry is unique to the United States and not found in other countries. Investors interested in the managed care segment of the industry can monitor the medical care ratio (MCR), Medicare and ex-Medicare membership growth, administrative service fees, and adjusted EPS growth.

Standard valuation metrics such as P/E, P/CF, and EV/EBITDA can be used to compare valuations of companies in this industry.

■ Life Science Tools and Services

Businesses		Relative Characteristics					
Company	Country		Sector			Market	
			Lower ≈ Higher			Lower ≈ Higher		
Agilent Technologies Inc. —————— United States		Valuation		●			●
BioMerieux ——————— France		Profitability		●			●
Danaher Corp. ——————— United States		Sales Growth		●			●
DiaSorin SpA ——————— Italy		Profit Growth		●			●
Illumina Inc. ——————— United States		Debt Levels	●			●	
Lonza Group AG ——————— Switzerland		Dividend Yield	●			●	
PerkinElmer Inc. ——————— United States		Payout Ratio	●			●	
Sartorius AG ——————— Germany		Dividend Growth		●			●
Sysmex Corp. ——————— Japan		Earnings Predictability	●				●
Thermo Fisher Scientific Inc. ———— United States		Share Price Volatility	●			●	

Data source: Bloomberg, as of March 18, 2022.

Companies in the life sciences and tools industry provide services and tools to support the development of drugs and medical devices. The industry is highly fragmented and experiencing consolidation across all segments. Biopharma, a segment within the industry, continues to lead end market growth driven by novel methods such as cell and gene therapies. Additionally, as drug modalities (methods of application) become more complex, outsourcing will continue to be an attractive option for biopharma companies, and benefit contract research and contract manufacturing organizations (CROs and CMOs) in the process. Within the diagnostics industry segment, new and innovative technologies such as liquid biopsy, early detection, and proteomics continue to remain a focus. Diagnostic companies typically only operate in their respective locale given restrictions related to shipping of biological samples. However, some companies have successfully implemented strategies to sell products outside of their local market that typically involve a kit solution. Economic factors that have a substantial influence on earnings and revenue for life science businesses include interest rates and general inflationary trends (such as commodity and labor costs), regulatory productivity (how quickly new tools and treatments are reviewed and approved), and biopharma and government funding, as well as hospital capital expenditures. Other primary drivers of growth for the industry include aging populations and government support for the academic market, where universities are engaged in developing new therapies. Important metrics for investors to track include sales growth, EBITDA growth, cash burn (how quickly cash is being depleted), revenue per unit, customer adds, volume, installed base, and pull-through. Commonly used measures to assess valuation in this industry include P/E, P/CF, and EV/EBITDA.

■ Pharmaceuticals

Businesses		Relative Characteristics						
Company	Country		Sector			Market		
			Lower	≈	Higher	Lower	≈	Higher
Abbvie Inc.	United States	Valuation	●			●		
AstraZeneca PLC	United Kingdom	Profitability			●			●
Bayer AG	Germany	Sales Growth	●			●		
GlaxoSmithKline PLC	United Kingdom	Profit Growth	●			●		
Johnson & Johnson	United States	Debt Levels		●			●	
Novartis AG	Switzerland	Dividend Yield			●		●	
Novo Nordisk A/S	Denmark	Payout Ratio			●			●
Pfizer Inc.	United States	Dividend Growth		●				●
Roche Holding AG	Switzerland	Earnings Predictability			●			●
Sanofi	France	Share Price Volatility	●			●		

Data source: Bloomberg, as of March 18, 2022.

Pharmaceutical (pharma) companies produce chemical compounds to treat disease and improve our health. These companies are considered defensive since many of the drugs produced are essential products for the people who need them. As a result, earnings are relatively predictable for these businesses. However, the earnings power of a pharma company can be materially impacted by the success or failure of a single compound. Drugs under development by the company form its drug pipeline (similar to the biotechnology industry). It is important for investors to monitor each compound as it progresses through clinical trials and is submitted for regulatory approval before it can be administered to patients. New drugs that address a large, unmet need may receive fast-track status and are reviewed more quickly, but most drugs take years to develop and test to ensure their safety and efficacy. Drugs with the potential to generate more than $1 billion in annual sales are often referred to as blockbusters. Existing drugs that are approaching patent expiration are potential risks, as competitors are likely to produce generic drugs at a lower price. Economic factors that have a significant impact on the industry include GDP growth, inflation, interest rates, government healthcare budgets, and changes to pricing and reimbursement rates. Strong and predictable cash flow generation from existing drugs allows most pharma companies to pay attractive dividends, although it is important for businesses in this industry to invest heavily in research and development (R&D) to strengthen their portfolio of patented compounds. Some helpful sites to monitor in the United States include clinicaltrials.gov and PubMed (pubmed.ncbi.nlm.nih.gov). Investors should track revenue by product, gross margins, SG&A margins, R&D, operating margins, EPS, and EPS growth. P/E is a commonly used metric to assess valuation in this industry.

CHAPTER 15

Industrials

The global industrials sector includes companies that provide goods and services tied to manufacturing and transportation and is perhaps the most diverse sector of the stock market. These companies produce a wide variety of goods including manufacturing equipment, aircraft, trucks, and building products. Services include building and maintaining roads, bridges, tunnels, and airports. Additionally, they operate shipping businesses that deliver goods to all corners of the globe and provide goods and services to support other businesses.

215

Sector Characteristics versus Market

	Lower	≈	Higher		Lower	≈	Higher
Valuation	●			Dividend Yield		●	
Profitability	●			Payout Ratio	●		
Sales Growth	●			Dividend Growth			●
Profit Growth	●			Earnings Predictability		●	
Debt Levels		●		Share Price Volatility		●	

Data source: Bloomberg, as of March 18, 2022.

Industrial companies listed in this chapter are mature businesses with a marginally lower underlying growth rate compared to the market. However, they have offered competitive dividend yields and above-average dividend growth in recent years.

These companies tend to be capital intensive and are sensitive to the economic cycle and changes in economic growth. That said, companies that produce high-ticket items, such as heavy equipment, factory automation equipment, and machinery, do not usually experience a pickup in customer orders until business confidence improves and the economic cycle is well under way. On the other hand, industries such as commercial services (which includes hiring services) are likely to experience increased demand for their services earlier in an economic recovery.

In this chapter we review the 16 primary industry groups in the industrial sector: (1) aerospace and defense, (2) air freight and courier services, (3) air travel, (4) building products, (5) commercial services, (6) construction and engineering, (7) electrical equipment, (8) environmental and facility services, (9) heavy equipment, (10) industrial conglomerates, (11) industrial machinery, (12) infrastructure management, (13) marine shipping, (14) railroads, (15) trading and distribution, and (16) trucking and logistics.

■ Aerospace and Defense

Businesses		Relative Characteristics						
Company	Country		Sector (Lower ≈ Higher)			Market (Lower ≈ Higher)		
			Lower	≈	Higher	Lower	≈	Higher
Airbus SE	France	Valuation		●		●		
BAE Systems PLC	United Kingdom	Profitability		●		●		
Boeing Co.	United States	Sales Growth	●			●		
General Dynamics Corp.	United States	Profit Growth	●			●		
Leonardo SpA	Italy	Debt Levels			●			●
Lockheed Martin Corp.	United States	Dividend Yield	●			●		
Raytheon Technologies Corp.	United States	Payout Ratio			●		●	
Rolls-Royce Holdings PLC	United Kingdom	Dividend Growth	●			●		
Safran SA	France	Earnings Predictability			●			●
Thales SA	France	Share Price Volatility		●			●	

Data source: Bloomberg, as of March 18, 2022.

The aerospace and defense industry is broadly split between military and commercial aerospace equipment. The defense-related segments of these businesses are highly dependent on government spending, and they tend to perform well when geopolitical tensions are rising, especially leading up to and during times of war. The sale of military products to foreign countries requires government approval, often limiting exports. Commercial aerospace, on the other hand, depends primarily on private sector spending, making it more sensitive to the economic cycle, particularly long-term demand for air travel. In defense, key themes include the expansion and modernization of militaries in China and NATO member countries, which are primarily being driven by heightened tensions between the United States, China, and Russia. A noteworthy trend in the aerospace industry is the development of new engine technology focused on decarbonization. Economic factors that impact the industry include inflation, interest rates, government defense budgets, air travel demand, and private sector spending. Aircraft deliveries drive the aerospace industry, distributing cash throughout the supply chain and allowing companies to invest in the next generation of aircraft. Air traffic demand, miles flown, the financial strength of operators and lessors, and jet fuel prices can all impact the aerospace industry. Higher fuel prices may also incentivize operators to buy newer, more fuel-efficient aircraft. Key factors for the defense segments of these companies include earnings and free cash flow, the geopolitical landscape, and government defense budgets. Other important metrics include commercial aircraft deliveries, business segment operating income and margin, free cash flow conversion rates, free cash flow (FCF) margin, R&D as a percentage of sales, capex as a percentage of sales, gross profit and gross margin, EBIT, EBITDA, and related margins. Primary valuation methods include P/E, EV/EBITDA, discounted cash flow (DCF), and FCF yield.

■ Air Freight and Courier Services

Businesses		Relative Characteristics						
Company	Country		Sector			Market		
			Lower	≈	Higher	Lower	≈	Higher
bpost SA	Belgium	Valuation		●		●		
Deutsche Post AG	Germany	Profitability	●			●		
DSV A/S	Denmark	Sales Growth			●			●
FedEx Corp.	United States	Profit Growth			●			●
Poste Italiane SpA	Italy	Debt Levels			●			●
Royal Mail PLC	United Kingdom	Dividend Yield	●			●		
SF Holding Co.	China	Payout Ratio	●			●		
United Parcel Service Inc.	United States	Dividend Growth			●			●
Yamato Holdings Co.	Japan	Earnings Predictability			●			●
YTO Express Group Co. Ltd.	China	Share Price Volatility	●			●		

Data source: Bloomberg, as of March 18, 2022.

Although it represents a relatively small portion of the total volume of goods shipped each year worldwide, the air freight industry remains a critical part of the global supply chain. Technological innovations continue to significantly impact this industry, including a shift toward improving logistical efficiencies, autonomous trucking, digital freight brokers, and the use of drones. There is also an ongoing trend toward reducing carbon emissions, which affects the composition of company aircraft and truck fleets. Financial health of consumers and their ability to spend, based partly on where we are in the economic cycle, is an important consideration when assessing future earnings prospects for the air freight industry. Other key economic considerations include GDP growth, inventory levels, labor costs, labor availability, inflation, interest rates, advances in technology and automation, economic activity, e-commerce penetration, fuel surcharges and the ability to pass higher fuel costs on to consumers, labor availability, as well as risks related to changes in tariffs and, in extreme cases, economic sanctions. The rapid growth in e-commerce has been a key driver of sales and profit growth for the industry. Important metrics for investors to follow include pricing, volumes, shipments per trading day, revenue per shipment, total shipments, volume growth by geographic region, utilization rates, fleet count, operating ratio (inverse of operating margins), and EBIT and EBITDA, as well as EPS. Standard valuation metrics such as P/E, P/CF, and EV/EBITDA can be used to compare valuations between companies in this industry.

◼ Air Travel

Businesses		Relative Characteristics						
Company	**Country**		**Sector**			**Market**		
			Lower	≈	Higher	Lower	≈	Higher
Air China Ltd. —————— China		Valuation			●	●		
Air France-KLM ————— France		Profitability	●			●		
American Airlines Group Inc. ————— United States		Sales Growth	●			●		
ANA Holdings Inc. ————— Japan		Profit Growth	●			●		
China Southern Airlines Co. Ltd. ————— China		Debt Levels		●				●
Delta Air Lines Inc. ————— United States		Dividend Yield	●			●		
Deutsche Lufthansa AG ————— Germany		Payout Ratio	●			●		
International Consolidated Airlines Group ——— United Kingdom		Dividend Growth	●			●		
Korean Air Lines Co. Ltd. ————— South Korea		Earnings Predictability		●				●
United Airlines Holdings Inc. ————— United States		Share Price Volatility			●			●

Data source: Bloomberg, as of March 18, 2022.

The air travel industry was hit hard by the 2020 global pandemic, forcing companies to suspend dividend payments and take on added debt to keep their operations going in a period where passenger volumes dropped by upwards of 90%. Notable industry themes include ESG initiatives whereby companies are upgrading their fleets to more fuel-efficient aircraft, managing capacity more effectively, and providing a wider assortment of premium products to entice customers and earn additional revenues. It remains to be seen whether some of the side effects of the pandemic, such as the reduction in business travel and move to a hybrid or work-from-home model, will last, or whether business travel will fully recover. Since the majority of revenue is derived from business travel, airlines may need to boost revenue from leisure passengers, most likely by adding premium services. Economic factors that have the biggest impact on industry participants include GDP growth, personal consumption expenditures (PCEs), fuel costs, labor costs, interest rates, inflation, jet fuel prices, international and corporate travel demand, and competitive price wars. Important metrics for the industry include available seat miles (ASMs), passenger revenue per available seat mile (PRASM), cost per available seat mile (CASM), CASM excluding fuel, load factor, fleet size, capex, free cash flow, EBITDA, EBITDAR, and EPS. Valuation comparisons can be made using P/E and EV/EBITDA, as well as discounted cash flow (DCF) analysis.

■ Building Products

Businesses			Relative Characteristics	Sector Lower	≈	Higher	Market Lower	≈	Higher
Company		**Country**							
AGC Inc.		Japan	Valuation		●		●		
Assa Abloy AB		Sweden	Profitability			●	●		
Carrier Global Corp.		United States	Sales Growth	●			●		
Cie de Saint-Gobain		France	Profit Growth	●			●		
Daikin Industries Ltd.		Japan	Debt Levels	●			●		
Johnson Controls International		United States	Dividend Yield	●			●		
Kone Oyj		Finland	Payout Ratio			●	●		
Lixil Corp.		Japan	Dividend Growth			●			●
Otis Worldwide Corp.		United States	Earnings Predictability			●			●
Trane Technologies		Ireland	Share Price Volatility	●			●		

Data source: Bloomberg, as of March 18, 2022.

Building products companies produce a wide range of finished products used in the construction of buildings. These include air conditioners, elevators, escalators, door lock systems, glass, insulation, roofing, furnaces, air cleaners, faucets, cabinets, plumbing, security systems, and architectural coatings. Although the housing industry is an important end market, companies in the building products industry also serve commercial construction needs and so benefit from a broad range of customers. Economic factors that have the greatest impact on revenue and earnings for this industry include inflation, changes in interest rates, M&A, and supply chain disruptions. Changes in interest rates can have a significant impact on building products companies since many commercial and residential construction projects are funded through mortgages or other forms of financing. A reduction in interest rates will typically result in an increase in building construction. Companies in this industry have generated below-average growth in sales and profits. In contrast, dividend growth has been strong due to above-average levels of profitability compared to the market. Important metrics that investors should track include commodity prices, EBIT and EBITDA margins, operating income and margins by business segment and region, orders backlog, free cash flow conversion, organic versus acquired sales growth, commercial and residential construction, utilization rates, and discretionary maintenance spending. Valuation metrics such as P/E, P/CF, and EV/EBITDA can be used to assess the valuations of companies in the building products industry.

220

GLOBAL SECTORS AND INDUSTRIES

■ Commercial Services

Businesses		Relative Characteristics					
Company	Country		Sector (Lower ≈ Higher)			Market (Lower ≈ Higher)	
Adecco Group AG	Switzerland	Valuation		●		●	
Aramark	United States	Profitability	●			●	
Bunzl PLC	United Kingdom	Sales Growth	●			●	
Dai Nippon Printing Co. Ltd.	Japan	Profit Growth	●			●	
ISS A/S	Denmark	Debt Levels	●			●	
ManpowerGroup Inc.	United States	Dividend Yield	●			●	
Randstad NV	Netherlands	Payout Ratio		●		●	
Recruit Holdings Co. Ltd.	Japan	Dividend Growth	●			●	
Securitas AB	Sweden	Earnings Predictability			●		●
Toppan Inc.	Japan	Share Price Volatility		●			●

Data source: Bloomberg, as of March 18, 2022.

Companies in the commercial services industry provide goods and services to other businesses that are often essential to their operations and serve to reduce costs. These include human resources, cleaning, laundry and uniform services, food services and facility management, delivery of nonfood items used to run and maintain facilities, as well as purchasing and supply chain outsourcing services. Economic factors that are most impactful for industry growth and profitability include GDP growth, inflation, interest rates, unemployment rate, labor-participation rates, and nonfarm payrolls (which indicate new hires). The industry is dependent on the general level of business activity and is therefore sensitive to the economic cycle. Recruitment companies are particularly sensitive to the economic cycle, as temporary staff are often employed by businesses at the preliminary stages of an economic recovery, when the sustainability of the expansion is still uncertain. These same companies can experience a dramatic drop in earnings during recessions as businesses cease hiring temporary employees completely and begin to lay off full-time employees. Companies that operate in multiple geographies and provide vital goods and services are likely to be less sensitive to the economic cycle. Important metrics for investors to follow include gross profit and gross margins, EBITDA and EBITDA margins, organic growth, and EPS growth. Valuation metrics such as P/E, P/CF, and EV/EBITDA are commonly used to compare valuations between companies in this industry.

■ Construction and Engineering

Company	Country
ACS SA	Spain
China Communications Construction Corp.	China
China Railway Group	China
Eiffage SA	France
Hochtief AG	Germany
Hyundai Engineering & Construction Co. Ltd.	South Korea
Kajima Corp.	Japan
Larsen & Toubro Ltd.	India
Power Construction Corp. of China	China
Vinci SA*	France

Relative Characteristics	Sector			Market		
	Lower	≈	Higher	Lower	≈	Higher
Valuation	●			●		
Profitability	●			●		
Sales Growth	●			●		
Profit Growth	●			●		
Debt Levels	●			●		
Dividend Yield			●			●
Payout Ratio		●		●		
Dividend Growth			●			●
Earnings Predictability		●			●	
Share Price Volatility			●			●

Data source: Bloomberg, as of March 18, 2022.

Construction and engineering companies design and construct buildings as well as infrastructure projects like airports, bridges, dams, tunnels, railways, roadways, and utility lines. Some of the companies in this industry operate concession businesses in which they manage infrastructure projects after they construct them (discussed separately within the infrastructure management industry). Key trends affecting the industry include increased levels of urbanization and the move toward decarbonization and renewable energy, as well as infrastructure upgrades in many countries around the world. Economic factors affecting this industry include GDP growth, infrastructure spending, and the ability of governments and other organizations to raise the capital needed to fund these projects. To the extent that these projects require financing, changes in interest rates can be a deciding factor on whether a project is undertaken. Falling interest rates typically cause an increase in new construction, while rising interest rates could delay the construction of new infrastructure projects. Since many large-scale projects are undertaken by government authorities, the construction and engineering industry is heavily influenced by the general level of government spending. Important metrics to track for this industry include organic and acquired growth, revenue and profit by segment and region, operating income and margins by segment and region, new orders and backlog, consulting service revenue and margins, gross and EBIT margins, days sales outstanding (DSOs), return on invested capital (ROIC), FCF and return on equity (ROE), as well as leverage (net debt to EBITDA). Standard valuation metrics such as P/E, P/CF, and EV/EBITDA can be used to compare valuations between companies in this industry.

■ Electrical Equipment

Businesses		Relative Characteristics	Sector			Market		
Company	Country		Lower	≈	Higher	Lower	≈	Higher
ABB Ltd.	Switzerland	Valuation		●		●		
Amphenol Corporation	United States	Profitability			●	●		
Emerson Electric Co.	United States	Sales Growth	●			●		
Legrand SA	France	Profit Growth	●			●		
Mitsubishi Electric Corp.	Japan	Debt Levels	●			●		
Prysmian SpA	Italy	Dividend Yield	●			●		
Schneider Electric SE	France	Payout Ratio	●			●		
Shanghai Electric Group	China	Dividend Growth		●				●
TE Connectivity Ltd.	United States	Earnings Predictability		●				●
Toshiba Corp.	Japan	Share Price Volatility		●				●

Data source: Bloomberg, as of March 18, 2022.

Companies in the electrical equipment industry produce equipment used in the manufacture of industrial goods. Examples include motors, drivetrain components, factory control and automation equipment, electrical cable, power systems, and robotics. Currently, the industry is benefiting from a trend toward automation as businesses search for ways to improve productivity and reduce costs. Some of these businesses manufacture cable and other products that are benefiting from the buildout of wireless and broadband communication systems globally, as well as energy management components that help reduce energy consumption. Economic factors that help drive industry sales growth and profitability include industrial production and capacity utilization, GDP growth, changes in the level of interest rates, freight costs, the cost and availability of labor, and the general level of employment. These businesses are likely to benefit in rising labor cost environments, which may prompt companies to increase investments in automation. The industry is sensitive to the economic cycle, in particular to changes in corporate capital expenditures. Companies in this industry have traded at lower valuations compared to the market in recent years, most likely due to lower sales and profit growth and lower profitability. Important metrics for investors to monitor include organic revenue growth by segment and region, operating and profit margins by segment and region, inventory levels, order backlog, and capital expenditure plans of key customers, as well as leverage (net debt to EBITDA) versus industry peers. Standard valuation metrics such as P/E, P/CF, and EV/EBITDA can be used to compare valuations between companies in this industry.

■ Environmental and Facility Services

Businesses		Relative Characteristics						
Company	Country		Sector			Market		
			Lower	≈	Higher	Lower	≈	Higher
ABM Industries Inc. — United States		Valuation			●	●		
China Everbright Environment Group — Hong Kong		Profitability	●			●		
China Tianying Inc. — China		Sales Growth			●			●
Derichebourg SA — France		Profit Growth			●			●
GFL Environmental Inc. — Canada		Debt Levels			●			●
Rentokil Initial PLC — United Kingdom		Dividend Yield	●			●		
Republic Services Inc. — United States		Payout Ratio	●			●		
Serco Group PLC — United Kingdom		Dividend Growth			●			●
Waste Connections Inc. — Canada		Earnings Predictability			●			●
Waste Management Inc. — United States		Share Price Volatility	●			●		

Data source: Bloomberg, as of March 18, 2022.

Environmental services companies engage in commercial, industrial, municipal, and residential waste collection and disposal. Facility service businesses supply janitorial, parking, security, and other outsourced services related to the management and maintenance of commercial and industrial buildings. The industry also includes companies that supply pest control, recycling services, and environmental remediation and restoration services. The industry has experienced above-average growth rates in recent years, benefiting from a strong trend toward environmental sustainability as businesses look for ways to reduce their environmental footprint. Economic factors that influence industry sales growth and profitability include GDP growth as well as variables that affect economic growth such as changes in interest rates and job growth. Important metrics that investors should monitor for businesses in the environmental service industry include volumes collected by segment and region (usually measured in tons), revenue per ton, gross profit per ton, EBITDA per ton, adjusted EBITDA margin, collection and disposal average yield, tipping fees, churn rate, SG&A expense ratios, capital expenditures as a percentage of sales, and free cash flow conversion. Size and composition of a company's truck fleet is worth noting, along with revenue per truck. Valuation measures such as P/E, P/CF, and EV/EBITDA can be used to compare valuations between companies in this industry.

■ Heavy Equipment

Businesses		Relative Characteristics						
Company	Country		Sector			Market		
			Lower	≈	Higher	Lower	≈	Higher
Caterpillar Inc.	United States	Valuation	●			●		
CRRC Corp. Ltd.	China	Profitability		●		●		
Cummins Inc.	United States	Sales Growth	●			●		
Daimler Truck Holding AG	Germany	Profit Growth			●		●	
Komatsu Ltd.	Japan	Debt Levels	●			●		
Mitsubishi Heavy Industries Ltd.	Japan	Dividend Yield		●			●	
PACCAR Inc.	United States	Payout Ratio		●		●		
Traton SE	Germany	Dividend Growth			●			●
Volvo AB	Sweden	Earnings Predictability			●			●
Weichai Power Co.	China	Share Price Volatility			●			●

Data source: Bloomberg, as of March 18, 2022.

Heavy equipment manufacturers produce commercial trucks and vehicles used in construction and mining. Noteworthy trends within the industry include a shift toward zero emissions technology in global commercial vehicle markets using electric batteries and fuel cells, and the development of precision and self-guided construction equipment technologies. Recent infrastructure spending announcements globally should also benefit heavy equipment manufacturers for the foreseeable future. Economic factors that have the greatest impact on revenue growth and profitability for the industry include GDP growth, industrial production, job growth, and changes in interest rates. Commodity prices act both as a driver of costs (steel, rubber) and end demand (iron ore, copper, gold). Since a weaker US dollar tends to increase demand for many commodities, fluctuations in the US dollar exchange rate can also impact the industry. Although sales have grown at a below-average rate compared to the market, the businesses listed here have managed to grow profits and dividends at an above-average rate in recent years. Important metrics to monitor for the industry include organic growth trends, incremental margins, and dealer inventory levels. Replacement demand, freight rates, nonresidential construction spending, industrial production, capacity utilization, and supply chain dynamics are also important variables to monitor. Common measures used to assess the valuations of companies in this industry include P/E, P/CF, and EV/EBITDA.

■ Industrial Conglomerates

Businesses		Relative Characteristics						
Company	Country		Sector			Market		
			Lower	≈	Higher	Lower	≈	Higher
3M Co.	United States	Valuation	●			●		
CITIC Ltd.	China	Profitability		●		●		
CK Hutchison Holdings	Hong Kong	Sales Growth	●			●		
General Electric Co.	United States	Profit Growth			●			●
Hitachi Ltd.	Japan	Debt Levels	●			●		
Honeywell International Inc.	United States	Dividend Yield		●				●
Jardine Matheson Holdings	Hong Kong	Payout Ratio	●			●		
Samsung C&T Corp	South Korea	Dividend Growth			●			●
Siemens AG	Germany	Earnings Predictability		●			●	
SK Inc.	South Korea	Share Price Volatility		●			●	

Data source: Bloomberg, as of March 18, 2022.

Like financial conglomerates, industrial conglomerates operate in a broad range of industries. As a result, these companies are best analyzed by looking at their individual business segments. Many of the trends taking place within the industrials sector will have an impact on industrial conglomerates. These include electrification, automation, digitization, building efficiency, and modernization. Economic factors with the greatest influence on firm earnings and sales in this industry include industrial production, the purchasing managers index (PMI), GDP growth, residential and nonresidential construction spending, and broader capex spending. Although sales have grown at a below-average rate compared to the market, these businesses have managed to grow dividends at an above-average rate in the past few years. Important metrics that investors should track include organic growth, operating and EBITDA margins, and incremental margins, as well as all financial and operating metrics that apply to their individual business segments. Although standard valuation metrics such as P/E, P/CF, and EV/EBITDA are often used to compare valuations between companies in this industry, a sum of the parts analysis is most appropriate for companies with diverse and distinct business segments.

■ Industrial Machinery

Company	Country		Sector (Lower ≈ Higher)			Market (Lower ≈ Higher)		
Atlas Copco AB	Sweden	Valuation			●	●		
China International Marine Containers	China	Profitability			●			●
Doosan Co. Ltd.	South Korea	Sales Growth	●			●		
Eaton Corp.	United States	Profit Growth			●		●	
Illinois Tool Works Inc.	United States	Debt Levels	●			●		
Keyence Corp.	Japan	Dividend Yield	●			●		
Kion Group AG	Germany	Payout Ratio			●	●		
Sandvik AB	Sweden	Dividend Growth			●			●
Stanley Black & Decker	United States	Earnings Predictability		●		●		
Techtronic Industries	Hong Kong	Share Price Volatility			●			●

Data source: Bloomberg, as of March 18, 2022.

Industrial machinery manufacturers primarily sell goods to companies within the industrial sector. These businesses produce compressors, electronic components, control equipment, logistics equipment, power tools, hydraulic products, fluid connectors, industrial fluids and adhesives, and vacuum and air treatment systems. One of the most notable trends impacting the industry is that of electrification, which could serve to transform the electrical network into a dynamic exchange of electricity and data. Electrification has the potential to provide ample energy in an environmentally friendly manner. Economic factors that have the greatest impact on earnings for the industrial machinery industry include commodity prices (primarily as inputs like steel), freight rates, nonresidential construction spending, replacement demand, industrial production, capacity utilization, and supply chain dynamics. Although industry sales growth has lagged the market, profitability levels and dividend growth have been above average. Important metrics for investors to monitor include organic growth trends, incremental operating margins, organic growth, orders and order backlog, adjusted EBIT, operating margins, and dealer inventory levels. Common measures used to compare valuations between companies in this industry include P/E, P/CF, and EV/EBITDA.

■ Infrastructure Management

Businesses		Relative Characteristics						
Company	Country		Sector (Lower ≈ Higher)			Market (Lower ≈ Higher)		
Aena SME SA	Spain	Valuation		●		●		
Aeroports de Paris	France	Profitability			●		●	
Atlantia SpA	Italy	Sales Growth	●			●		
Downer EDI Ltd.	Australia	Profit Growth	●			●		
Ferrovial SA	Spain	Debt Levels		●			●	
Fraport AG	Germany	Dividend Yield			●			●
Ningbo Zhoushan Port Co. Ltd.	China	Payout Ratio		●		●		
Qingdao Port International Co. Ltd.	China	Dividend Growth	●			●		
Shanghai International Port Group Co. Ltd.	China	Earnings Predictability			●			●
Vinci SA*	France	Share Price Volatility	●			●		

Data source: Bloomberg, as of March 18, 2022.

While businesses in the construction and engineering industry design and construct infrastructure projects like airports, bridges, tunnels, roads, and buildings, the infrastructure management industry operates and maintains those assets after they are built. Some companies compete in both the construction and engineering and infrastructure management industries by designing and building infrastructure projects and operating them after completion. These companies are benefiting from a trend by governments to outsource the task of managing and maintaining public infrastructure.

Economic factors that have the greatest impact on industry revenue and earnings growth include fuel prices, which can influence travel volumes (both by air and by car), GDP growth, and the level of employment, which helps determine the number of people commuting for work. Under normal circumstances these businesses generate comparatively stable earnings and cash flows, but the industry could be negatively affected should the recent trend toward working from home and associated reductions in business travel persist. Since the industry depends on overall levels of travel (commuting for work as well as leisure travel), the 2020 global pandemic was detrimental for the industry and resulted in below-average sales, profit, and dividend growth rates. Important metrics for investors to track include road and airline traffic volumes, expected government spending on infrastructure, average toll revenues per trip, average toll price inflation, EBIT margin, and FCF yield. Valuation measures such as P/E, P/CF, and EV/EBITDA can be used to compare valuations between companies in this industry.

◾ Marine Shipping

Businesses		Relative Characteristics						
Company	Country		Sector			Market		
			Lower	≈	Higher	Lower	≈	Higher
AP Moller - Maersk A/S	Denmark	Valuation		●		●		
Cosco Shipping Holdings Co.	China	Profitability	●			●		
Evergreen Marine Corp.	Taiwan	Sales Growth		●				●
Hapag-Lloyd AG	Germany	Profit Growth		●				●
HMM Co. Ltd.	South Korea	Debt Levels		●				●
HNA Technology Co. Ltd.	China	Dividend Yield		●				●
Mitsui OSK Lines Ltd.	Japan	Payout Ratio	●			●		
Nippon Yusen KK	Japan	Dividend Growth		●				●
Orient Overseas International Ltd.	Hong Kong	Earnings Predictability	●			●		
Yang Ming Marine Transport	Taiwan	Share Price Volatility		●				●

Data source: Bloomberg, as of March 18, 2022.

Businesses in the marine shipping industry transport a wide range of goods by sea. As discussed in Chapter 3, the maritime shipping industry is responsible for transporting roughly 80% of the total volume of world trade. Marine shipping companies are impacted by the type of goods being transported since ships are built to carry a specific type of cargo. Ships carrying oil or iron ore, for example, are not equipped to carry shipping containers. This results in serious inefficiencies, as a ship carrying oil from Australia to China or Japan must return empty of cargo, or a ship moving autos or electronics from Japan to Africa may likewise return with no cargo. In fact, it is estimated that roughly 40% of all ships at sea are traveling with no cargo at any given point in time. For this reason, there is a significant effort being made to improve logistical processes and software, and to develop more fuel-efficient vessels. A primary driver for the industry is increasing globalization and corresponding growth in global trade. Economic factors that have the biggest impact on sales growth and profitability for the industry include regional and global GDP growth, labor costs and availability, and fuel costs. As a key beneficiary of global economic growth and increased trade volumes, sales and profit growth for the industry have been strong. Marine shipping companies tend to maintain high levels of debt needed to fund the purchase of new vessels, which can cost over US$100 million each to build. Important metrics that investors should monitor for the marine shipping industry include shipping prices or day rates (the Baltic Dry Index is one such indicator), shipping volumes, utilization rates, fleet count, new fleet builds and ship order backlog, operating ratio (inverse of operating margins), EBIT and EBITDA margins, and EPS. Standard valuation measures such as P/E, P/CF, and EV to EBITDA can be used to compare valuations between companies in this industry.

■ Railroads

Businesses		Relative Characteristics					
Company	Country		Sector			Market	
			Lower ≈ Higher			Lower ≈ Higher	
Aurizon Holdings Ltd.	Australia	Valuation	●			●	
Canadian National Railway Co.	Canada	Profitability		●			●
Canadian Pacific Railway Ltd.	Canada	Sales Growth	●			●	
CSX Corp.	United States	Profit Growth		●			●
Daqin Railway Co.	China	Debt Levels		●			●
East Japan Railway Co.	Japan	Dividend Yield		●			●
Gmexico Transportes SAB de CV	Mexico	Payout Ratio		●		●	
Norfolk Southern Corp.	United States	Dividend Growth		●			●
Tokyu Corp.	Japan	Earnings Predictability		●			●
Union Pacific Corp.	United States	Share Price Volatility	●			●	

Data source: Bloomberg, as of March 18, 2022.

Railroads are a cost-effective method for shipping goods over great distances by land but are seldom able to deliver goods directly to their final destination. Nevertheless, railroads form a critical component of the global supply chain. A prevalent theme within the railroad industry has been the development of precision scheduled railroading, which tries to maximize the asset utilization (and minimize the operating ratio) of a railroad system by focusing on point-to-point movement of individual freight cars. Rail operators currently view the rapidly evolving autonomous truck market as a potential threat to their business models. Economic factors with the biggest influence on sales growth and profitability for the railroad industry include GDP growth, interest rates, availability and relative cost of competing freight modes (air, truck, and pipeline), inventory levels in major segments of the economy (such as autos), labor costs, and fuel costs. The rail industry has generated comparatively strong profit margins and delivered above-average profit and dividend growth in the past few years due to strong economic growth and shipping volumes. Important metrics for investors to track include total carloads, carloads by segment, carload growth, revenue ton miles (RTM) per carload, gross ton miles (GTM) per carload, revenue per carload, operating income and operating margin, operating ratio, operating ratio ex-fuel surcharge, capital expenditures, free cash flow, pricing, volumes, utilization, fleet count, asset turnover, EBIT and EBITDA margins, and leverage (net debt to EBITDA ratio). Valuation measures such as P/E and EV to EBITDA as well as discounted cash flow analysis are commonly used to compare valuations between companies in this industry.

■ Trading and Distribution

Businesses		Relative Characteristics						
Company	**Country**		**Sector**			**Market**		
			Lower	≈	Higher	Lower	≈	Higher
Adani Enterprises Ltd.	India	Valuation		●		●		
Brenntag SE	Germany	Profitability	●			●		
Ferguson PLC	United Kingdom	Sales Growth			●			●
ITOCHU Corp.	Japan	Profit Growth			●		●	
Mitsubishi Corp.	Japan	Debt Levels	●			●		
Mitsui & Co. Ltd.	Japan	Dividend Yield	●			●		
Posco International Corp.	South Korea	Payout Ratio		●			●	
Wuchan Zhongda Group Co. Ltd.	China	Dividend Growth			●			●
W.W. Grainger Inc.	United States	Earnings Predictability			●			●
Xiamen ITG Group	China	Share Price Volatility		●				●

Data source: Bloomberg, as of March 18, 2022.

Trading and distribution companies conduct import and export operations. Many of these companies resemble conglomerates in that they operate in multiple segments of the economy. Economic factors that can affect sales growth and profitability of the industry include inflation (and the ability of the company to pass through higher costs to customers), GDP growth in the regions in which they operate, construction spending, housing construction, infrastructure spending, and freight costs. To the extent trading companies can pass through higher costs, they can serve as a hedge against inflation. Since these companies are primarily trading goods rather than manufacturing them, they have tended to produce somewhat lower profit margins compared to the industrial sector but make up for this with high and growing sales volumes. This has allowed these businesses to grow their dividends at an above-average rate. Important metrics for investors to track include the split between commodity and noncommodity revenues, revenues and operating margins by segment and region, inventory levels, commodity prices, operating margins, capital expenditures, SG&A expenses, tax rates, growth in EBIT and EBITDA margins, supply chain dynamics, and leverage (net debt to EBITDA). Valuation measures such as P/E, P/CF, and EV/EBITDA or discounted cash flow analysis can be used to compare valuations between companies in this industry.

■ Trucking and Logistics

Businesses		Relative Characteristics						
Company	Country		Sector			Market		
			Lower	≈ Higher		Lower	≈ Higher	
CH Robinson Worldwide — United States		Valuation		●		●		
Cia de Distribucion Integral Logista Holdings — Spain		Profitability	●			●		
Expeditors International — United States		Sales Growth		●				●
Hyundai Glovis Co. Ltd. — South Korea		Profit Growth		●				●
JD Logistics Inc. — China		Debt Levels	●			●		
Kerry Logistics Network Ltd. — Hong Kong		Dividend Yield		●				●
Kuehne + Nagel International AG — Switzerland		Payout Ratio	●			●		
Nippon Express Holdings Inc. — Japan		Dividend Growth		●				●
Sinotrans Limited — China		Earnings Predictability	●			●		
XPO Logistics Inc. — United States		Share Price Volatility	●			●		

Data source: Bloomberg, as of March 18, 2022.

While railroads are very cost-effective for shipping goods over great distances by land, trucks are often required to get products to their final destination. Goods transported by rail must usually be unloaded and put into trucks for delivery to customers that are not conveniently located directly on rail lines. Fortunately, shipping containers make this a simple task. It is becoming increasingly difficult to attract sufficient truck drivers to keep up with growing demand. Labor availability therefore has been a particularly big challenge for trucking companies in recent years, and a primary motivation for the development of autonomous trucking technologies. Newly emerging companies are attempting to create trucks that can operate without human intervention, but this technology is still in its infancy and must undergo a great deal of testing before it is presumed safe for widespread use. In addition to autonomous trucking, the trucking industry is being impacted by a shift to more fuel-efficient trucks, growth of digital freight brokers, improvements in logistic software, and the potential introduction of competing delivery methods, such as drones. Although profit margins for the industry have lagged the market, growth rates in sales, profits, and dividends have been strong. Economic factors with the greatest influence on the trucking industry's sales growth and profitability include GDP growth, interest rates, trade flows, personal consumption, industrial production and capacity utilization, inventory levels, unemployment levels, labor costs and availability, and fuel costs. Important metrics for investors to monitor include pricing, volumes, utilization, fleet count, operating ratio, EBIT and EBITDA, and EPS. Standard valuation measures such as P/E, P/CF, and EV to EBITDA can be used to compare valuations between companies in this industry.

CHAPTER 16

Information Technology

The global technology sector includes companies providing software, electronic equipment, semiconductors, and IT services used in every corner of the globe and is the driving force behind the digital economy. The technology sector has played a leading role in improving human productivity over the past few decades. Every sector of the global economy relies on the technology sector to run its operations effectively. The invention of the semiconductor was central to this revolutionary process, but semiconductors alone did not achieve this feat. Corresponding advancements in software and other electronic devices also played critical roles in enhancing productivity.

233

Sector Characteristics versus Market

	Lower	≈	Higher		Lower	≈	Higher
Valuation			●	Dividend Yield	●		
Profitability		●		Payout Ratio	●		
Sales Growth			●	Dividend Growth			●
Profit Growth			●	Earnings Predictability	●		
Debt Levels	●			Share Price Volatility			●

Data source: Bloomberg, as of March 18, 2022.

Like the financial sector, many companies in the technology sector are interest rate sensitive; however, there is an important distinction. Businesses in the financial sector are primarily affected operationally by changes in interest rates, but in the case of technology companies, valuations may also be impacted. This is especially true for tech companies trading at high valuations. As previously noted in Chapter 5, rising interest rates have a larger, negative impact on long-dated bonds and the share prices of companies whose cash flows are expected to occur further into the future. The reason the technology sector is especially vulnerable to rising interest rates is because it contains a larger proportion of early-stage businesses with little or no earnings and high expected future growth rates. That being said, not all companies in the technology sector would be considered long-duration assets since they already generate strong earnings.

The technology sector usually outperforms the market throughout the entire bull market but is especially vulnerable late in the cycle due to rising interest rates and is often the weakest-performing sector in bear markets.

In this chapter we review eight main industry groups that together comprise the technology sector: (1) communications equipment, (2) electronic components, (3) fintech and payment processing, (4) IT consulting, (5) semiconductors, (6) semiconductor equipment, (7) software, and (8) technology hardware.

■ Communications Equipment

Businesses		Relative Characteristics	Sector			Market		
Company	Country		Lower	≈	Higher	Lower	≈	Higher
Cisco Systems Inc.	United States	Valuation	●			●		
Commscope Holding Co Inc.	United States	Profitability	●			●		
Corning Inc.	United States	Sales Growth	●					●
Fujikura Ltd.	Japan	Profit Growth	●			●		
Jiangsu Zhongtian Techology Co.	China	Debt Levels	●			●		
Telefonaktiebolaget LM Ericsson	Sweden	Dividend Yield		●		●		
Motorola Solutions Inc.	United States	Payout Ratio			●	●		
Nokia Oyj	Finland	Dividend Growth	●			●		
Xiaomi Corp.	China	Earnings Predictability			●			●
ZTE Corp.	China	Share Price Volatility		●				●

Data source: Bloomberg, as of March 18, 2022.

Software and equipment (hardware) produced by the communications equipment industry forms the backbone of both the internet and the world's telecommunications infrastructure. These businesses produce switches, routers, and various other components. Initial advancements in the industry came from hardware development, but now efficiency gains are increasingly coming from improvements in the software needed to run the equipment. According to the United Nations Conference on Trade and Development (UNCTAD), communications equipment was the second-most widely traded good globally in 2020, representing nearly US\$2 trillion in value.[1] The industry tends to be somewhat regionalized, with US firms having the greatest presence in the United States and Europe and a smaller footprint in Asia, where Chinese vendors are dominant. Notable industry trends include the deployment of 5G networks, a shift to hybrid office environments, supply chain bottlenecks, and cloud hyperscale (the ability to scale data center capacity as demand is added to the system), as well as the continuing migration of enterprises (businesses) to the cloud. Economic factors with the greatest impact on sales growth and profitability include business confidence (which is an important driver of IT budgets), commodity, labor, and component costs (important to gross margins). In its infancy, the communications equipment industry grew strongly and generated extremely high profit margins. As the industry matured, however, growth rates and profitability have fallen as many of the products have become commoditized. Important metrics that investors should track include revenue, margin, and earnings growth, cash flow, capital allocation (R&D, share repurchases, dividends and acquisitions), subscription revenue growth for communication software segment, and gross margins. Valuation measures such as P/E and EV/EBITDA as well as discounted cash flow analysis are commonly used to compare valuations between companies in this industry.

■ Electronic Components

The electronic component industry produces a wide variety of products, including optical network equipment, semiconductor parts, sensors, digital displays, connectors, cables, power supplies, inductors, transformers, and capacitors, just to name a few. These components are used in a multitude of devices, such as appliances, airplanes, automobiles, computers, and mobile phones. Many of the products created by this industry are commoditized (do not differ significantly between companies in terms of functionality). Like

Businesses		Relative Characteristics						
Company	Country		Sector			Market		
			Lower	≈	Higher	Lower	≈	Higher
AU Optronics Corp.	Taiwan	Valuation	●			●		
BOE Technology Group Co.	China	Profitability	●			●		
Innolux Corp.	Taiwan	Sales Growth		●				●
Kyocera Corp.	Japan	Profit Growth			●			●
LG Display Co.	South Korea	Debt Levels	●			●		
LG Innotek Co.	South Korea	Dividend Yield	●			●		
Luxshare Precision Industry Co. Ltd.	China	Payout Ratio			●	●		
Murata Manufacturing Co. Ltd.	Japan	Dividend Growth			●			●
Nidec Corporation	Japan	Earnings Predictability	●			●		
TDK Corp.	Japan	Share Price Volatility		●				●

Data source: Bloomberg, as of March 18, 2022.

other commoditized industries, pricing power is limited, and manufacturers rely on scale and strong supply chains and distribution networks to remain competitive. Economic factors with the greatest impact on earnings and sales growth include business confidence (an important driver of IT budgets), industrial production, capacity utilization, ISM purchasing manager survey, as well as commodity, labor, and component costs (important for gross margins). Similar to the communication equipment industry, profit margins for electric components have been below average; however, growth rates for the industry remain strong, as end market demand for electric components has remained robust. Important company metrics that investors should track include revenue and operating margins by product or segment, capital expenditures, product or segment market share, fab (fabrication plant) utilization, product shipments and order backlog (where available), as well as demand for consumer electronics. Standard valuation measures such as P/E, P/CF, and EV/EBITDA or discounted cash flow analysis are commonly used to assess company valuations in this industry.

◼ Fintech and Payment Processing

The fintech and payment processing industry is a rapidly evolving segment of the technology sector. Fintech (financial technology) companies provide systems and software that allow businesses and individuals to complete

Businesses		Relative Characteristics					
Company	Country		Sector			Market	
			Lower	≈	Higher	Lower	≈ Higher
Adyen NV	Netherlands	Valuation	●				●
Block Inc.	United States	Profitability		●			●
Global Payments Inc.	United States	Sales Growth		●			●
Mastercard Inc.	United States	Profit Growth		●			●
Network International Holdings PLC	UAE	Debt Levels	●			●	
Nexi SpA	Italy	Dividend Yield	●			●	
PayPal Holdings Inc.	United States	Payout Ratio	●			●	
Tencent Holdings Ltd.	China	Dividend Growth		●			●
Visa Inc.	United States	Earnings Predictability		●			●
Worldline SA	France	Share Price Volatility		●			●

Data source: Bloomberg, as of March 18, 2022.

financial transactions. High barriers to entry allowed credit card companies, such as Visa and Mastercard, along with payment processors like Global Payments, to dominate this industry for years. However, technological improvements have made it easier for new entrants to introduce disruptive solutions and compete for market share. These disruptive technologies, combined with inexpensive, readily available capital, have enhanced competition and structurally impaired return on investment for the industry's incumbents. There are significant differences in both interchange economics (fees received for processing transactions) and the regulatory treatment of fintech companies, across countries. The industry has experienced a shift in consumer preferences away from using cash to cards and online transactions, a trend that has served to disrupt the financial service offerings of banks. Economic factors with the greatest influence on sales growth and profitability include nominal GDP growth, personal consumption expenditures, e-commerce growth, cross-border volume growth, international travel, interest rates, changes in employment levels, and loan delinquency rates. Strong global economic growth in recent years is reflected in the industry's above-average profit margins and its strong sales and earnings growth, while high reinvestment requirements have restricted the ability of these companies to pay dividends. Important metrics that investors should monitor include TPV, take rate, user growth, and EBITDA margins. Common measures used to compare valuations between companies in this industry include P/E, P/CF, and EV/EBITDA.

IT Consulting

Businesses		Relative Characteristics						
Company	**Country**		**Sector**			**Market**		
			Lower	≈	Higher	Lower	≈	Higher
Accenture PLC	Ireland	Valuation	●			●		
Capgemini SE	France	Profitability	●			●		
Cognizant Technology Solutions Corp.	United States	Sales Growth	●			●		
Fujitsu Ltd.	Japan	Profit Growth	●			●		
Hewlett Packard Enterprises	United States	Debt Levels	●			●		
International Business Machines Corp.	United States	Dividend Yield	●			●		
Infosys Ltd.	India	Payout Ratio		●		●		
NEC Corp.	Japan	Dividend Growth		●				●
NTT Data Corp.	Japan	Earnings Predictability		●				●
Tata Consultancy Services Ltd.	India	Share Price Volatility	●				●	

Data source: Bloomberg, as of March 18, 2022.

The information technology (IT) consulting industry helps companies advance into the digital era, designing and implementing complex technological solutions that improve organizational efficiencies. Some of these solutions include intelligent systems, cloud technologies, automation, application development, systems integration, analytics, and cybersecurity. End market customers are found in every segment of the world economy, including healthcare, financial services, manufacturing, telecommunications, media, and retail. IT consulting companies have benefited from both a strong desire to improve business productivity across many industries, as well as the increasing complexity of corporate IT infrastructure and the high costs of in-house management. Economic factors that affect their customers can impact IT consulting businesses, since a reduction in IT spending (especially if it is outsourced) is a quick way for companies to cut costs in periods of economic weakness. To illustrate, reduced demand for automobiles may prompt auto OEMs to reduce capital expenditures by postponing or eliminating IT projects. Projects that are mission-critical or that deliver significant operational efficiencies are less prone to cutbacks. Although their sales and profit growth has lagged, these companies have grown their dividends more than the market in recent years. Important metrics that investors should monitor include labor availability, employee count, utilization rates, revenue per employee, revenue, and margins by business segment, adjusted operating margins, and gross margin growth. Standard valuation measures such as P/E, P/CF, and EV/EBITDA are commonly used to compare valuations between companies in this industry.

■ Semiconductors

Businesses		Relative Characteristics						
Company	Country		Sector			Market		
			Lower	≈	Higher	Lower	≈	Higher
Broadcom Inc.	United States	Valuation	●				●	
Intel Corp.	United States	Profitability			●			●
MediaTek Inc.	Taiwan	Sales Growth		●				●
Micron Technology Inc.	United States	Profit Growth		●				●
NVIDIA Corp.	United States	Debt Levels	●			●		
Qualcomm Inc.	United States	Dividend Yield		●		●		
Samsung Electronics	South Korea	Payout Ratio		●		●		
SK Hynix Inc.	South Korea	Dividend Growth	●					●
Taiwan Semiconductor	Taiwan	Earnings Predictability	●			●		
Texas Instruments Inc.	United States	Share Price Volatility		●				●

Data source: Bloomberg, as of March 18, 2022.

Companies in the semiconductor industry design and manufacture computer chips, including NAND (flash memory), DRAM (temporary data storage in computers and other devices), graphic chips (GPUs), core processors (CPUs), and logic controllers, among others. Many of the semiconductors produced today are designed to serve a specific purpose. Once designed, computer chips are manufactured in a fab. Accordingly, companies that outsource the manufacturing process of the chips they design are referred to as fabless semiconductor companies. Manufacturing semiconductors is highly capital intensive and requires advanced machinery and knowledge. New fabs being constructed today cost upwards of US$10 billion each to build. For this reason, there are very few semiconductor companies that focus only on fabrication, with Taiwan Semiconductor being one example. Most successful semiconductor companies design chips that improve on previous designs, making them smaller, faster, or consume less energy. Recent supply chain problems and rising geopolitical tensions have resulted in a trend toward onshoring or nearshoring production, which is driving investment in domestic manufacturing capacity. Other important themes include increased electric vehicle (EV) production, data center growth, artificial intelligence (AI), machine learning (ML), as well as the Internet of Things (IoT). These trends are serving as long-term structural tailwinds for the industry. Natural disasters such as earthquakes have the potential to disrupt the chip supply if they occur where fabs are located. Economic factors with the biggest influence on sales growth and profitability include commodity prices, freight, and logistics costs. Economies of scale are critical for fabs, but less so for fabless companies who can maintain high margins through continual design innovations. The industry is still growing quickly and generates above-average profit margins. However, these companies tend to have lower dividend yields than the market because significant reinvestment is required to stay competitive. Important financial metrics that investors should track include inventory levels, gross margin, and lead times. Semiconductor companies can usually be valued using the P/E multiple, but for younger, faster-growing companies that need to reinvest the vast majority of their cash flows, a P/CF ratio or discounted cash flow analysis would be more appropriate. A useful source for information on the industry is the Semiconductor Industry Association website at www.semiconductors.org.

■ Semiconductor Equipment

Businesses		Relative Characteristics		
Company	**Country**		**Sector** (Lower ≈ Higher)	**Market** (Lower ≈ Higher)
Applied Materials Inc.	United States	Valuation	Lower	≈
ASE Technology	Taiwan	Profitability	Higher	Higher
ASM Pacific Technology Limited	Hong Kong	Sales Growth	Higher	Higher
ASML Holding NV	Netherlands	Profit Growth	Higher	Higher
KLA Corp.	United States	Debt Levels	Lower	Lower
Lam Research Corp.	United States	Dividend Yield	Lower	Lower
SCREEN Holdings Co. Ltd.	Japan	Payout Ratio	≈	Lower
SUMCO Corp.	Japan	Dividend Growth	Higher	Higher
Teradyne Inc.	United States	Earnings Predictability	Higher	Higher
Tokyo Electron Ltd.	Japan	Share Price Volatility	Higher	Higher

Data source: Bloomberg, as of March 18, 2022.

Semiconductor equipment companies build the tools needed to design, manufacture, package, and ship semiconductor chips. These goods are at the forefront of advanced technology, where billions of circuits as small as two nanometers in width are etched into thin layers of wafers made from silicon using a process known as extreme ultraviolet lithography. In fact, all aspects of semiconductor manufacturing, even packaging, require technological expertise and advanced manufacturing capabilities. The high growth rate of the semiconductor industry feeds into the equipment industry. This is especially true today, with a worldwide shortage of semiconductor chips leading to calls for greater local production of semiconductors (onshoring). This means that more fabs are being built around the globe, which should keep industry demand strong for years to come. As is the case with semiconductors the growth in electric vehicles (EVs), data centers, artificial intelligence (AI), machine learning (ML), and the Internet of Things (IoT) creates a strong backdrop for semiconductor equipment demand. Economic factors influencing sales growth and profitability for the industry include commodity prices, as well as freight and logistics costs. Demand for semiconductors, and by extension semiconductor equipment, is cyclical and share prices can be volatile. Like semiconductors, semiconductor equipment companies have generated profit margins and growth rates above that of the market. Important metrics that investors should monitor include inventory levels, gross margin, fab capital expenditure budgets, lead times, and chip pricing. Valuation ratios such as P/E, P/CF, and EV/EBITDA can be used to compare valuations between companies in this industry.

■ Software

Businesses		Relative Characteristics						
Company	Country		Sector			Market		
			Lower	≈	Higher	Lower	≈	Higher
Adobe Inc.	United States	Valuation			●			●
Constellation Software Inc.	Canada	Profitability			●			●
Dassault Systemes SE	France	Sales Growth			●			●
Micro Focus International PLC	United Kingdom	Profit Growth	●					●
Microsoft Corp.	United States	Debt Levels	●			●		
Oracle Corp.	United States	Dividend Yield	●			●		
Salesforce.com Inc.	United States	Payout Ratio	●			●		
SAP SE	Germany	Dividend Growth	●			●		
Shopify Inc.	Canada	Earnings Predictability		●				●
VMware Inc.	United States	Share Price Volatility	●			●		

Data source: Bloomberg, as of March 18, 2022.

Software companies offer a broad range of computing-based platforms that give electronic devices functionality. The software industry can be divided into two broad categories, system software and application software. Systems software refers to the underlying software needed to operate a device, while application software acts as a second layer of functionality that is focused on a specific use. Since software development is carried out primarily by people rather than machinery, capital investment is lower than for hardware manufacturers, resulting in higher levels of profitability. A key industry trend has been the prioritization of software spending on digital transformation, cloud computing, artificial intelligence (AI), machine learning (ML), and automation. Economic factors that have the greatest impact on sales growth and profitability for the industry include GDP growth, employment growth, wage growth, and corporate IT budgets across the economy. Software companies selling primarily to small and mid-sized businesses are typically more sensitive to the economic cycle and to trends in new business formations, while enterprise software (which generates revenue from large businesses) is more resilient. Enterprise software has little to no supply chain disruption risk, and in some cases, software is viewed as an inflation hedge since it makes employees more productive, reducing the need to hire additional staff. Important metrics for companies in the software industry include subscriber numbers, net revenue, customer retention rate, average revenue per user (ARPU), billings, changes in remaining performance obligations (RPO), and annual recurring revenue (ARR). Software companies can usually be valued using the P/E ratio, but for younger, faster-growing companies that need to reinvest their cash flows, a P/CF ratio or discounted cash flow analysis would be more suitable.

■ Technology Hardware

Businesses		Relative Characteristics						
Company	**Country**		**Sector**			**Market**		
			Lower	≈	Higher	Lower	≈	Higher
Apple Inc.	United States	Valuation	●			●		
Canon Inc.	Japan	Profitability	●			●		
Compal Electronics Inc.	Taiwan	Sales Growth	●			●		
Dell Technologies Inc.	United States	Profit Growth	●			●		
HP Inc.	United States	Debt Levels		●				●
Lenovo Group Ltd.	China	Dividend Yield		●				●
Pegatron Corp.	Taiwan	Payout Ratio		●		●		
Quanta Computer Inc.	Taiwan	Dividend Growth	●			●		
Samsung Electronics	South Korea	Earnings Predictability		●			●	
Western Digital Corp.	United States	Share Price Volatility	●				●	

Data source: Bloomberg, as of March 18, 2022.

Technology hardware companies build mobile devices, laptops, personal computers, and hard-disk drives, among many other products. Hardware refers to the physical components that make up a device while software refers to the programming or coding that is needed for the device to function. Trends affecting the industry include the buildout of cloud infrastructure, enterprise data management, and the rapid development of artificial intelligence (AI) and machine learning (ML). Economic factors that have the greatest impact on industry sales growth and profitability include GDP growth, employment growth, and corporate IT budgets across the global economy. Profitability varies significantly within the industry, where businesses that distinguish their products (often through added layers of software that improve functionality) can generate higher profit margins. Other segments of the hardware industry produce goods that are commoditized, meaning that the products are similar regardless of who manufactures them. In these instances, profit margins tend to be lower and overall profits of the firm are determined more by the number of units sold. In both cases, though, supply chain management as well as manufacturing efficiency and scale are primary determinants of a company's success. Important metrics for investors to track include customer inventory levels, cost inflation, product and replacement cycles, new product deployments by competitors, capex budgets, capacity additions in the industry, operating profits and margins, gross margins, and revenue growth by segment or product line. Standard valuation measures such as P/E, P/CF, and EV/EBITDA can be used to compare valuations between companies in this industry.

CHAPTER 17

Materials

S upplying both finished products and the raw materials used as inputs in
manufacturing processes worldwide, the global materials sector feeds
global supply chains. Most businesses in this sector are cyclical due to their
sensitivity to changes in economic growth. Some companies within the sector are less sensitive to the economic cycle than others, such as companies
that provide industrial gases to the healthcare sector. Another more defensive segment of the materials sector is the container and packaging industry,
which manufactures packaging and cans for both the beverage and packaged
food industries. End-user demand for certain industrial gases, packaging,
and containers is relatively consistent when compared to many other goods
produced by companies in the materials sector. It is important to note the
operations of some companies within the materials sector are heavily influenced by events taking place in other industries. Paint and lumber producers, for example, are largely dependent on the strength of the housing market. Since the housing market is tied to changes in mortgage rates (which
are derived from interest rates), changes in interest rates could eventually
flow through to affect businesses in the materials sector as well. Some companies within the sector benefit from rising commodity prices and therefore
perform well during inflationary periods. Operational scale is important
for most of the businesses in this sector, since there is little differentiation
between products and there are generally large, fixed costs associated with

extracting and processing raw materials. Both product scarcity and transportation costs play a key role in determining industry dynamics, including barriers to entry, degree of competition, and pricing power.

Sector Characteristics versus Market

	Lower	≈	Higher		Lower	≈	Higher
Valuation	●			Dividend Yield			●
Profitability	●			Payout Ratio	●		
Sales Growth			●	Dividend Growth			●
Profit Growth			●	Earnings Predictability	●		
Debt Levels	●			Share Price Volatility			●

Data source: Bloomberg, as of March 18, 2022.

Companies in this sector have generated strong sales and profit growth compared to the market in recent years. Additionally, they have strong balance sheets and have grown their dividends at an above-average rate. Despite this valuations for the sector have been lower than the market.

Companies within the materials sector tend to outperform immediately following bear market bottoms and in the late stage of the bull market cycle as prices start to rise and demand for base materials is strongest. On the other hand, materials companies tend to underperform the market during bear markets and in the mid-cycle portion of bull markets.

In this chapter we take a close look at the seven main industry groups within the sector: (1) agricultural products, (2) chemicals, (3) construction materials, (4) containers and packaging, (5) industrial metals, (6) mining, and (7) paper and forest products.

■ Agricultural Products

The agricultural industry represents approximately 4% of world GDP.[1] The companies in this industry provide farmers with everything they need to feed the world, including farm equipment and machinery, fertilizers, and food processing. The businesses listed here can be split into three distinct groups, namely food processing, farm products (seed and fertilizer), and

Businesses		Relative Characteristics						
Company	Country		Sector			Market		
			Lower	≈	Higher	Lower	≈	Higher
Archer-Daniels-Midland Co. ———— United States		Valuation	●			●		
Bunge Ltd. ———— United States		Profitability	●			●		
CNH Industrial NV ———— United Kingdom		Sales Growth	●				●	
Corteva Inc. ———— United States		Profit Growth	●				●	
Deere & Co. ———— United States		Debt Levels	●			●		
Kubota Corp. ———— Japan		Dividend Yield	●					●
Mosaic Co. ———— United States		Payout Ratio		●		●		
Nutrien Ltd. ———— Canada		Dividend Growth	●					●
Wilmar International Ltd. ———— Singapore		Earnings Predictability		●				●
Yara International ASA ———— Norway		Share Price Volatility	●				●	

Data source: Bloomberg, as of March 18, 2022.

farm equipment. While they are all tied to the agricultural cycle, these three segments differ substantially. Farm product companies produce large volumes of relatively inexpensive goods that are purchased by farmers on a regular basis, while farm equipment manufacturers produce fewer units of high-priced products, which are purchased infrequently. Fertilizer producers are dependent on feedstock (natural gas) in their manufacturing process, while farming equipment manufacturers require steel and electronic components (among other items) as inputs in manufacturing. In addition to food for human consumption, many food processing companies produce animal feed as well as nonedible products such as biodiesel and ethanol. Advancements in machinery, fertilizers, and farming techniques, along with the consolidation of agricultural land, have led to significant improvements in farming productivity. These productivity gains are necessary if we are to feed the world's population while limiting the amount of farmland created through deforestation. The global positioning system (GPS) has also dramatically impacted farming productivity. GPS and data collection sensors on farming equipment enable farmers to work in poor visibility and apply fertilizers and pesticides more selectively, reducing expenses and improving crop yields. Emerging industry trends include the proliferation of precision agriculture technology, a shift to zero emission vehicles (electrification), and the production of more environmentally friendly ammonia-based fertilizers. Economic factors that have the greatest impact on the industry include labor costs, population growth, and income growth. Important industry metrics that investors should monitor include dealer inventory levels, commodity input prices (steel, copper, ilmenite/rutile ore, chlorine, sulfur, and natural gas), freight costs, interest rates (financing costs), and operating and profit margins. Other key metrics include realized product pricing, cost of goods sold per tonne, sales volumes, and utilization rates (both for individual companies and the industry as a whole). Cost competitiveness for fertilizer producers is dependent on availability of feedstock (such as natural gas used to produce nitrogen). Standard valuation measures such as P/E, P/CF, and EV/EBITDA are commonly used to compare valuations between companies in this industry.

■ Chemicals

Businesses

Company	Country
Air Liquide SA	France
BASF SE	Germany
Dow Inc.	United States
Hengli Petrochemical Co. Ltd.	China
LG Chem Ltd.	South Korea
Linde PLC	United Kingdom
LyondellBasell Industries NV	United States
Mitsubishi Chemical Holdings	Japan
Saudi Basic Industries	Saudi Arabia
Wanhua Chemical Group Co. Ltd.	China

Relative Characteristics

	Sector			Market		
	Lower	≈	Higher	Lower	≈	Higher
Valuation		●		●		
Profitability			●	●		
Sales Growth			●			●
Profit Growth	●					●
Debt Levels	●			●		
Dividend Yield	●					●
Payout Ratio			●	●		
Dividend Growth			●			●
Earnings Predictability	●			●		
Share Price Volatility		●				●

Data source: Bloomberg, as of March 18, 2022.

The chemical industry produces a wide range of products, including plastics, paint and other coatings, batteries, glue, solvents and cleaners, food additives, inputs for personal care products (like cosmetics and shampoo), refinery additives, as well as gases used in industrial processes and healthcare settings. According to the United Nations Conference on Trade (UNCTAD), chemicals were the most widely traded good globally in 2020, representing more than US$2 trillion in value.[2] The continuing struggle to reduce carbon emissions is impacting businesses in the industry as they strive to produce goods with smaller carbon footprints. Economic factors that have the greatest impact on sales growth and profitability of the industry include industrial demand and capacity utilization, interest rates, and GDP growth, as well as any factors that impact the end markets of these businesses. Companies that produce industrial gases, paint, and cleaning and solvent manufacturers are more defensive in nature and generate relatively consistent earnings throughout the economic cycle, whereas companies that manufacture base and specialty chemicals are more sensitive to economic conditions and have greater variability in earnings. Important metrics for investors to track include realized pricing, cost of goods sold per tonne, sales volumes, utilization rates, commodity prices (such as natural gas and chlorine), as well as EBITDA, and EBITDA margins by product type or segment. Each firm's relative position on the cost curve depends on the availability of feedstock in the regions in which they operate. For example, plastic producers that have easy access to an inexpensive supply of natural gas are lower on the cost curve than others that rely on natural gas imports or shipments. Standard valuation measures such as P/E, EV/DACF, and EV/EBITDA can be used to compare valuations between companies in this industry.

■ Construction Materials

Businesses			Relative Characteristics						
Company		**Country**		**Sector**			**Market**		
				Lower	≈	Higher	Lower	≈	Higher
AGC Inc.		Japan	Valuation		●		●		
Anhui Conch Cement Co. Ltd.		China	Profitability		●		●		
BBMG Corp.		China	Sales Growth		●				●
Cemex SAB de CV		Mexico	Profit Growth	●					●
China National Building Material Co.		China	Debt Levels	●			●		
CRH PLC		Ireland	Dividend Yield			●			●
HeidelbergCement AG		Germany	Payout Ratio	●			●		
Holcim Ltd.		Switzerland	Dividend Growth	●					●
Siam Cement		Thailand	Earnings Predictability			●			●
Sika AG		Switzerland	Share Price Volatility	●				●	

Data source: Bloomberg, as of March 18, 2022.

The construction materials industry produces many of the materials needed to build large-scale infrastructure projects, such as roads, tunnels, and bridges. This includes cement (the second most widely used material in the world after water), resins, sealants and adhesives, mortar, aggregates, and asphalt. Note that although steel is used extensively in construction, it has been included in the industrial metal industry. To the extent that large infrastructure projects are financed, changes in interest rates are important to consider. Keep in mind that large projects are usually planned and funded well in advance of construction, and once started they are likely to be completed regardless of economic conditions. Emerging themes affecting the construction materials industry include decarbonization of cement as well as planned upgrades to infrastructure in many countries around the globe. Economic factors that have the greatest impact on sales growth and profitability for the industry include interest rates, GDP growth, building construction, and government spending on infrastructure. These businesses have generated above-average growth in sales, earnings, and dividends in the past few years compared to the market. Important metrics for the industry include inventories, realized pricing, cost of goods sold per tonne, sales volumes, utilization rates, commodity prices (such as cement), fuel and freight costs, leverage (net debt to EBITDA), operating cash flow, free cash flow (FCF) to net income, as well as EBITDA and EBITDA margins in each region or business segment. Standard valuation measures such as P/E, P/CF, and EV/EBITDA are commonly used to compare valuations between companies in this industry.

■ Containers and Packaging

Businesses		Relative Characteristics						
Company	Country		Sector Lower	Sector ≈	Sector Higher	Market Lower	Market ≈	Market Higher
Amcor PLC	United Kingdom	Valuation		●		●		
Ball Corp.	United States	Profitability	●			●		
Berry Global Group Inc.	United States	Sales Growth	●			●		
Crown Holdings Inc.	United States	Profit Growth	●					●
DS Smith PLC	United Kingdom	Debt Levels			●			●
International Paper Co.	United States	Dividend Yield	●				●	
Mondi PLC	United Kingdom	Payout Ratio			●	●		
Nine Dragons Paper Holdings Ltd.	Hong Kong	Dividend Growth	●					●
Smurfit Kappa Group	Ireland	Earnings Predictability			●			●
Westrock Co.	United States	Share Price Volatility		●				●

Data source: Bloomberg, as of March 18, 2022.

The containers and packaging industry manufactures beverage cans and bottles, packaging materials for food and personal care products, as well as containerboard materials used to create boxes used to ship goods. A firm's relative position on the cost curve depends on the availability of feedstock in the regions in which they operate. For example, containerboard producers that have easy access to a supply of timber are lower on the cost curve (more cost competitive) than others that rely on pulp or paper imports or shipments. Packaging companies tend to have good pricing power and can pass through inflationary costs to customers, in part due to the relatively low cost of packaging compared to the total cost of the good being produced. ESG concerns continue to affect the packaging industry, with an increasing focus on recycling and reducing carbon emissions. Economic factors that have the greatest impact on sales growth and profitability for the industry include interest rates, GDP growth, population growth, commodity costs and availability, and shipping volumes. Despite having generated below-average growth in sales over the past few years, these businesses have grown profits and dividends at a higher rate than the market. Important metrics for companies in this industry include realized pricing, cost of goods sold per tonne, sales volume by product or segment, capacity utilization rates, cost of goods sold, commodity prices (aluminum, natural gas, polypropylene, polyethylene resin, kraft paper, and pulp), capital expenditure budgets, capacity additions, and EBITDA margin. P/E, P/CF, and EV/EBITDA can be used to compare valuations between companies in this industry.

■ Industrial Metals

Businesses		Relative Characteristics						
Company	**Country**		**Sector**			**Market**		
			Lower	≈	Higher	Lower	≈	Higher
Aluminum Corp. of China ——— China		Valuation	●			●		
ArcelorMittal SA ——— Luxembourg		Profitability	●			●		
Auribus AG ——— Germany		Sales Growth		●				●
Baoshan Iron & Steel Co. ——— China		Profit Growth			●			●
Hunan Valin Steel Co. Ltd. ——— China		Debt Levels	●			●		
JFE Holdings Inc. ——— Japan		Dividend Yield		●				●
Nippon Steel Corp. ——— Japan		Payout Ratio	●			●		
Nucor Corp. ——— United States		Dividend Growth	●					●
POSCO Holdings Inc. ——— South Korea		Earnings Predictability	●			●		
Tata Steel Ltd. ——— India		Share Price Volatility		●				●

Data source: Bloomberg, as of March 18, 2022.

The industrial metals industry processes raw materials to produce steel, aluminum, and other metals used to manufacture a vast array of machinery and durable goods. Similar to other businesses within the materials sector, each company's relative position on the cost curve depends on the availability of feedstock in the regions in which they operate. For example, steel producers that have access to an inexpensive supply of iron ore are lower on the cost curve than others that rely on imports for which they must absorb costly shipping fees. Economic factors that have the largest impact on industry earnings and sales include GDP growth, industrial production and utilization rates, freight costs, industrial and agricultural machinery demand, heavy equipment demand, demand for durable goods (i.e., autos, appliances and aircraft), and construction activity. Although these businesses have generated above-average growth in sales, earnings, and dividends compared to the market over the past few years, they have traded at below-average valuations. Important metrics for investors to track include realized pricing, cost of goods sold per tonne, sales volumes, capacity utilization rates, steel and aluminum prices, shipments, commodity (such as energy, iron ore, nickel, copper, alumina, and ilmenite/rutile ore) prices, adjusted EBITDA, as well as adjusted EBITDA margins. Standard valuation measures such as P/E, P/CF, and EV/EBITDA may be used to compare valuations between companies in this industry.

■ Mining

Businesses		Relative Characteristics						
Company	Country		Sector			Market		
			Lower	≈	Higher	Lower	≈	Higher
Anglo American PLC	United Kingdom	Valuation		●		●		
BHP Group Ltd.	Australia	Profitability			●			●
Fortescue Metals Group Ltd.	Australia	Sales Growth			●			●
Freeport-McMoran Inc.	United States	Profit Growth			●			●
Glencore PLC	Switzerland	Debt Levels	●			●		
Grupo Mexico SAB	Mexico	Dividend Yield			●			●
Jiangxi Copper Co. Ltd.	China	Payout Ratio			●	●		
Rio Tinto PLC	United Kingdom	Dividend Growth			●			●
Southern Copper Co.	Peru	Earnings Predictability			●			●
Teck Resources Ltd.	Canada	Share Price Volatility			●			●

Data source: Bloomberg, as of March 18, 2022.

The mining industry extracts raw materials from the earth, such as coal, iron ore, copper, nickel, zinc, and precious metals. Mining companies may also process raw materials to a limited degree, but these materials are typically turned into finished goods by businesses in other industries. ESG concerns are becoming increasingly important, prompting mining companies to focus on reducing energy consumption, water usage, CO_2, NO_x, and SO_x emissions, minimize the environmental damage caused by certain activities like strip mining, and limiting the waste generated from operations. Investors should closely monitor company ESG ratings and regulatory risks. Economic factors that have the largest impact on industry sales growth and profitability include GDP growth, industrial production and capacity utilization rates, freight costs, industrial and agricultural machinery demand, heavy equipment demand, demand for durable goods (i.e., autos and aircraft), and demand for building and construction materials. Although these businesses have generated above-average growth in sales, earnings, and dividends over the past few years, they have traded at below-average valuations, possibly because of ESG concerns. Important metrics for investors to track include realized pricing by product type, cost of goods sold per tonne, sales volumes, utilization rates, commodity (such as oil, metallurgical coal, iron ore, ilmenite and rutile ore, nickel, copper, zinc, and gold) prices, operating costs, capital expenditures, tax expense, reserve life, exploration optionality, off-balance-sheet liabilities, tax structure, leverage (debt/EBITDA), as well as EBIT and EBITDA margins. P/FCF and EV/EBITDA are frequently used to compare valuations between companies in the mining industry, but price to net asset value (P/NAV), adjusted for off-balance-sheet items, may provide better insights into the valuation of companies whose value is largely dependent on reserves of raw materials.

■ Paper and Forest Products

Businesses		Relative Characteristics	Sector			Market		
Company	Country		Lower ≈ Higher			Lower ≈ Higher		
Boise Cascade Co.	United States	Valuation	●			●		
Canfor Corp.	Canada	Profitability		●		●		
Empresas CMPC SA	Chile	Sales Growth	●					●
Oji Holdings Corp.	Japan	Profit Growth			●			●
Sappi Ltd.	South Africa	Debt Levels	●			●		
Stora Enso Oyj	Finland	Dividend Yield	●			●		
UFP Industries Inc.	United States	Payout Ratio	●			●		
UPM-Kymmene Oyj	Finland	Dividend Growth	●					●
West Fraser Timber Co. Ltd.	Canada	Earnings Predictability			●			●
Weyerhaeuser Co.	United States	Share Price Volatility			●			●

Data source: Bloomberg, as of March 18, 2022.

The paper and forest products industry comprises one of the largest components of global trade. Companies within the industry produce lumber and plywood used in building construction, paper used for printing, and pulp, which is used to make containerboard, the primary component of boxes and other packaging materials. While pulp demand is dependent on the need for packaging materials and paper, lumber demand is driven by the homebuilding and home renovation markets. Deforestation remains a concern due to climate change and the beneficial impact trees have on absorbing CO_2 emissions from the atmosphere, so it is crucial that companies implement sustainable forestry practices. Economic factors that have the greatest impact on industry sales growth and profitability include the age of housing inventory, housing permits, housing starts, mortgage rates (which influence housing starts), tariffs, containerboard production, GDP growth, and employment levels. Despite having generated above-average growth in sales, earnings, and dividends compared to the market over the past few years, these businesses have traded at below-average valuations. Important metrics for investors to monitor include pulp, paper, and lumber sales volumes, cost of goods sold, EBITDA per mfbm (thousand board feet) shipped for lumber and EBITDA per mt (metric ton) for pulp and paper, cash costs per mfbm for lumber or per mt for pulp and paper, sales volumes, production and utilization rates, average net selling prices (pulp and lumber), adjusted EBIT and EBITDA margins, operating leases, as well as pulp, paper and lumber inventories. Commonly used measures to compare valuations between companies in the industry include P/E, price to book (P/B), EV/EBITDA, and EV/mfbm for lumber producers (or EV/mt for pulp and paper producers).

CHAPTER 18

Real Estate

The global real estate sector includes companies that predominately own and manage real estate assets across a variety of property types from distribution centers to office skyscrapers, business parks, multi-family residential properties, shopping malls, data centers, cell towers, and self-storage facilities. Real estate offers unique characteristics that can enhance the risk-and-return profile of an investor's portfolio. It is generally regarded as a separate asset class from stocks and bonds, as real estate has historically exhibited relatively low correlations with other sectors of the market.

Publicly traded real estate companies are a preferred way for investors to gain access to real estate properties capable of generating consistent income and attractive capital gains. Investing in real estate through the public markets has four main benefits over private (direct) real estate investing. First, private real estate is illiquid. In addition to the lengthy sales process for an individual property, many fund investments in private real estate have a multi-year lockup period preventing investors from exiting. On the other hand, publicly traded real estate securities are exchange traded and can be transacted on during regular market hours. Second, most private investors limit themselves to more traditional property types like office, residential, industrial, and retail, but there are more niche opportunities in the public markets for emerging property types. These include data centers, cell towers, life sciences, and self-storage assets that can generate outsized growth.

Third, the investment, asset, and property management of private real estate investing is specialized by property type and geography. Accessing best-in-class management for multiple property types and across multiple regions is therefore only feasible through the public markets. Finally, assembling a diversified portfolio of real estate requires a tremendous amount of capital. Well-diversified portfolios can be created through the public markets almost instantaneously and at a very modest cost.

Publicly traded real estate comes in two forms, a real estate investment trust (REIT) and a real estate operating company (REOC). A REIT is a corporation or business trust that combines the capital of many investors to buy properties or supply financing for income-producing real estate. In most countries, a REIT is not required to pay corporate income tax if it distributes the majority of its taxable income to shareholders. A REOC is a company whose primary business is similarly the ownership and/or operation of commercial real estate properties; however, the company has elected not to be taxed as a REIT.

Accounting methods employed by companies within the real estate sector are another important distinction from companies in other sectors. Cash flow does not equal accounting income because of depreciation, amortization, and straight-lining of leases. REITs use straight-line rents because generally accepted accounting principles (GAAP) requires it. Straight-lining averages the tenant's rent payments over the life of the lease but does not necessarily reflect the cash payments received during each period due to tenant concessions or other issues. Furthermore, company balance sheets reflect the acquisition price of the underlying assets, not their current market value.

Data source: Bloomberg, as of March 18, 2022.

Sales and EBITDA growth in the real estate sector are typically higher and steadier than the market, given normally low vacancy rates and contractual rental rates (leases contractually bind both property owner and tenant to both rents and term). Higher earnings stability supports strong dividend yields and results in higher-than-normal earnings predictability, which facilitates financing at both the property and corporate level. However, it should be noted that consolidated company debt levels often vary by country. For example, the average debt-to-equity level of a REIT domiciled in the United States is much lower than that of a Canadian REIT.

Long-term trends affecting the real estate sector include housing shortages, the increasing need for senior living establishments, a shift to e-commerce from traditional retailing, working from home and the move toward smaller office spaces, offshoring or onshoring of manufacturing, urban and suburban office space demand shifts, and just-in-time manufacturing.

Companies within this sector vary in sensitivity to the economic cycle, and investors should note that since real estate assets are stationary, they are subject to economic events and demographic trends specific to that geographic region. When interest rates rise quickly, companies within the sector typically underperform and correlations between REITs and the universe of common stocks increase. Real estate companies tend to have a higher beta than the market average, reflecting the reactionary nature of investor sentiment on economic expectations, high fixed costs, high leverage, and thin operating margins. Real estate company performance during bear markets is influenced by the factor(s) that precipitated the bear market in relation to their underlying exposures. In general, during deteriorating economic conditions, REITs that are focused on residential properties and grocery-anchored shopping centers are a safer segment within the sector. However, these companies are often priced more aggressively (expensive) heading into a recession.

REIT operating performance is usually assessed by reviewing a company's funds from operations (FFO). FFO is equal to net income excluding gains or losses from sales of property plus depreciation, and it is considered a better measure of earnings than EPS. Adjusted funds from operations (AFFO) is another useful measure of operating performance. AFFO attempts to quantify cash flow generated by operations and is calculated by subtracting recurring expenditures (necessary to maintain a REIT's properties and its revenue) from FFO. It also straight-lines rents to spread rental rate incentives common to new tenants across the term of the lease. Investors can identify sector and industry income multiples, make any necessary adjustments, and apply that multiple to forecasted FFO and AFFO for a particular REIT to arrive at a fair value estimate.

Another commonly used valuation measure is net asset value (NAV), which is the net market value of a REIT's assets after subtracting its liabilities and obligations. Since most jurisdictions require REITs to only report book value, which likely differs substantially from market value, estimates of NAV vary widely by geographic region. Further, individual property or even aggregate net operating income (NOI) is not reported and has to be estimated. Investors must then attempt to apply a market capitalization rate (the inverse of a P/E multiple) to the aggregate NOI. Capitalization rates (commonly referred to as cap rates) are calculated by dividing a property's NOI by its current market value, and they reflect the estimated expected annual income return on a real estate investment.

In this chapter we take a closer look at eight main industry groupings within the real estate sector: (1) diversified REITs, (2) industrial REITs, (3) office REITs, (4) residential REITs, (5) retail REITs, (6) real estate development, (7) real estate services, and (8) specialty REITs.

■ Diversified REITs

Businesses		Relative Characteristics						
Company	Country		Sector			Market		
			Lower	≈	Higher	Lower	≈	Higher
CapitaLand Investment Limited —————— Singapore		Valuation	●			●		
China Fortune Land Development Co. Ltd. —— China		Profitability	●					●
Daiwa House Industry Co. Ltd. —————— Japan		Sales Growth	●			●		
Land Securities Group PLC —————— United Kingdom		Profit Growth	●			●		
Lexington Realty Trust —————— United States		Debt Levels	●				●	
Mitsubishi Estate Co. —————— Japan		Dividend Yield			●			●
Mitsui Fudosan Co. —————— Japan		Payout Ratio	●			●		
New World Development Co. Ltd. —————— Hong Kong		Dividend Growth	●			●		
Sun Hung Kai Properties Limited —————— Hong Kong		Earnings Predictability		●				●
Swiss Prime Site AG —————— Switzerland		Share Price Volatility		●			●	

Data source: Bloomberg, as of March 18, 2022.

Diversified REITs include those companies that have been in business for many years and after focusing on a single property type, have expanded their operations. As a result, these companies own and manage a wide array of property types, making them suitable for investors looking for diversified sector exposure. As these firms hold multiple property types, their performance is primarily determined by the economic strength of the geographies in which they operate and the types of properties they own. Diversified REITs typically generate more stable cash flows than property-specific REITs over the economic cycle. As a result, earnings predictability and dividend yields are typically higher than market. Further, the more stable cash flow allows them to invest in out-of-favor properties when REITs that focus on a single property type cannot. Management teams try to exploit their industry knowledge by concentrating on a limited geographic area or leveraging some other potential advantage. Important metrics for investors to monitor vary by the types of properties held, but often include occupancy, same-store sales growth, FFO, and AFFO. Investors can use a combination of valuation approaches including DCF, P/FFO and P/AFFO, and NAV.

■ Industrial REITs

Businesses		Relative Characteristics						
Company	**Country**		**Sector**			**Market**		
			Lower	≈	Higher	Lower	≈	Higher
AB Sagax	Sweden	Valuation		●				●
Ascendas REIT	Singapore	Profitability		●				●
CTP NV	Netherlands	Sales Growth		●				●
Duke Realty Corp.	United States	Profit Growth		●				●
First Industrial Realty Trust, Inc.	United States	Debt Levels	●			●		
Goodman Group	Australia	Dividend Yield	●			●		
Nippon Prologis REIT	Japan	Payout Ratio	●			●		
Prologis Inc.	United States	Dividend Growth		●				●
Segro PLC	United Kingdom	Earnings Predictability		●				●
STAG Industrial Inc.	United States	Share Price Volatility	●			●		

Data source: Bloomberg, as of March 18, 2022.

Although companies within this segment are classified as industrial, many of the underlying real estate assets are warehouses or bulk distribution facilities. Compared to other industries within the real estate sector, industrial REITs can increase supply very quickly as the zoning, building, and leasing for warehouses are straightforward compared to all other property types. Furthermore, buildings constructed on "spec" (without a tenant) are more common, as warehouse space is often less expensive to construct per square foot versus other types of real estate. Land is typically inexpensive and leasing costs are also lower because of a reduced requirement for tenant improvements. Industrial REIT performance is highly correlated to GDP growth, since demand for warehouse and distribution space heavily depends on economic growth. The demand for warehouse space also depends on import and export activity in the region. Warehouse demand has increased because of trade restrictions, disruptions in global trade, and a shift by consumers to purchase goods online. This has led to increased demand for distribution facilities closer to population centers driving outsized EBITDA growth, exceedingly low vacancies, and rapidly increasing rents, all of which are positively skewing the segment metrics. Other macroeconomic factors that affect the industry include goods moving through the supply chain (shipping volumes), inventory levels, retail sales, industrial production and capacity utilization, population growth, and wage growth. Business confidence is also an important indicator. Important operational and financial metrics for investors to track include funds from operations (FFO) and adjusted funds from operations (AFFO). Investors can use a combination of approaches to value companies within the industry, including DCF, P/FFO, P/AFFO, and NAV.

■ Office REITs

Businesses		Relative Characteristics						
Company	Country		Sector			Market		
			Lower	≈	Higher	Lower	≈	Higher
Alexandria Real Estate Equities Inc.	United States	Valuation	●			●		
Aroundtown SA	Luxembourg	Profitability			●			●
Boston Properties Inc.	United States	Sales Growth		●				●
Dexus	Australia	Profit Growth	●			●		
Gecina SA	France	Debt Levels			●			●
Hongkong Land Holdings Ltd.	Hong Kong	Dividend Yield			●			●
IWG PLC	Switzerland	Payout Ratio	●			●		
Kilroy Realty Corp.	United States	Dividend Growth	●			●		
Nippon Building Fund Inc.	Japan	Earnings Predictability			●			●
Swire Properties Ltd.	Hong Kong	Share Price Volatility		●			●	

Data source: Bloomberg, as of March 18, 2022.

Office REITs are unique within the real estate sector because the factors that drive office property performance are highly localized. A building in

Frankfurt may perform quite differently than the exact same quality of building in Berlin or the building across the street. Despite swings in REIT prices, occupancy (and therefore cash flows) changes very little for office REITs because of the long-term nature of the leases (with 10-year terms being common) and the high (70–90%) probability of lease renewal. Rents, tenant improvement allowances (paid by the landlord to entice a new tenant), and other lease terms like rights and options vary through property cycles and by local custom. One important trend affecting the industry is a shift toward a smaller average amount of space per employee. In addition, new supply is typically state of the art with better amenities, design, and lower operating costs, weakening the demand for dated or poorly located buildings. Economic recessions are most harmful to office properties located outside major urban central business districts, as regional and satellite offices are often the first to be eliminated to cut costs. Office occupancy levels in urban centers are relatively stable when compared to suburban locations, particularly for strong assets in markets with significant supply constraints and barriers to entry. Since it is the local environment that drives the supply and demand for office space, it is essential to monitor local economies and their key industries. Macroeconomic factors that have the greatest impact on the industry include employment growth and changes in the level of interest rates. Office REITs often trade below NAV despite delivering above-average profitability and dividend yields. Important industry metrics that investors should track include new supply, tenant contraction or expansion, changes in the amount of office space available for sublease and changes in tenant improvement allowances (a component of net effective rent), and changes in the face or asking rent. Other metrics for investors to track include funds from operations (FFO) and adjusted funds from operations (AFFO). Investors can use a combination of approaches to value companies in the industry, including DCF, P/FFO, P/AFFO, and NAV.

■ Residential REITs

Residential is considered the most stable property type, given the ability to accurately forecast demand and supply. High earnings predictability supports high loan-to-value levels and dampens share price volatility. The demand for multi-family space depends on population growth and household formation, which is often regional in nature. Demand also depends

Businesses		Relative Characteristics						
Company	**Country**		**Sector**			**Market**		
			Lower	≈	Higher	Lower	≈	Higher
Altarea SCA	France	Valuation	●			●		
AvalonBay Communities Inc.	United States	Profitability		●				●
Country Garden Holdings Co. Ltd.	China	Sales Growth		●				●
Deutsche Wohnen SE	Germany	Profit Growth		●		●		
Equity Residential	United States	Debt Levels	●			●		
Invitation Homes Inc.	United States	Dividend Yield		●				●
Kojamo Oyj	Finland	Payout Ratio	●			●		
LEG Immobilien SE	Germany	Dividend Growth		●				●
Poly Developments and Holdings Group	China	Earnings Predictability		●				●
Vonovia SE	Germany	Share Price Volatility	●			●		

Data source: Bloomberg, as of March 18, 2022.

on the cost of renting compared to the cost of owning. Higher interest rates will make homeownership more expensive, causing a shift toward renting. Therefore, mortgage rates are a key indicator of future performance. Geography is also critically important, since rental regulations and barriers to new supply vary significantly by country, state, and city. Multi-family properties typically have short-term leases, with one year being most common, so rents adjust to market quickly in an unregulated environment, which is an attractive feature in inflationary times. Tenants often pay utilities, but landlords have responsibility for building maintenance, capital expenditures, insurance, and taxes. Economic factors that have the greatest effect on the industry include interest and mortgage rates, employment and wage growth, property availability and affordability, median rent versus median income, geography (high barrier to entry markets versus low barrier to entry markets), government-imposed rental regulations, new unit construction, the inventory of unsold homes, immigration, and household formations. Residential REITs have generated strong profit and dividend growth over the past decade due to strong demand for housing aided by low-cost mortgages. Important operational and financial metrics for investors to track include funds from operations (FFO) and adjusted funds from operations (AFFO). Investors can use a combination of approaches to value companies in the industry, including DCF, P/FFO, P/AFFO, and NAV.

Retail REITs

Businesses		Relative Characteristics						
Company	**Country**		**Sector**			**Market**		
			Lower	≈	Higher	Lower	≈	Higher
Aeon Mall Co. Ltd.	Japan	Valuation	●			●		
Kimco Realty Corp.	United States	Profitability	●					●
Klepierre SA	France	Sales Growth	●			●		
Link REIT	Hong Kong	Profit Growth	●			●		
Regency Centers Corp.	United States	Debt Levels		●				●
Riocan REIT	Canada	Dividend Yield		●				●
Scentre Group	Australia	Payout Ratio		●				●
Simon Property Group Inc.	United States	Dividend Growth	●			●		
Unibail-Rodamco-Westfield	France	Earnings Predictability		●				●
Wharf REIC	Hong Kong	Share Price Volatility		●				●

Data source: Bloomberg, as of March 18, 2022.

Retail REITs are somewhat more insulated than their retailer tenants due to intermediate- to long-term lease durations. Retail is relatively management intensive compared to other property types and the perception of management skill is often reflected in differing FFO/AFFO multiples. Properties owned by retail REITs vary significantly in size and tenancy, resulting in differing performance for categories within this segment. Nonessential retail describes regional shopping centers or malls with large department stores or big-box retailers as anchors and numerous smaller in-line stores (focused on fashion or discretionary spending) between those anchors. These are the retail REITs that can experience high share price volatility, as nonessential retail performance is heavily influenced by GDP growth. Neighborhood shopping centers tend to have smaller anchor tenants and in-line tenants with a reduced focus on high-end retailers. Stand-alone properties usually represent grocery stores, home improvement stores, pharmacies, or restaurants. Grocery-anchored retail centers outperform in a recession due to stability of cash flows and strong covenants. Key economic factors that affect the industry include consumer confidence and job growth. On a relative basis, retail REITs have been trading at below-average valuations but have also delivered below-average growth and profitability in recent years. Important metrics for investors to track include same-store sales growth for key tenants, funds from operations (FFO), and adjusted funds from operations (AFFO). Investors can use a combination of approaches to value companies in this industry, including DCF, P/FFO, P/AFFO, and NAV.

■ Real Estate Development

Businesses		Relative Characteristics						
Company	Country		Sector			Market		
			Lower	≈	Higher	Lower	≈	Higher
China Evergrande Group — China		Valuation	●			●		
China Overseas Land — Hong Kong		Profitability	●					●
China Resources Land — Hong Kong		Sales Growth		●				●
Daito Trust Construction Co. Ltd. — Japan		Profit Growth	●			●		
DLF Ltd. — India		Debt Levels	●			●		
Emaar Properties PJSC — UAE		Dividend Yield			●			●
Hongkong Land Holdings — Hong Kong		Payout Ratio	●			●		
Longfor Group Holdings — China		Dividend Growth			●			●
Nexity SA — France		Earnings Predictability		●				●
SM Prime Holdings — Philippines		Share Price Volatility			●			●

Data source: Bloomberg, as of March 18, 2022.

Companies within the real estate development industry construct buildings commissioned by a specific user or by multiple users. The latter is categorized as "build to sell" (also called a merchant builder) or "build to hold." Condo developers are merchant builders, fixing their selling price early in the process and often receiving a significant portion of their revenues upfront and prior to completion. In an inflationary environment, condo developers bear risks associated with escalating construction costs (labor and materials) and delays (interest expense). In contrast, the construction of a large new office building may only be feasible once a large portion of the building is preleased, reflecting the massive, long-term capital required for development. Few developers have sufficient funds to self-finance construction, but even for those that do, equity returns are usually enhanced by the use of debt. Lenders usually regard preleasing as a condition for financing a new development, but in periods of high demand and limited new supply, buildings may be financed and constructed before preleasing. Development companies that need to retain earnings for new projects and cannot meet the REIT distribution thresholds choose to list as REOCs, discussed earlier. Economic factors affecting the industry include economic growth, employment growth, interest rates, construction costs (such as labor and materials), and business confidence. Balance sheet values and cash flows are highly variable given the lack of liquidity of the assets, which makes FFO and AFFO calculations of limited use. Land values, for example, are dependent on marketability, which improves once density increases are approved by the local municipality. Companies within the industry have high variability of cash flows and differences in the riskiness of strategy, product type, and geography, which makes earnings-multiple comparisons of little use. Therefore, investors should use DCF and NAV to assess valuations.

■ Real Estate Services

Businesses		Relative Characteristics						
Company	Country		Sector			Market		
			Lower	≈	Higher	Lower	≈	Higher
CBRE Group Inc.	United States	Valuation			●			●
Colliers International	China	Profitability	●			●		
Compass Inc.	United States	Sales Growth			●			●
Cushman & Wakefield PLC	United States	Profit Growth			●		●	
Evergrande Property Services Group Ltd.	China	Debt Levels	●			●		
FirstService Corp.	Canada	Dividend Yield	●			●		
Newmark Group Inc.	United States	Payout Ratio	●			●		
Relo Group Inc.	Japan	Dividend Growth			●			●
Savills PLC	United Kingdom	Earnings Predictability			●			●
Sodexo SA	France	Share Price Volatility			●			●

Data source: Bloomberg, as of March 18, 2022.

Companies within the real estate services industry provide sales and leasing brokerage, property management services, equity and mortgage brokerage, due diligence and appraisal work, and other consulting or advisory services related to real estate. The cash flow volatility of these companies varies depending on the portion of income that is generated from highly profitable but highly volatile fees and commissions from property sales, but all are susceptible to periods in which transaction volumes fall. Interestingly, when the property market experiences a downturn, a portion of the service company's revenues grow because lenders need third-party expertise to appraise, operate, and sell foreclosed real estate. Most property management agreements base their fee (which is a fixed percentage) on effective gross income, a revenue measure that reflects not just rental income (lease rates and occupancy) but other ancillary income (parking and laundry), vacancy, and credit losses. Therefore, service company valuations are sensitive to expectations about the general health of the real estate business and are dependent on economic growth to increase both occupancy and rental rates. Companies within the industry often compete on cost for service agreements since many landlords seek to minimize the cost of these services to entice new tenants from competitors. Property management fees are passed through to tenants for offices, retail, and warehouse properties. Third-party appraisals are required regularly, providing a highly predictable, though low-margin, earnings stream. The volume of ad hoc work, such as sales and leasing brokerage work and consulting, is the main driver of earnings and share price volatility. Important operational and financial metrics for investors to track include funds from operations (FFO) and adjusted funds from operations (AFFO). Investors can use a combination of approaches to value companies in this industry, including DCF, P/FFO, P/AFFO, and NAV.

■ Specialty REITs

Businesses		Relative Characteristics						
Company	Country		Sector			Market		
			Lower	≈	Higher	Lower	≈	Higher
American Tower Corp.	United States	Valuation			●			●
Crown Castle International Corp.	United States	Profitability	●					●
Digital Realty Trust	United States	Sales Growth	●				●	
Equinix Inc.	United States	Profit Growth		●		●		
Extra Space Storage Inc.	United States	Debt Levels		●				●
Klepierre SA	France	Dividend Yield	●			●		
Public Storage	United States	Payout Ratio		●				●
SBA Communications Corp.	United States	Dividend Growth		●				●
Shurgard Self Storage SA	Luxembourg	Earnings Predictability		●				●
Ventas Inc.	United States	Share Price Volatility	●			●		

Data source: Bloomberg, as of March 18, 2022.

Companies within the specialty REIT segment include those focused on hospitals, medical office buildings, life science laboratories, self-storage, student housing, cell towers, and data centers. The ability to invest in these growing, niche areas is one of the attractive features of REITs. One potential caution to investors is that the higher returns typically associated with specialty REITs reflect the fact that the physical assets are usually built for a specific use and have a higher cost of construction (in most cases). The limited number of tenants for a location (and their unique design needs) increases the risk of long periods of negative cash flow and even the probability that the property cannot easily be leased to a new tenant. While the chance of vacancy is low, the cost of vacancy can be significant. This low vacancy, especially when averaged over a larger portfolio of properties, contributes to the lower share price volatility and higher earning predictability that the sector is known for. Economic factors that have the greatest effect on the industry are diverse and specific to the underlying properties. Population growth can be particularly impactful since population growth is a primary driver of economic growth. For example, a growing city will need more hospitals, student housing, cell towers, and self-storage units. Specialty REITs target assets in markets experiencing high population growth that should translate into higher economic growth. Important metrics for investors to track include funds from operations (FFO) and adjusted funds from operations (AFFO). Investors can use a combination of approaches to value companies in this industry, including DCF, P/FFO, P/AFFO, and NAV.

CHAPTER 19

Utilities

U tility companies around the world deliver natural gas, electricity, and water needed to run our businesses and households. Electricity may be generated by wind, solar, nuclear power, hydroelectric power, or coal. Since the cost of building these plants is exceedingly high, utility companies tend to hold a monopoly in the markets in which they operate. For this reason, and in order to ensure that all citizens have access to these necessities, utility companies are often regulated by government authorities, who determine the prices that can be charged to consumers. Population growth is another important macro variable since it drives demand for electricity, gas, and water. Keep in mind that every country (and sometimes each state or territory) has its own regulatory agency and so returns, allowed equity ratios, regulatory timelines for rate increases, stance on renewables energy investments, and so forth can vary significantly by location.

269

Sector Characteristics versus Market

	Lower	≈	Higher		Lower	≈	Higher
Valuation	●			Dividend Yield			●
Profitability		●		Payout Ratio		●	
Sales Growth		●		Dividend Growth	●		
Profit Growth	●			Earnings Predictability			●
Debt Levels			●	Share Price Volatility	●		

Data source: Bloomberg, as of March 18, 2022.

Since it is difficult for most people to live without these services, utility companies tend to have very stable earnings, generating consistent profits regardless of economic conditions. Utility companies usually have a limited ability to grow their business and so they also tend to pay out a higher portion of their earnings to investors in the form of dividends. As a result, they tend to have higher dividend yields, but lower dividend growth rates. There are cases, however, where a utility is able to grow through acquisition or by investing in new regions or innovative technologies. This is especially true today in the renewable energy segment, as investments in new projects are being made at a rapid pace to help meet the world's energy needs while combating climate change.

Rising interest rates tend to increase borrowing costs for utilities, which typically have high debt levels due to their high capital-intensive projects. These costs can generally be passed through to customers, although there could be a lag between when the financing occurs and when higher rates become effective. Inflationary pressures (such as rising commodity and labor costs) are also passed through to customers, but there could be a lag that affects cash flow in the short-term but may not affect earnings. Utilities also tend to hedge their fuel costs and carry storage positions (of gas, for example) so spikes in prices will not necessarily affect customer rates immediately. Rising interest rates and inflationary pressure do present a challenge if costs rise materially and stay elevated for an extended period of time, given that increases in customer bills reduce the potential for rate increases that could be used to fund capital expenditures.

The relatively predictable nature of utility company earnings causes most investors to view these businesses as defensive. This means that when economic conditions are expected to worsen, investors will move money into the sector as a way to preserve capital. It is therefore the late stage of a bull market as well as bear markets when utility stocks exhibit the best relative performance. Lower growth rates for most utility companies leads investors to move money out of the sector once economic conditions improve, instead favoring businesses in industries that will benefit more from resurging economic growth.

There are five main industry groups to explore in this sector: (1) electric utilities, (2) gas utilities, (3) multi-utilities, (4) renewable energy, and (5) water utilities.

Electric Utilities

Businesses		Relative Characteristics						
Company	**Country**		**Sector**			**Market**		
			Lower	≈	Higher	Lower	≈	Higher
BW Energie Baden-Wuerttember AG	Germany	Valuation		●		●		
Electricite de France SA	France	Profitability	●			●		
Exelon Corp.	United States	Sales Growth			●			●
Fortum Oyj	Finland	Profit Growth		●		●		
Huaneng Power International	China	Debt Levels		●				●
Korea Electric Power	South Korea	Dividend Yield		●				●
NTPC Ltd.	India	Payout Ratio			●			●
Red Electrica Corporacion S.A	Spain	Dividend Growth	●			●		
Saudi Electricity Co.	Saudi Arabia	Earnings Predictability	●				●	
Tokyo Electric Power Co. Holdings	Japan	Share Price Volatility		●		●		

Data source: Bloomberg, as of March 18, 2022.

Electric utilities can be broadly segmented into regulated and unregulated companies (also referred to as independent power producers or IPPs), with regulated companies being the most common and for which pricing is decided by regulatory authorities. There is an increasing focus on ESG within the industry (especially for decarbonization of coal-fired power plants, which is driving coal plant closures), operations (safety and ethics), and the risk of losing customers to distributed energy (energy produced directly onsite, such as solar or fuel cells). The choice to move to distributed energy is dependent not only on government incentives to use renewable energy, but also on the stability of the local electrical grid. Another trend in some jurisdictions is to place restrictions around the use of coal and natural gas as fuels for thermal power generation. This is largely due to the higher carbon emissions they produce. Population and GDP growth are fueling demand for electricity around the globe and are key economic drivers for the industry. These businesses tend to operate with above-average debt levels and pay higher dividend yields since they typically generate strong free cash flow. For regulated utilities, key drivers of earnings include weather, allowed ROE, earned ROE, regulatory asset, or capital value (RAV/RCV), capital expenditures that drive growth in the company's "rate base" (regulatory asset book value), allowed equity ratio, projected cost structure (creates room to increase billing), projected changes to customer demand, equity needs, and FFO/debt for credit rating purposes. Since utilities generate earnings based on the allowed equity ratio of their rate base, investors should pay close attention to regulatory dynamics, including rate cases, which ultimately drive rate base and EPS growth. For unregulated electric utilities, important drivers include energy demand and capacity, electricity pricing, state or federal subsidies (such as those for nuclear plants or other competing power sources), operational performance of power plants, and debt/EBITDA. Important drivers for independent power producers include power prices, commodity costs, and interest rates to the extent companies have large capital expenditure plans. Regulated utilities tend to be valued using P/E, whereas unregulated utilities (IPPs) are generally valued on EV/EBITDA and to a lesser extent FCF/equity (expressed as a yield).

■ Gas Utilities

Businesses		Relative Characteristics						
Company	Country		Sector			Market		
			Lower	≈	Higher	Lower	≈	Higher
Altagas Ltd.	Canada	Valuation		●		●		
China Gas Holdings Ltd.	Hong Kong	Profitability	●			●		
ENN Energy Holdings Ltd.	China	Sales Growth			●			●
Gail India Limited	India	Profit Growth			●			●
Korea Gas Corp.	South Korea	Debt Levels	●				●	
Kunlun Energy Co. Ltd.	Hong Kong	Dividend Yield		●				●
Naturgy Energy Group	Spain	Payout Ratio			●			●
Osaka Gas Co. Ltd.	Japan	Dividend Growth			●			●
Snam SpA	Italy	Earnings Predictability			●			●
Tokyo Gas Co. Ltd.	Japan	Share Price Volatility		●		●		

Data source: Bloomberg, as of March 18, 2022.

Natural gas is widely used by consumers in many countries to heat their homes and run household appliances, in addition to serving as fuel in thermal power plants. Although natural gas prices are driven by supply (production) and demand (power generation, heating, weather, industrial activity) fundamentals, demand for natural gas is highly seasonal and prices are very regional. Companies realize different prices based on a spread to major pricing hubs, also known as differentials. Trends affecting the industry include a greater focus on ESG factors, including decarbonization, operational improvements (safety and ethics), and the risk of losing customers to distributed energy. Some jurisdictions are placing restrictions around the use of natural gas, due to higher carbon emissions. However, some gas utilities are investigating the possibility of blending hydrogen and renewable natural gas. If these technologies become economical, they could reduce the risk of stranded natural gas assets. Population and GDP growth are fueling demand for electricity around the globe and are important economic drivers for the industry. Factors that affect earnings of regulated gas utilities include weather, the company's asset (or capital) base, allowed return on assets, capital expenditures (that drive growth in the asset base), allowed equity ratio, projected cost structure and equity needs, projected changes to customer demand, and funds from operations (FFO)/debt for credit rating purposes. Since utilities generate earnings on the allowed equity ratio of their asset base, investors should pay close attention to regulatory dynamics, which ultimately drive rate base and EPS growth. For unregulated gas utilities (also referred to as independent power producers or IPPs), important factors include weather, state or federal subsidies for competing fuels and power sources, operational performance of power plants, and debt/EBITDA. Unregulated gas utilities are generally valued on EV/ EBITDA and to a lesser extent FCF/equity (expressed as a yield), while regulated utilities tend to be valued using P/E.

■ Multi-Utilities

Businesses		Relative Characteristics						
Company	Country		Sector			Market		
			Lower	≈	Higher	Lower	≈	Higher
A2A SpA	Italy	Valuation	●			●		
Abu Dhabi National Energy Company	UAE	Profitability	●			●		
AGL Energy Ltd.	Australia	Sales Growth	●			●		
Centrica PLC	United Kingdom	Profit Growth	●			●		
Dominion Energy Inc.	United States	Debt Levels		●				●
DTE Energy Company	United States	Dividend Yield		●				●
Engie SA	France	Payout Ratio	●			●		
Hera SpA	Italy	Dividend Growth	●			●		
RWE AG	Germany	Earnings Predictability			●			●
Sembcorp Industries Limited	Singapore	Share Price Volatility		●		●		

Data source: Bloomberg, as of March 18, 2022.

Multi-utilities are essentially utility conglomerates, providing both electricity and gas to their customers. As previously mentioned, natural gas prices are driven by supply (production) and demand (power generation, heating, weather, industrial activity). However, demand for natural gas is highly seasonal and prices are very regional. Companies realize different prices based on the spread to major pricing hubs, also known as differentials. Multi-utilities face the same challenges with respect to a growing emphasis on ESG and operational effectiveness. Population and GDP growth are fueling demand for electricity around the globe and are important economic drivers for the multi-utility industry. Over the past few years, these businesses have grown sales and profits at a below-average rate but have generated strong free cash flow, allowing them to pay attractive dividends. For regulated multi-utilities, key drivers of earnings include asset or rate base, weather, allowed and earned ROE, capital expenditures that drive growth in the rate base (regulatory asset book value), allowed equity ratio, projected cost structure (as this creates bill headroom), projected changes to customer demand, equity needs, and funds from operations (FFO)/debt for credit rating purposes. Since multi-utilities earn on the allowed equity ratio of their rate base, investors should pay close attention to regulatory dynamics (such as rate cases and how much is recovered via trackers), which ultimately drive rate base and EPS growth. For unregulated multi-utilities (also referred to as independent power producers, or IPPs), important drivers include energy and capacity markets, state or federal subsidies (such as those for nuclear plants, production tax credit for wind, and investment tax credit for solar), operational performance of power plants, and debt/EBITDA. Regulated utilities are commonly valued using P/E, while IPPs are generally valued on EV/EBITDA and to a lesser extent FCF/equity (expressed as a yield).

■ Renewable Energy

Renewable energy companies are the biggest beneficiaries of the move to reduce carbon emissions and mitigate climate change. The renewable energy sector includes companies generating electricity primarily through solar, wind, geothermal, nuclear, and hydroelectric power. Some of the businesses listed here, while still producing electricity through traditional means, are considered leaders in the field of renewable energy. In areas where customers face high and rising utility costs, there is greater risk of them moving to

Businesses		Relative Characteristics						
Company	**Country**		**Sector**			**Market**		
			Lower	≈	Higher	Lower	≈	Higher
E.ON SE	Germany	Valuation			●	●		
Endesa SA	Spain	Profitability		●				●
Enel SpA	Italy	Sales Growth	●			●		
Energias de Portugal SA	Portugal	Profit Growth	●			●		
Iberdrola SA	Spain	Debt Levels	●					●
National Grid PLC	United Kingdom	Dividend Yield		●				●
NextEra Energy Inc.	United States	Payout Ratio	●			●		
Orsted A/S	Denmark	Dividend Growth			●			●
Siemens Energy AG	Germany	Earnings Predictability			●			●
SSE PLC	United Kingdom	Share Price Volatility		●		●		

Data source: Bloomberg, as of March 18, 2022.

distributed, renewable energy sources (such as rooftop solar and fuel cells). In some regions, like the Southern and Midwestern United States, replacing carbon-intensive generation with renewables is more economic and therefore utilities in these regions should be able to continue to grow without dramatically increasing customer rates. Regions that are place restrictions on the use of natural gas are most likely to see growth in renewable energy investments. Economic drivers that have the greatest impact on sales growth and profitability for the industry include population and GDP growth, as well as government incentives used to promote renewable energy usage. For businesses that operate as regulated utilities, key drivers of earnings include allowed and earned ROE, regulatory asset, or capital value (RAV/RCV), capital expenditures that drive growth in the rate base or RAV/RCV (regulatory asset book value), allowed equity ratio, projected cost structure (allows for rate increases), projected changes to customer demand, equity needs, and FFO/debt for credit rating purposes. Since utilities earn on the allowed equity ratio of their rate base, it is important for investors to pay close attention to regulatory dynamics, which ultimately drive rate base and EPS growth. Unregulated utilities (also referred to as independent power producers or IPPs) are most impacted by energy and capacity markets, state or federal subsidies, operational performance of power plants, and metrics such as debt/EBITDA. Regulated utilities tend to be valued using P/E, whereas unregulated utilities (IPPs) are generally valued on EV/EBITDA and to a lesser extent FCF/equity (expressed as a yield).

■ Water Utilities

Businesses		Relative Characteristics						
Company	**Country**		**Sector**			**Market**		
			Lower	≈	Higher	Lower	≈	Higher
American Water Works Co. ———— United States		Valuation	●			●		
Beijing Capital Eco-Enviro. Protection ——— China		Profitability	●			●		
Beijing Enterprises Water Group Ltd. ——— Hong Kong		Sales Growth		●			●	
Manila Water Company Inc. ———— Philippines		Profit Growth			●			●
Severn Trent PLC ———— United Kingdom		Debt Levels	●			●		
SIIC Environment Holdings Ltd. ———— Singapore		Dividend Yield		●				●
TTW PCL ———— Thailand		Payout Ratio	●			●		
United Utilities Group ———— United Kingdom		Dividend Growth	●			●		
Veolia Environment SA ———— France		Earnings Predictability	●			●		
Yunnan Water Investment Co. Ltd. ——— China		Share Price Volatility		●		●		

Data source: Bloomberg, as of March 18, 2022.

Water utility companies help to clean wastewater and deliver clean drinking water to homes and businesses. Water scarcity is becoming a critical concern in certain regions of the world. According to the United Nations, "[w]ater scarcity already affects every continent. Water use has been growing globally at more than twice the rate of population increase in the last century, and an increasing number of regions are reaching the limit at which water services can be sustainably delivered, especially in arid regions."[1] In total, it is estimated that 1.42 billion people live in areas of high or extremely high water vulnerability.[2] Due to climate change and the necessity to provide clean drinking water to a growing population, water utilities are likely to continue to benefit from steady growth in demand over the foreseeable future. Important metrics for investors to track include regulatory capital value (RCV), regulatory asset value (RAV—also referred to as the regulated asset base), inflation rates (such as CPI, RPI, and CPIH), embedded debt and cost of embedded debt, revenue by segment, operating expense ratio, EBIT and EBITDA margins by segment, allowed return, and free cash flow. Valuation methods for businesses in this industry include P/E and EV/EBITDA, as well as net present value to regulatory capital value (RVC premium) and FCF/P (free cash flow yield).

PART VI

Own the Best
and Leave
the Rest

CHAPTER 20

Portfolio Construction

W e have reviewed the world's major sectors and industries and the environment in which global businesses operate, along with the risks we are exposed to when investing in foreign companies. We now explore how an investor can construct a portfolio of good global businesses and build wealth in a safe and effective way. Since we are concerned with building business ownership, we exclude corporate-issued debt as well as preferred shares, both of which represent claims on the cash flows of the business rather than equity ownership. Depending on age and financial circumstances, it may be appropriate for investors to hold bonds or preferred shares in their portfolio (if this is the case, please refer to *The Handbook of Fixed Income Securities* by Frank Fabozzi, and *Financial Statement Analysis* by Martin Fridson). This approach assumes that the investor has a long-term investment horizon and will not need to access this money for many years. Additionally, it assumes that the investor has a high-risk tolerance, meaning they have the ability and willingness to endure periods of volatile and/or declining share prices. We begin with a discussion on the types of investment instruments you can buy to obtain ownership in the businesses you like.

■ Types of Investment Instruments

Common shares of publicly traded companies are my preferred investment instrument because they represent a direct ownership stake in a specific company and can be traded easily on a stock exchange. For some investors, however, buying shares on a foreign stock exchange may be difficult or even impossible. In those situations, investors may be able to buy depositary receipts instead. A depositary receipt is where a third party (often a bank or trust company) holds shares of a foreign company in trust and issues receipts for those shares that will trade on an exchange where the trustee is domiciled. The bank or trust company issuing the depositary receipts acts as a trustee and periodically charges a fee for providing this service. While the fee charged by the trustee is generally small, investors should confirm the fee size prior to purchasing the receipts, as it can be high in some cases. This information is typically available in the depositary receipt's prospectus or on the trustee's website.

A depositary receipt that is listed on a US exchange is known as an American depositary receipt (ADR), and a depositary receipt listed on a European exchange is known as a European depositary receipt (EDR). Other depositary receipts are commonly referred to as global depositary receipts (GDRs). Depositary receipts are equivalent to a prespecified number of common shares of the underlying company, which is known as the conversion ratio. For example, if the depositary receipt's conversion ratio were 20:1, the investor would own 20 shares of the underlying security for each receipt they purchase. This highlights the importance of knowing the conversion ratio for the depositary receipt of any company under consideration.

ADRs can be either sponsored or unsponsored. Sponsored depositary receipts are supported by the issuer of the underlying common shares, while unsponsored receipts are not. Companies with sponsored ADRs must file annual reports with the SEC in the United States, and therefore financial data is readily available (in the English language) for those companies. In comparison, foreign companies tied to unsponsored ADRs are subject to less regulatory scrutiny in the United States and are not required to file annual reports. As a result, there may be less information available about these companies, making them more difficult for investors to analyze. In these instances, investors may need to rely on regulatory filings and company disclosures issued by the company in its home country.

Investors should also understand that dividend payments for ADRs are paid in the currency the receipt is issued in (e.g., US dollars for ADRs and euros for EDRs) and that they may be subject to withholding tax in the same manner as a foreign stock. Investors should consider dividend withholding tax before they invest in a foreign company regardless of whether they purchase a depositary receipt or the company's underlying shares. Dividends that are paid by the company are initially received by the trustee, who then converts the funds into the currency the receipt is denominated in and provides payment to the investor. For example, an ADR representing a Japanese-domiciled company would trade on a US exchange in US dollars and would pay dividends in US dollars even though the underlying cash flows received by the trustee are denominated in Japanese yen. It is important to remember that the returns generated by depositary receipts are affected by the currency the receipt is denominated in as well as by the base currency used by the underlying company. For example, the price of German industrial giant Siemens AG's ADR is affected by exchange rate fluctuations of the company's underlying base currency, the euro, as well as the currency the ADR is traded in, the US dollar.

One of the benefits of owning common shares rather than depositary receipts is better liquidity, which means a higher number of shares are traded each day. The amount of trading that takes place in a company's shares helps determine the ease with which one can transact in the security without impacting the share price. While some depositary receipts trade daily in large volumes, many are thinly traded with only a fraction of the daily trading volume compared to the underlying shares. There are situations when a depositary receipt trades in greater volumes than does the underlying security, but these instances are rare. Avoid investing in securities when the average daily trading volume is so low that it will be difficult for you to sell the shares quickly if you must. Another benefit to owning common shares over depositary receipts relates to voting rights. Readers should note that some depositary receipts do not allow the holder of the receipt to vote the underlying shares. Should the ability to vote on company matters be important to you, it is best to confirm whether owning the receipt will allow you to vote.

Depositary receipts are unfortunately not available for all foreign-listed companies, which may serve as an additional constraint for investors. That said, if an investor is unable to invest directly in a particular business, an ETF or index fund may be their only viable option. As mentioned earlier, buying a passive ETF or index fund means you are investing in substandard businesses at the same time you are investing in the best businesses.

■ Stick to the Basics (of Investing)

The first step in portfolio construction is to recall the basics of global investing set out in Chapter 8. Own businesses with defensible, leading market positions in growing industries, astute management teams, strong balance sheets, and a strong social conscience, and buy them at attractive prices. When deciding which businesses to own, comparing their relative characteristics to close competitors in their industry and the broader market will provide you with better insights into the company and allow you to make more informed investment decisions.

As outlined in Part Two, avoid investing in countries that do not protect shareholder rights and where reliable financial statements are not readily available. Avoid buying companies that are in countries that have high levels of sovereign or consumer debt, and that are experiencing high or rapidly increasing levels of inflation combined with an overheated housing market. While a good starting point is to set a minimum sovereign credit rating for the countries you invest in (such as an investment-grade rating), continuous monitoring of economic and political events in each country is essential. If that country's regulatory structure is lacking or if shareholder rights are not protected, avoid investing in that country. Also, it is critical that investors fully understand the business they propose to invest in, so having access to information about the company in a language they understand is vital. If this is not possible, then do not invest in the company.

■ Be Innovative

If you really like the fundamental backdrop for a sector or industry but the companies appear too expensive to warrant an investment, think outside the box and consider alternative ways to take advantage of the opportunity. For example, assume you like the internet retail industry but company valuations are too expensive; you could instead look to the transportation industry and invest in a company positioned to benefit from strengthening e-commerce fundamentals. Similarly, owning a railroad company might be a better way to take advantage of an increased demand outlook for coal as opposed to buying a coal mining company. This is because railroad company shipping volumes would increase since a substantial portion of coal is transported via rail. The same logic can be applied within the commodity space as well. In the case of energy, you might make a direct investment in an energy company with large oil reserves rather than buying oil directly through an ETF or in the futures market. Think of the industry's supply and value chains to look for the most efficient manner to capture the opportunity.

■ Healthy Diversification

If we knew exactly where we were in the market cycle, the job of building a portfolio would be much easier. The reality is that there is always a degree of uncertainty to investing, and unlikely events occur more often than you would imagine. For this reason, it is prudent to own a variety of businesses that generate sales and earnings in a range of economic sectors as well as different regions of the world. Having a diversified portfolio of complementary businesses will smooth out the underlying earnings stream, not to mention the aggregate price fluctuations in their share prices. This approach, combined with not overpaying for good businesses, will help protect you when stocks enter a bull market correction or a bear market.

In Chapter 8 we discussed how investment risk can be divided into fundamental risk and share price volatility. Share price volatility can be further separated into market risk (also known as systematic risk) and firm-specific risk (also called unsystematic risk). Investors are only compensated for market risk since firm-specific risk can be eliminated by owning a diversified basket of stocks. Many studies have been performed to determine the optimal number of stock holdings needed to eliminate unsystematic risk within a portfolio. While results of those studies varied, there is a widespread belief that investors should own approximately 20 companies in their portfolio. Personally, I have found that owning 20–30 companies in equal weightings provides adequate portfolio diversification. Given the sheer size of the global stock market, I recommend that a globally focused investor hold closer to 30 businesses at any given point in time. As an investor adds incremental companies to their portfolio, it dilutes their research efforts, adds trading costs, and increases the difficulty of monitoring the portfolio. Conversely, owning too few companies within a portfolio may cause the value of the portfolio to fluctuate more than necessary, tempting the investor to succumb to emotion and sell stocks at the wrong time and wrong price.

■ You Own a Conglomerate

Now picture yourself as the owner of a global business empire. Your business is comprised of the individual companies you have selectively purchased, and you can drill down to see the subcomponents and business lines of your new company. By investing in 20–30 good businesses, you have effectively built a conglomerate that generates revenue from numerous sectors, industries, and countries, providing more consistent sales and earnings power now and into the future. There will be times when some parts of your business empire will perform well while others may be weak. This is not necessarily bad or a sign of a poorly constructed portfolio, since it is difficult to predict which parts of your business empire will do well each year. If you had certainty, then you would divest the businesses that will underperform in the coming year and only hold those that will outperform. Looking at sources of revenue and earnings for your conglomerate, you can now assess how the fundamental earnings power of your company will fare in good and bad economic times. Is the combined business you built sufficiently diversified so that it captures significant areas of growth while still being able to endure weak economic times? Are the individual business components of your conglomerate reasonably valued, or are some of them overpriced and pose a risk to the overall portfolio?

Figures 20.1 and 20.2 illustrate the importance of owning a diversified group of businesses from differing industries. Since the earnings of companies in each industry group are affected by the same factors, owning several

Company	Industry	2011	2012	2013	2014	2015	2016	2017	2018	2019	2020	2021
A	Banking	4.01	5.16	5.43	5.57	5.44	5.04	5.69	6.49	6.58	5.82	8.79
B	Banking	0.19	0.23	0.26	0.30	0.36	0.38	0.44	0.55	0.59	0.70	0.78
C	Beverages	4.41	4.10	4.51	4.03	4.63	4.85	5.53	5.52	5.53	5.53	6.26
D	Capital Markets	-0.52	1.93	1.99	1.53	2.61	2.98	3.86	4.71	5.19	6.74	8.29
E	Chemicals	3.05	-0.20	4.03	3.58	4.34	2.32	2.19	2.24	3.10	3.76	4.23
F	Convenience Stores	1.66	2.41	2.10	2.15	1.97	1.75	2.05	2.60	2.62	2.63	2.25
G	Electric Utilities	2.55	2.65	2.70	2.80	2.89	2.91	3.31	3.12	2.98	3.25	3.41
H	Fintech and Payment Processing	0.88	1.14	1.72	1.95	2.75	3.06	3.67	5.05	5.96	5.53	6.42
I	Hotels	1.20	2.48	2.85	3.74	3.06	3.61	4.49	5.14	3.95	-0.02	3.46
J	Household and Personal Products	3.95	3.80	3.91	3.91	4.08	3.76	3.82	4.17	4.37	5.12	5.76
K	Industrial Machinery	1.63	1.69	1.51	1.51	1.16	1.63	1.24	1.46	1.49	1.37	1.73
L	Life Insurance	2.14	1.89	2.31	2.35	2.19	2.05	1.15	4.42	-2.16	-0.92	1.44
M	Integrated Oil and Gas	4.83	4.62	3.04	2.92	1.37	1.04	1.97	2.51	2.10	0.40	2.85
N	Interactive Entertainment	-0.28	0.55	0.34	0.24	1.59	2.27	3.18	3.36	3.44	10.40	2.96
O	Media	0.76	0.96	1.25	1.49	1.63	1.74	4.68	2.41	2.76	2.21	3.09
P	Medical Devices	3.43	3.32	3.62	3.77	3.26	3.32	3.53	3.67	4.14	3.50	3.32
Q	Packaged Foods	3.52	3.54	3.96	3.68	3.43	3.51	3.79	3.68	4.37	4.42	7.67
R	Pharmaceuticals	1.63	1.63	1.70	1.78	1.67	2.10	2.06	2.26	1.27	1.78	4.30
S	Semiconductors	2.11	2.00	1.99	2.14	3.03	3.50	4.33	5.65	5.25	5.72	8.28
T	Software	2.61	2.68	2.66	2.63	2.43	2.59	3.06	3.67	4.68	5.80	7.84

FIGURE 20.1   Annual EPS for 20 Large Global Companies (USD)

businesses in the same industry will not deliver the diversification benefits you are striving for. Figure 20.1 provides actual reported earnings from 20 large companies from around the world in differing industries. The mix of industries used in this fictitious portfolio is not meant to provide the reader with an investable portfolio but is intended only to highlight the need to diversify.

As an investor, it is important to stay focused on the combined earnings stream of your portfolio rather than share prices of individual securities or even the current market value of your portfolio. When you aggregate the earnings of all the companies in Figure 20.1, you achieve a more consistent stream of earnings in the same way a large, diversified conglomerate does. The dark line in Figure 20.2 shows how the average earnings per share (EPS) over a 10-year period was much more stable for the diversified portfolio of 20 large companies compared to a concentrated portfolio consisting of only the four financial companies (A, B, D, and L) in Figure 20.1.

Figure 20.2 shows that the diversified portfolio provided a more consistent level of earnings than did the concentrated portfolio and illustrates the importance of diversification to create a stable and growing stream of earnings. So long as earnings continue to rise, share prices will eventually follow. Remember from Chapter 6 that owning a basket of different currencies will also help create a more stable earnings stream.

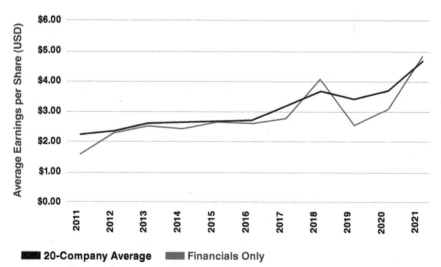

FIGURE 20.2 Single-Sector versus Diversified Portfolio Average EPS

Data source: Bloomberg.

◼ Stay Fully Invested

Even with everything we know about the possible warning signs of bull market peaks and bear market bottoms, timing the market has been an elusive goal for even the savviest professional investors around the world. Cash can significantly reduce portfolio returns when share prices are rising. For this reason, when I have raised cash to protect client capital, I ended up detracting value from the portfolio, with only a handful of exceptions. My preference therefore is to stay fully invested, always owning good businesses. Buy stocks for good times and bad, businesses that you think have sustainable earnings growth and are priced attractively. If a company becomes overvalued compared to its historical range, its sector, and the market, reassess why you own it and consider selling it and switching the proceeds into another stock. It is exceedingly difficult to time the market, but investors should always be prepared to sell companies with deteriorating fundamentals and redeploy the proceeds into good companies.

◼ Saying Goodbye Is Always the Hardest Part

Buying a business can be relatively straightforward but knowing when to sell it can be extremely difficult. Valid reasons to sell a business include the loss of a key member of the management team, a significant increase in the competitiveness of the industry in which it operates, falling profit margins that cannot be reversed by management, or if valuation becomes expensive relative to the company's earnings prospects. In the case of a drop in earnings, the best way to think of it is as an owner of the business. Determine whether the earnings prospects of the company are permanently impaired or whether they will recover. If earnings are expected to recover, stay the course and hold on, or potentially add, to your position. As mentioned previously, another reason to sell a business is if the credit rating of the country in which the company is domiciled is downgraded below investment grade, or if you believe the geopolitical or currency risks are rising excessively in that country or region.

One helpful practice is to set an upper limit on the number of businesses owned. For example, if an investor were at their self-imposed maximum number of businesses (e.g., 25 or 30) and wanted to add a new holding, they would want to identify the weakest holding in their portfolio and sell it to make room for the new, better business. In this sense, active investors are best served by always looking for better investment opportunities, and I refer to the process as "high grading" the portfolio.

■ Rebalancing

Investors should also revisit their portfolio periodically and rebalance it. Since certain industries perform better or worse at various stages of the market cycle, the percentage weight of each company in your portfolio will fluctuate over time. It is best practice to reduce your winners and, assuming your investment thesis for them is still intact, add to your losing positions on an infrequent but regular basis. Most pension fund managers follow this procedure by shifting money from the best-performing asset classes or regions into those that have lagged. This technique is based on the idea that stocks, bonds, and other asset classes will revert to their long-term average valuations over time, a phenomenon known as mean reversion. Rebalancing forces you to buy low and sell high and can add tremendous value to your portfolio over the long run.

The frequency of rebalancing should depend partly on trading costs. If you pay a high commission rate for trades, then less frequent rebalancing is recommended. There is also something to be said for letting your winners run. Finding the right balance between letting your winners run and locking in profits can be tricky. For example, if you own 25 equally weighted stocks in your portfolio (i.e., 4% each), you may want to set a specific threshold at which you trim a position that has outperformed and reallocate the proceeds to stocks that have underperformed and whose relative weighting in your portfolio has fallen. In practice, if that threshold were, for example, 7%, when a stock rose above 7% of your portfolio you would reduce it back down to a 4% weight and add the proceeds of the sale to stocks that have lagged, bringing them back up to the original 4% weight. The decision on when and how to rebalance is yours. Optimal approaches to rebalancing typically involve employing a mechanical (unemotional) process. It is critical that you follow it precisely to prevent yourself from making random changes to your portfolio. If you find that your rebalancing process could be improved, make incremental adjustments while adhering to your existing plan, no matter how uncomfortable it may feel to do so at the time.

Tax may also play a role in your decision of when to rebalance your portfolio. If your portfolio is in a tax-sheltered account, there are no tax implications when you sell a security. However, since realized gains on the sale of a stock are usually subject to capital gains tax in an open (nonsheltered) account, investors should consider the tax implications when rebalancing their portfolio. My advice to investors is "do not let the tail wag the dog" when it comes to taxation. After all, paying tax means that you made money on your investment. I have seen investors delay the sale of a security purely for tax reasons, only to watch the security fall in value and their unrealized gain disappear completely. However, for transactions that would generate a particularly large taxable gain it would be best to consult a tax professional prior to executing the trade. In some cases, it may be better to sell the security over two or more taxation years.

As discussed in Chapter 5, signs of sector rotation and an assessment of where we are in the market cycle are a means to help improve your investment returns, but I would caution you that these should be considered over weeks and months rather than days. The shorter the time the more vulnerable the stock market is to random noise. A single day (or even week or month) of an apparent change in stock market leadership does not, in and of itself, confirm sector rotation or indicate an important inflection point in the market cycle. Bull market corrections and bear market rallies are notorious for fooling investors into thinking an inflection point has occurred when in fact the trend is still intact. Even if you can accurately identify sector rotation early enough to take advantage of it, it is simply not necessary to act on it if your portfolio has been appropriately constructed. If you own good businesses over a long time period, you should be able to generate sufficient wealth to fund your retirement needs. This means generating solid returns by diminishing the impact of negative performance through diversification, maximizing long-run success by choosing good companies, staying fully invested, and rebalancing to take advantage of reversion to the mean for your good companies.

■ Advanced Investment Strategies

The basic premise behind this book is that one can create a portfolio of great businesses that will perform well over a full market cycle, through both good and bad times. There are some investment strategies, however, that may be appropriate for more experienced investors who are able to devote the time necessary to monitor the markets continually. One such strategy could be to create two baskets of great businesses, one for good economic times and one for bad economic times. To illustrate the concept, I created two hypothetical portfolios based on sector returns only; therefore, no individual stocks were chosen. The market sectors are broken into two groups: cyclical and noncyclical. The cyclical sectors are more sensitive to economic growth and include consumer discretionary, energy, financials, industrials, materials, and technology. The noncyclical sectors are less sensitive to economic growth and include consumer staples, telecom, healthcare, and utilities. Real estate is excluded here because it was only recently broken out as a separate sector of the stock market and so historical data is limited.

Next, I created two portfolios, simply allocating between the cyclical and noncyclical sectors using an 80/20 split, as shown in Figure 20.3.

In Figure 20.4, Portfolio A is our "offensive" portfolio and is built for strong economic growth and bull markets, while Portfolio B is our "defensive" portfolio and is built for recessions and bear markets. Note that the securities do not change when we switch between the two portfolios, only the amount we invest in each of them.

In this example, the decision of which portfolio to own at any point in time is simple. First, choose a broad stock market index that is most

| Portfolio A (Offensive) | 80% Cyclical Sectors | 20% Noncyclical Sectors |
| Portfolio B (Defensive) | 20% Cyclical Sectors | 80% Noncyclical Sectors |

FIGURE 20.3 Sample Cyclical versus Noncyclical Sector Portfolios

	Sectors	Portfolio A (Offensive)	Portfolio B (Defensive)
Noncyclical	Telecom	5.0%	20%
	Staples	5.0%	20%
	Healthcare	5.0%	20%
	Utilities	5.0%	20%
Cyclical	Discretionary	13.3%	3.3%
	Energy	13.3%	3.3%
	Financials	13.3%	3.3%
	Industrials	13.3%	3.3%
	Materials	13.3%	3.3%
	Technology	13.3%	3.3%

FIGURE 20.4 Sample Offensive and Defensive Portfolio Sector Weights

reflective of your portfolio. If the stock market index is trading above its 18-month moving average, you own the offensive portfolio (Portfolio A), and if it is trading below the 18-month moving average, you own the defensive portfolio (Portfolio B). The 18-month moving average is the average month-end closing price for the index for the preceding 18 months. The benefit of this type of rebalancing approach is its simplicity since anyone can easily calculate and track the moving average of a broad market index. Moving averages can often be added easily on a price chart, depending on the service provider. I have found that the 18-month moving average provides a relatively consistent level of support for a bull market (and therefore can act as an effective trigger point for when to switch between an offensive and defensive posture), but there are no guarantees it will work in the future. Accordingly, investors may be best served by using a long-term moving average (like the 18-month moving average) in conjunction with the signs described in Chapter 5 that have been known to provide an early warning sign for bear market bottoms and bull market tops.

The results of an approach as simplistic as this may surprise you. Merely rebalancing between our offensive and defensive portfolios can add significant value over a buy-and-hold strategy. Figure 20.5 shows the value of $1,000 invested at the beginning of 1990 under each scenario, namely reallocating between offensive and defensive portfolios versus simply holding the broad market index.

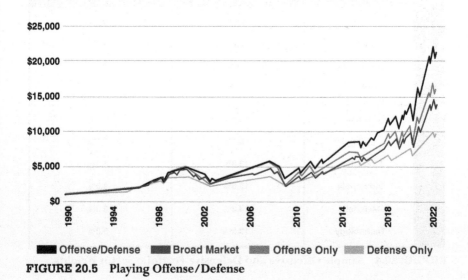

FIGURE 20.5   Playing Offense/Defense

In this example, owning the broad stock market from the beginning of 1990 to March 2022 would have generated an ending portfolio value of $13,767. Compared to the broad stock market, the defensive portfolio generated a lower return, with an ending value of $9,691, while the offensive portfolio generated a higher return, with an ending value of $15,994. These results make sense when we consider the fact that despite interim recessions and bear markets, economic growth and equity markets for the full period were both strong.

What is most interesting, though, is when we adjust our weights between the offensive and defensive portfolios in the manner just described. The straightforward process of rebalancing our weights between Portfolio A and Portfolio B based solely on whether the broad stock market traded above or below its 18-month moving average resulted in an ending portfolio value of $21,279. That amounts to a 54% higher portfolio value over 30 years compared to passively owning the broad market. Although these results do ignore trading costs (which would reduce the strategy's return), investors should be able to offset these costs by selecting good businesses since the offensive and defensive portfolios are based only on passive sector returns. Furthermore, while this example is based on price appreciation only, dividends are likely to augment the effectiveness of this strategy since dividend-paying stocks tend to perform better in bear markets from a total return perspective. Keep in mind, though, that these results are based on a single time frame and a single stock market and that the results will vary based on the time period and index chosen. Nevertheless, this helps to illustrate how an investor can generate superior returns and provide some downside protection for their portfolios when stock prices fall while remaining fully invested throughout the market cycle.

Admittedly, dividing sectors into cyclical and defensive (noncyclical) groups is an oversimplification. Cyclical sectors contain businesses that could be considered defensive, and defensive sectors contain businesses that could be considered cyclical. You can also think of your businesses in terms of being low-beta (noncyclical) or high-beta (cyclical). As an investor, you should therefore consider how the stocks you own will behave in a given market environment and in each stage of the market cycle. Similar to the previous sector-based example, investors could therefore rebalance a portfolio of individual stocks using a moving average or some other mix of indicators. When you believe that market risks are elevated based on the criteria set out in Chapter 5, or otherwise decide to get defensive, reduce the weights of stocks that are cyclical or high-beta, and move the proceeds to your low-beta, defensive stocks. Conversely, if you believe a bear market bottom has been reached, reduce weights in defensive stocks and add to the cyclical, higher-beta stocks.

In a similar fashion, I created offensive and defensive portfolios, each made up of 25 equally weighted large, global stocks. All 50 stocks were randomly chosen from a pool of stocks that I regard as good businesses and that have remained attractively valued. The defensive portfolio consisted of stocks in the communication services, consumer staples, healthcare, real estate, and utilities sectors, while the offensive portfolio consisted of businesses primarily in the technology, industrials, energy, materials, financials, and consumer discretionary sectors. From the end of 1999 to the end of April 2022, and with no rebalancing, the offensive portfolio returned 12.5% annually while the defensive portfolio was not far behind, generating a 12.2% annual return. This suggests that it is most important to own good businesses and stay fully invested, regardless of whether you are positioned for a bull or bear market. Keep in mind that, while you can add value by being incrementally more defensive in a bear market and offensive in a bull market, you can also reduce your returns significantly if you time these changes poorly.

■ Advanced Portfolio Structures

The way we have structured our portfolio, buying a diverse group of good businesses, is known as a "long-only" investment strategy and the stocks you own are referred to as long positions. As you become comfortable with the process of building and rebalancing portfolios, and your understanding of the global financial markets grows, you may want to consider a more advanced form of portfolio structure, known as a "long-short" strategy. The benefit of a long-short strategy over a long-only strategy is improved risk management through the addition of short selling. Recall that a short seller is an investor who borrows shares in a company and sells them, with the intention of buying them back later in the future at a lower price and then returning the borrowed shares. The short seller thinks that the price of the stock today is too high and that it will fall soon. Long-short strategies are particularly useful in bull market corrections and in bear markets when stock prices are falling, since gains in the short positions will help offset losses in the long positions. Be aware that in order for you to short-sell a stock, you need to borrow the stock first through a broker. To do so you must provide collateral (usually in the form of your long positions) and you must pay the owner of the shares interest based on a borrow rate to compensate them for loaning you the shares.

There are numerous ways to structure a long-short portfolio. Hedge funds and market-neutral funds are both variations of the long-short strategy. You may have also heard of a "130/30" fund, which refers to a portfolio that is 130% long and 30% short. In this case, the investor short-sells stocks that total 30% of the portfolio's value and then uses the proceeds of those sales to add to the "long" portion of the portfolio. The expectation is that the short positions will fall in value while the long positions will increase in value. For example, using the shares they own as collateral, an investor with a $1,000,000 portfolio could short-sell $300,000 worth of shares of businesses they dislike and use the $300,000 cash proceeds to add to their existing long positions. The investor is now long $1,300,000 in stock but short $300,000, so the net long position (total market exposure) is still $1,000,000. Numerous studies have been done to compare the efficacy of long-short strategies, and these often indicate that a long-short strategy such as this will provide superior, long-term risk-adjusted returns compared to long-only strategies.

Short selling, especially when done using individual company stocks, is not for the faint of heart. Volatility in a single stock can be remarkably high and cause significant, even unlimited, losses for anyone who is short the stock. In addition, short selling requires a different skill set from long-only investing. One way to capture the benefits of short selling without the risk of shorting the shares of individual companies is to short index or sector-based ETFs. By shorting broad market ETFs, investors are essentially reducing the market risk (beta) in their portfolio. If the investor is unable to short stocks in their investment account, there are a number of inverse index ETFs that can be purchased "long" that provide the same benefit of a short position because they move in the opposite direction from the index. One limitation of buying inverse ETFs, however, is that there are no short sale proceeds that can be used to add to your individual long positions.

There are many approaches to portfolio construction beyond what has been outlined here. Regardless of the approach you choose, your investment decisions should be based on careful analysis of the businesses purchased, including how the earnings profiles of those companies are affected by different stages of the economic cycle, and how their share prices will move relative to one another (correlation) and the broad market (beta) during the market cycle.

Common shares of publicly traded companies are a preferred investment instrument since they represent a direct ownership stake in a specific company and can be traded easily on a stock exchange. It is best practice to rebalance your portfolio by reducing your winners and using the proceeds to add to your losing positions on an infrequent but regular basis. This is based on the idea that stocks will revert to their long-term average valuations over time, a phenomenon known as mean reversion. Investors can create a portfolio of great businesses that will perform well through both good and bad times. However, some investment strategies may be appropriate for more experienced investors, including adjusting security weights to make the portfolio incrementally offensive or defensive based on some mechanical (unemotional) process, as well as long/short strategies. Regardless of the approach chosen, portfolios should be constructed based on careful analysis of the businesses purchased, including how the earnings profiles of those companies are affected by different stages of the economic cycle, and how their share prices will move relative to one another (correlation) and the broad market (beta) during the market cycle.

The best way to build wealth is through business ownership, and for most people buying the publicly traded shares of great businesses from around the world is the most efficient means of achieving business ownership. While bonds can provide stable income and reduce the volatility of portfolio returns (a good idea when investors reach retirement age and need to begin withdrawing money), owning great businesses over a long period of time could be all that is needed to achieve financial success. By taking a global approach to investing, investors expand the number of investment opportunities available to them, enhance their knowledge of the global financial markets, and reach a better comprehension of the risks they face. Investors also gain considerable benefits from currency diversification. Searching the globe for businesses that are consistently able to create wealth and then weighing that against the price you pay for the business is the best way to allocate your capital.

The reality is that investing successfully is a complex and time-consuming task. Understanding the myriad factors that can impact the performance of an investment requires great effort and constant vigilance on the part of the investor. At a minimum, investors are required to assimilate vast amounts of information. To be successful, investors must also quickly understand the context and implications of new information. For the global investor who must monitor the entire world, the job of gathering and analyzing market data is even more challenging. Investors who are keen to take advantage of all the world's financial markets have to offer will find the effort to be both intellectually stimulating and financially rewarding. Whether we recognize it or not, we live in a global financial system. Many businesses that we consider domestic or local are affected by developments that take place around the world. Therefore, whether investing globally or not, any investor will benefit by thinking globally. Investors who take a global perspective will be better equipped to understand and mitigate investment risks.

The most essential element of investment success is to buy good businesses and own them for a long period. Own companies that you believe will continue to generate strong earnings and cash flows regardless of the economic environment. These are businesses that operate in growing industries with predictable pricing and have a dominant and defensible industry position, a strong balance sheet, an astute management team whose interests are aligned with investors, and a positive image in society. Businesses with these attributes are best able to withstand and perhaps even take advantage of periods of economic weakness. Not overpaying for the business is vitally important when you invest. Valuation is often overlooked by investors, who tend to think of share prices more in absolute terms than in relation to the earnings or cash flow of a business. Remember, common shares of a company priced at $20 may be more expensive than a company whose shares are trading at $100 when you consider the earnings and cash flow of each business. Own businesses that you think have sustainable earnings growth and that are priced attractively. If a company becomes overvalued relative to its historical range, its sector, and the market, reassess why you own it and consider selling it and investing the proceeds in another stock.

Most businesses participate to some degree on the global economic stage, competing for resources and customers with both domestic and foreign competitors. Furthermore, the global economy is infinitely complex, resulting from the interactions of nearly 7.8 billion people who inhabit the earth as well as the multitude of businesses they operate. It is critical for investors to understand how the businesses they invest in generate profits as well as the risks associated with those earnings. The global economy is constantly evolving, with cycles created by the normal ebb and flow of the economic environment that can last many months or years.

Understanding how the global economy affects the businesses we invest in requires knowledge of global trade and the risks inherent in the global trade system. Global trade has evolved tremendously in the past several decades, propelled by trade agreements and transformed by advancements in shipping and logistics. When investing in a company it is crucial to understand its business relationships, including its supply chain and the risks they pose to earnings. We noted the majority of global trade is conducted by sea, and that geographical constraints force strict adherence to specific shipping routes that often contain bottlenecks or "chokepoints." These shipping routes often represent the shortest distance between two points, but in some cases, they may be deemed the safest passage. These chokepoints are therefore of strategic importance and represent significant risks to global trade due to their vulnerability to accidents and acts of aggression. The interconnectedness of the global economy and business supply chains has made globalization inexorable. Globalization has led to widespread prosperity around the world, but also gives rise to new business risks.

Developments in the global economy manifest themselves in the global financial markets. Global financial markets are the engine that powers the global economy. Companies use both local and global markets to access the capital required to fund and grow their businesses, while investors provide needed capital in the form of loans (debt) or in exchange for business ownership (equity). Financial markets employ security exchanges to facilitate transactions including trading in currencies and commodities and the issuance and trading of debt and equity securities. Financial markets are also where companies go to complete the vast number of transactions that drive corporate earnings and comprise global trade. Efficient financial markets are therefore a vital part of a country's continuing economic development and serve as a conduit to global markets. To be effective, these markets should be structured and governed in a way that allows capital to flow easily to its most productive use. Regulations must exist and be enforced to protect investor rights and ensure that investor capital is adequately rewarded. Should foreign capital be needed to fund domestic businesses, the rights of foreign investors must be protected on par with domestic investors. Trust in a country's financial system, the rule of law, and the way business is carried out is essential for sustainable, long-term economic growth. Investors should remember that the global capital markets are closely connected and can impact one another in the form of a financial contagion.

Perhaps the most pervasive risk faced by investors comes in the form of market cyclicality. Market cycles stem from fluctuations in economic growth, that flow through and cause variability on corporate earnings. For this reason, all investors are subject to market cycle risk, whether they invest globally or not. Market cycle risk may be heightened for global investors at times due to the interconnectedness of the world's capital markets. This is especially true for investments held in regions experiencing economic weakness, or when there is an increased risk of financial contagion. The benefits afforded global investors are improved diversification and enhanced flexibility, allowing them to access economies that are growing and avoid economies that are weak.

Having an approximate idea of where we are in the market cycle can provide an investor with a tremendous advantage. Different asset classes and businesses perform well or poorly depending on where we are in the market cycle. Having this knowledge can be a powerful tool when it comes to managing risk in a portfolio and seizing opportunities when they arise. It is impossible to know exactly when stocks will switch between bull and bear markets, and therefore "timing the market" is never perfect. As a result, wholesale changes to portfolios are not recommended. Instead, it is best to stay fully invested and remain vigilant for signs indicating which stage of the market cycle we are currently in. Doing so will allow us to prepare ourselves mentally for what is likely to come and deploy available cash in times of market weakness. For investors who are more engaged with the markets and able to devote the necessary time and resources, identifying market cycle stages may allow them to shift weights modestly between defensive and cyclical holdings to generate incrementally higher returns. Always thinking about events in context (why something is happening) will provide investors with better insights into the market cycle and enable them to make more informed investment decisions. This simple step can help investors understand how market participants are viewing a particular situation or help gauge the amount of risk appetite that exists in the market.

Exposure to foreign currencies poses risks and provides significant benefits for global investors. Owning securities that are based in a variety of currencies helps lower the volatility of portfolio returns. Safe haven currencies, such as the US dollar, Japanese yen, and Swiss franc, tend to strengthen during periods of market weakness, helping to offset the corresponding but temporary losses in stocks. Conversely, some currencies, such as the Canadian and Australian dollars, act as risk assets, boosting portfolio returns during bull markets. However, exposure to foreign currencies creates risk for the global investor, especially over shorter time periods. Capital gains generated by foreign stock holdings could be offset by foreign currency losses when the investment returns are translated into your home currency.

Most currency exchange rate fluctuations are modest and reverse over time, as they contain a self-correcting mechanism. The primary concern for investors is to avoid exposing themselves to currencies that are vulnerable to significant depreciation. Currency crises often occur because of a banking crisis. Since banking crises are often preceded by a large, unsustainable increase in home prices, monitoring the housing market and housing afford-ability around the world is an easy step to protect your portfolio. An eco-nomic crisis or decrease in economic activity may negatively impact people's ability to pay their mortgage. If house prices are artificially high and then subject to a downward correction, the underlying collateral for the mort-gages may not be sufficient and the banks could suffer losses. This can rever-berate through the entire economy, causing widespread financial losses that lead to a strong rotation out of risk assets.

Of course, not all housing booms lead to a banking crisis. As an investor you must determine whether home price increases are based on sound and sustainable lending standards and what effect a deteriorating economic envi-ronment might have on the ability of homeowners to continue to make their mortgage payments. Low housing affordability combined with elevated lev-els of consumer debt and rising mortgage rates stands out as a high-risk scenario. Countries with extremely high debt levels and a history of high inflation are more likely to weaken their currency deliberately to deal with an unmanageable debt load, and should be avoided.

All investors face some degree of geopolitical risk, but this risk is espe-cially relevant for global investors. Geopolitical risk can be broadly sepa-rated into two types: internal and external risks. Internal geopolitical risk refers to events occurring within an individual country while external geo-political risk refers to events involving two or more countries. Internal risks include regulation, changes to restrictions on foreign ownership, changes to tax regimes, or other laws that can affect the profitability of a given business or industry. External risks include civil strife, diplomatic and economic sanctions, trade wars, and, in extreme situations, military conflicts. Shocks to global supply chains also pose a risk. To stay abreast of internal risks, investors must continuously observe social and political developments in the countries in which they are invested. Government policy can change quickly, requiring investors to be aware of statements made by government authorities that could foreshadow upcoming tax or regulatory changes. Perhaps the most dramatic events result from an outright change in political leadership, where a political party comes to power with radically different policy agendas. Social unrest is a potential precursor to significant political change. While many such changes may have only a modest impact on the businesses you own, it is important for investors to monitor these develop-ments closely.

Although globalization has led to greater integration and alignment of economic interests, incentivizing countries to favor diplomacy as a tool of foreign policy, it has also served to increase the frequency of contact between countries and increased competition for scarce goods, raising the possibility of disagreements and conflict. The geopolitical landscape is in a constant state of change and always marked by areas where conflict is more likely. These are today's geopolitical hotspots—regions where a significant disagreement between two or more countries exists and where tensions are already high. Among these are Eastern Europe, Iran and the Middle East, Taiwan and the South China Sea, the Kashmir regions of Pakistan and India, and North Korea. These areas require our attention, as an accident or misstep by one party could readily escalate into a military confrontation.

The first step to managing geopolitical risk is to stay vigilant. Investing globally requires investors to monitor world affairs, noting potential areas of concern as they arise and observing them. One simple step to manage geopolitical risk is to set a strict minimum sovereign credit rating for each country as a criteria for investing. Avoid buying companies located in countries with high levels of sovereign or consumer debt, or that are experiencing high or rapidly rising inflation (especially when combined with an overheated housing market). Also avoid investing in countries that are not business-friendly (do not protect shareholder rights), or where reliable financial statements are not readily available. Geopolitical risk may also be mitigated by ensuring your portfolio is properly diversified and that you own businesses whose revenues or supply chains are not excessively reliant on regions or countries whose economies are at risk of deteriorating due to severe fiscal mismanagement, economic coercion, or wars. Proper portfolio construction is a critical part of risk mitigation and successful investing.

There are many approaches to building and rebalancing a portfolio. Regardless of the method you choose, your investment decisions should be based on careful analysis of the businesses purchased, including how earnings are affected by different stages of the economic cycle and what factors pose a risk to those earnings streams. It is also crucial for investors to understand how the share prices of the companies they own correlate to one another and the broad market during the market cycle. Think of your portfolio as a single diversified business and focus on its underlying sales and earnings power. Rebalancing your portfolio to a target allocation at regular but infrequent intervals can add value to your portfolio over time and should help you avoid a buildup of excessive risk associated with large, single-stock positions. As investors gain experience and become more comfortable with the process of building and rebalancing their portfolio, a more active approach that allows one to capitalize on market cycles may be justified.

In my experience, the most common mistakes made by investors (professional or otherwise) include an underappreciation of business risks, overpaying for a business, focusing on short-term share price movements instead of long-term earnings fundamentals, and of course not considering the full set of global investment opportunities available to them. Last, a lack of preparation and failure to consider how companies perform in various stages of the economic and market cycles can lead investors to react emotionally and make poor investment decisions.

I hope that this book has provided its readers with the knowledge and tools necessary to construct and maintain a portfolio of great businesses to help them achieve their financial goals. For many people, the task of building and maintaining their own investment portfolio may require more time and resources than they can spare, or perhaps more time than they want to commit to the endeavor. In those cases, I hope that this book has provided you with an informative framework to engage with your financial advisor more effectively. Beware of advisors who cannot explain what you own or why you own it, as well as those who have invested your capital in so many companies that some of them must necessarily be inferior businesses. One final piece of advice: never be afraid to ask questions out of fear of appearing foolish or unknowledgeable. This is your hard-earned life savings, and you have every right to know how your money is being invested. If your financial advisor cannot or will not take the time to explain this to you, then you should find an advisor who will.

The availability of information and the sharing of ideas made possible by the digital age is both enabling and encouraging investors to shift their thinking and invest globally, a trend that is likely to persist well into the future. By analyzing and building ownership of foreign businesses, global investors serve to deepen economic and social ties between the people of different countries. In this way they help ensure more people around the world share in economic prosperity and thereby strengthen mankind's desire to choose economic and political cooperation over economic and military coercion. Aside from capitalizing on the world's best financial opportunities, by thinking and investing globally, we can hope to improve our understanding of the world we live in and gain a deeper appreciation of other people.

Thank you for reading my book. I hope you found it helpful, and I wish you amazing success in your investing journey.

NOTES

▪ Preface

1. International Monetary Fund, IMF DataMapper, https://www.imf.org/external/datamapper/NGDP_RPCH@WEO/OEMDC/ADVEC/WEOWORLD, as of April 2022, accessed April 28, 2022.
2. The Securities Industry and Financial Markets Association, "Global Equity Markets Primer," https://www.sifma.org/resources/research/insights-global-equity-markets-primer/, accessed November 14, 2021.
3. Howard Marks, *The Most Important Thing: Uncommon Sense for the Thoughtful Investor* (Harper, 2018).

▪ Chapter 1

1. Data sourced from Bloomberg and Yahoo Finance.

▪ Chapter 2

1. International Monetary Fund, "World Economic Outlook Update, July 2021: Fault Lines Widen in the Global Recovery," https://www.imf.org/en/Publications/WEO/Issues/2021/07/27/world-economic-outlook-update-july-2021.
2. International Monetary Fund, "World Economic Outlook Update, July 2021."
3. Mark Overton, *Agricultural Revolution in England: The Transformation of the Agrarian Economy: 1500–1850* (Cambridge University Press, 1966).

4. Ray Dalio, *Principles for Dealing with the Changing World Order: Why Nations Succeed and Fail* (Simon & Schuster, 2021), p. 28.

5. Graham Allison, *Destined for War: Can America and China Escape Thucydides's Trap?* (First Mariner Books, 2018), p. 111.

6. Data from World Bank Group, https://data.worldbank.org/.

7. World Bank, "World Bank Group President Says China Offers Lessons in Helping the World Overcome Poverty," September 15, 2010, http://www.worldbank.org/en/news/press-release/2010/09/15/world-bank-group-president-says-china-offers-lessons-helping-world-overcome-poverty (sourced from Allison, p. 15).

8. Allison, *Destined for War*, p. 7.

9. The World Intellectual Property Organization, "World Intellectual Property Indicators 2020," https://www.wipo.int/publications/en/details.jsp?id=4526, accessed July 25, 2021.

10. International Monetary Fund, "World Economic Outlook Update, July 2021."

11. International Monetary Fund, IMF DataMapper, https://www.imf.org/external/datamapper/NGDP_RPCH@WEO/OEMDC/ADVEC/WEOWORLD, May 1, 2022.

12. Boston Consulting Group, "Global Wealth 2021: When Clients Take the Lead," https://web-assets.bcg.com/d4/47/64895c544486a7411b06ba4099f2/bcg-global-wealth-2021-jun-2021.pdf.

13. World Bank, World Bank Data Bank, https://databank.worldbank.org/reports.aspx?source=2&series=SH.XPD.CHEX.GD.ZS&country=, accessed May 1, 2022.

14. Boston Consulting Group, "Global Wealth 2021."

15. Michelle Weaver, Michael Wilson, Adam Virgadamo, and Andrew Pauker, "Global Exposure Guide 2021—US," Morgan Stanley Research, 2021. Source: FactSet financial data and analytics.

16. Data from World Semiconductor Trade Statistics, Historical Billings Report 35, https://www.wsts.org/67/Historical-Billings-Report.

17. International Monetary Fund, IMF DataMapper.

18. Jeremy Siegel, *Stocks for the Long Run: The Definitive Guide to Financial Market Returns and Long-Term Investment Strategies* (McGraw-Hill, 2002), p. 94.

■ Chapter 3

1. World Ocean Review, https://worldoceanreview.com/en/wor-1/transport/global-shipping/, accessed November 7, 2021.

2. Britannica, "Shipping in the Nineteenth Century," https://www.bri
tannica.com/technology/ship/Shipping-in-the-19th-century, accessed
December 26, 2021.

3. World Shipping Council, https://www.worldshipping.org/building-
prosperity, accessed December 26, 2021.

4. GlobalSecurity.Org, "Container Ship Types," https://www.global
security.org/military/systems/ship/container-types.htm, accessed
December 26, 2021.

5. World Shipping Council, "Liner Shipping, The Backbone of World
Trade," December 7, 2021, https://static1.squarespace.com/static/
5ff6c5336c885a268148bdcc/t/61af42321c8a8b68c5408b9c/1638
875715637/Liner+Shipping_Whitepaper_English.pdf.

6. World Shipping Council, "The Top 50 Container Ports," https://www.
worldshipping.org/top-50-ports, accessed December 26, 2021.

7. GlobalSecurity.org, https://www.globalsecurity.org/military/systems/
ship/container-types.htm, accessed December 26, 2021.

8. The World Bank, https://data.worldbank.org/indicator/IS.SHP.GOOD.
TU, accessed December 26, 2021.

9. International Air Transport Authority, "World Air Transport Statistics,
Plus Edition 2021," https://www.iata.org/contentassets/a686ff624550
453e8bf0c9b3f7f0ab26/wats-2021-mediakit.pdf, accessed December 26,
2021.

10. The World Bank, "Air Freight: A Market Study with Implications for
Landlocked Countries," https://www.worldbank.org/en/topic/trans
port/publication/air-freight-study, accessed December 26, 2021.

11. World Integrated Trade Solution, https://wits.worldbank.org/Country
Profile/en/Country/WLD/Year/LTST/TradeFlow/Export/Partner/
by-country/Product/Total#, accessed November 7, 2021.

12. US Energy Information Administration, "Today In Energy," August 18,
2017, https://www.eia.gov/todayinenergy/detail.php?id=32552.

13. US Energy Information Administration, "The Strait of Malacca, a Key
Oil Trade Chokepoint, Links the Indian and Pacific Oceans," August 11,
2017, https://www.eia.gov/todayinenergy/detail.php?id=32452.

14. GlobalSeecurity.org, "Worldwide Chokepoints," https://www.global
security.org/military/world/chokepoints.htm#:~:text=Examples
%20include%3A%20Strait%20of%20Hormuz%20%E2%80%93%20
provides%20transit,12%20percent%20of%20the%20American%20
international%20seaborne%20trade, accessed June 1, 2022.

15. US Energy Information Administration, "Today in Energy."

16. Suez Canal Authority, https://www.suezcanal.gov.eg/English/Navigation/Pages/NavigationStatistics.aspx, accessed November 7, 2021.

17. US Energy Information Administration, "The Strait of Hormuz Is the World's Most Important Oil Transit Chokepoint," December 27, 2019, https://www.eia.gov/todayinenergy/detail.php?id=42338.

18. US Energy Information Administration, "The Strait of Hormuz."

19. World Bank, "Regional Trade Agreements," https://www.worldbank.org/en/topic/regional-integration/brief/regional-trade-agreements, accessed January 17, 2022.

20. World Bank, "Regional Trade Agreements."

21. Government of Canada, "Canada-United States-Mexico Agreement," https://www.international.gc.ca/trade-commerce/trade-agreements-accords-commerciaux/agr-acc/cusma-aceum/index.aspx?lang=eng, accessed January 17, 2022.

22. The European Union, "Facts and Figures on the European Union Economy," https://european-union.europa.eu/principles-countries-history/key-facts-and-figures/economy_en#:~:text=The%20European%20Union%20operates%20as%20a%20single%20market,around%2015%25%20of%20the%20world%E2%80%99s%20trade%20in%20goods, accessed May 16, 2022.

23. The ASEAN Secretariat, "ASEAN Statistical Yearbook 2021," https://www.aseanstats.org/wp-content/uploads/2021/12/ASYB_2021_All_Final.pdf, accessed May 16, 2022.

24. MERCOSUR, https://www.mercosur.int/en/, accessed May 16, 2022.

25. Grace Ho, "A Trade Pact Nearly 10 Years in the Making: 5 Things to Know about RCEP," *The Straits Times*, November 15, 2020, https://www.straitstimes.com/asia/a-trade-pact-nearly-10-years-in-the-making-5-things-to-know-about-rcep.

26. The World Trade Organization, https://www.wto.org/index.htm, accessed January 23, 2022.

27. The Organisation for Economic Co-operation and Development, https://www.oecd.org/about/members-and-partners/, accessed January 23, 2022.

28. The Bank for International Settlements, https://www.bis.org/about/index.htm?m=1_1, accessed January 23, 2022.

29. Data sourced from Bloomberg, as of November 7, 2021.

Chapter 4

1. The Securities Industry and Financial Markets Association, "Capital Markets Fact Book, 2021," https://www.sifma.org/resources/research/fact-book/, accessed November 14, 2021.
2. World Federation of Exchanges, "The Role of Stock Exchanges in Fostering Economic Growth and Sustainable Development," United Nations Conference on Trade and Development, 2017.
3. The Securities Industry and Financial Markets Association, "Global Equity Markets Primer," https://www.sifma.org/resources/research/insights-global-equity-markets-primer/, accessed November 14, 2021.
4. The Securities Industry and Financial Markets Association, "Global Equity Markets Primer."
5. Carmen Reinhart and Kenneth Rogoff, *This Time Is Different: Eight Centuries of Financial Folly* (Princeton University Press, 2009).
6. Roger Ibbotson and Gary Brinson, *Global Investing: The Professionals Guide to the World's Capital Markets* (McGraw-Hill, 1993), p. 87.

Chapter 5

1. Howard Marks, *Mastering the Market Cycle: Getting the Odds on Your Side* (Houghton Mifflin Harcourt, 2018), p. 289.
2. National Bureau of Economic Research, "US Business Cycle Expansions and Contractions," https://www.nber.org/research/data/us-business-cycle-expansions-and-contractions, accessed January 16, 2022.
3. Britannica, "Great Depression," https://www.britannica.com/event/Great-Depression, accessed January 16, 2022.
4. Britannica, "Great Recession."
5. Carmen Reinhart and Kenneth Rogoff, *This Time Is Different: Eight Centuries of Financial Folly* (Princeton University Press, 2009), p. 279.
6. Morgan Stanley, "A Spotter's Guide to Bull Corrections and Bear Markets," March 4, 2018.
7. Morgan Stanley, "A Spotter's Guide."
8. Morgan Stanley, "A Spotter's Guide."

Chapter 6

1. Carmen Reinhart and Kenneth Rogoff, *This Time Is Different: Eight Centuries of Financial Folly* (Princeton University Press, 2009), p. 189.
2. Jeremy Siegel, *Stocks for the Long Run: The Definitive Guide to Financial Market Returns and Long-Term Investment Strategies* (McGraw-Hill, 2002), p. 175.

Chapter 7

1. K. J. Holsti, *International Politics: A Framework for Analysis* (Prentice-Hall, 1988), p. 191.
2. Mark Armbruster, "What Happens If America Goes to War?," CFA Institute, September 25, 2013, https://blogs.cfainstitute.org/inside investing/2013/09/25/u-s-capital-market-returns-during-periods-of-war/.
3. Graham Allison, *Destined for War: Can America and China Escape Thucydides's Trap?* (First Mariner Books, 2018).

Chapter 11

1. World Health Organization, "WHOI Launches New Report on Global Tobacco Use Trends," December 19, 2019, https://www.who.int/news/item/19-12-2019-who-launches-new-report-on-global-tobacco-use-trends.

Chapter 12

1. U.S. Energy Information Administration, "An Introduction to Crack Spreads," https://www.eia.gov/todayinenergy/detail.php?id=1630, accessed March 31, 2022.

Chapter 16

1. United Nations Conference on Trade and Development, "Key Statistics and Trends in International Trade 2021," https://unctad.org/system/files/official-document/ditctab2022d3_en.pdf, accessed April 3, 2022.

■ Chapter 17

1. Food and Agricultural Organization of the United Nations, "World Food and Agriculture—Statistical Yearbook 2021," https://www.fao.org/documents/card/en/c/cb4477en/.
2. United Nations Conference on Trade and Development, "Key Statistics and Trends in International Trade 2021," https://unctad.org/system/files/official-document/ditctab2022d3_en.pdf.

■ Chapter 19

1. United Nations, UN Water Conference, https://www.unwater.org/water-facts/scarcity/, accessed May 30, 2022.
2. UNICEF, "Water Security for All," https://www.unicef.org/media/95241/file/water-security-for-all.pdf, accessed May 30, 2022.

This chapter acts as a guide to some of the best resources available to you as an investor. If you want to maximize your chances for investment success, I encourage you to check each of these out.

■ Recommended Books on Investing

Bogle, John. *The Little Book of Common Sense Investing*. John Wiley & Sons, 2017.

Browne, Christopher H. *The Little Book of Value Investing*. John Wiley & Sons, 2007.

Cunningham, Lawrence, Torkell T. Eide, and Patrick Hargreaves. *Quality Investing: Owning the Best Companies for the Long Term*. Harriman House, 1988.

Dalio, Ray. *Principles for Dealing with the Changing World Order*. Simon & Schuster, 2021.

Dalio, Ray. *Principles: Life and Work*. Simon & Schuster, 2017.

Ellis, Charles. *Winning the Loser's Game: Timeless Strategies for Successful Investing*. McGraw-Hill, 2002.

Fabozzi, Frank J. (ed.). *The Handbook of Fixed Income Securities*. 9th ed. McGraw-Hill, 2021.

Fridson, Martin, and Fernando Alvarez. *Financial Statement Analysis: A Practitioner's Guide*. 5th ed. John Wiley & Sons, 2022.

Graham, Benjamin. *The Intelligent Investor: The Definitive Book on Value Investing*. Harper Collins, 2006.

Graham, Benjamin, and David L. Dodd. *Security Analysis: Principles and Technique*. McGraw-Hill, 2009.

Greenblatt, Joel. *The Little Book That Beats the Market*. John Wiley & Sons, 2010.

Greenwald, Bruce, Judd Kahn, Paul D. Sonkin, and Michael van Biema. *Value Investing: From Graham to Buffett and Beyond*. John Wiley & Sons, 2001.

Horan, Stephen, Robert Johnson, and Thomas Robinson. *Strategic Value Investing: Practical Techniques of Leading Value Investors*. McGraw-Hill Education, 2014.

Ibbotson, Roger G., and Gary P. Brinson. *Global Investing: The Professional's Guide to the World's Capital Markets*. McGraw-Hill, 1993.

Malkiel, Burton G. *A Random Walk Down Wall Street*. W.W. Norton & Company, 1985.

Montier, James. *The Little Book of Behavioral Investing: How to Not Be Your Own Worst Enemy*. John Wiley & Sons, 2010.

O'Glove, Thomas L. *Quality of Earnings: The Investor's Guide to How Much Money a Company Is Really Making*. The Free Press, a Division of Macmillan, 1987.

Marks, Howard. *Mastering the Market Cycle: Getting the Odds on Your Side*. Houghton Mifflin Harcourt, 2018.

Marks, Howard. *The Most Important Thing: Uncommon Sense for the Thoughtful Investor*. Harper Business, 2018.

Reinhart, Carmen, and Kenneth Rogoff. *This Time Is Different: Eight Centuries of Financial Folly*. Princeton University Press, 2011.

Siegel, Jeremy. *Stocks for the Long Run: The Definitive Guide to Financial Market Returns and Long-Term Investment Strategies*. McGraw-Hill, 2002.

Solnik, Bruno. *International Investments*. Addison Wesley, 1991.

■ Recommended Books on International Politics

Allison, Graham. *Destined for War: Can America and China Escape Thucydides's Trap?* Mariner Books, 2017.

Brzezinski, Zbigniew. *The Grand Chessboard: American Primacy and Its Geostrategic Imperatives*. Basic Books, 1997.

Holsti, K.J. *International Politics: A Framework for Analysis*. Prentice-Hall, 1988.

Kennedy, Paul. *The Rise and Fall of the Great Powers*. William Collins, 2017.

Waltz, Kenneth. *Theory of International Politics*. Waveland Press, 2010.

■ Websites: Market Data and Commentary

AlphaStreet (https://news.alphastreet.com/) is a one-stop shop for financial news, data, and investment resources. AlphaStreet offers a wealth of insightful research and detailed company analysis.

Bloomberg (https://www.bloomberg.com/) provides timely financial market news and features stories of interest to investors (paid subscription required).

Google Finance (https://www.google.com/finance/) is a source for market-related data, including stock charts and basic historical company data.

Investopedia (https://www.investopedia.com/) is a leading provider of financial news: original studies, research, data analysis offering an abundance of investment dictionaries, advice, reviews, ratings, and comparisons of financial products. Includes an up-to-date news section covering the latest from corporations, global markets, and politics.

Pitchbook (https://pitchbook.com/) is a provider of the key financials of global, public, and private companies. This includes access to the balance sheets, cash flow statements, income statements, financial ratios, and more from 3,343,263 private companies and 59,374 public companies worldwide. Access requires a paid subscription.

Seeking Alpha (https://seekingalpha.com/) is a paid service providing company analysis from independent analysts.

Yahoo Finance (https://finance.yahoo.com/) is a source for market-related data, including stock charts and detailed historical company data. Yahoo Finance even provides some basic ESG rating information.

■ Stock Chart Services

StockCharts (https://stockcharts.com/) is a paid service that makes it easy to create high-quality financial charts in just a few simple clicks. It allows users to run custom scans to find new trades or investments, and set automatic alerts for your unique technical criteria, and provides daily market commentary from industry-leading technicians.

Symbolik (https://www.symbolik.com/) is a paid service offering access to indicators developed over a period of decades by famed investor Tom DeMark. The DeMark indicators have a wide following and can be helpful in identifying the beginning and end of trends in stock prices.

■ Ratings and Analytics

MSCI Inc. (https://www.msci.com/) is a leading provider of global market data, offering a wealth of insightful research and market commentary, including ESG ratings for over 2,900 publicly traded companies.

IHS Markit (https://ihsmarkit.com/index.html) is a leading provider of information and analytics. While most of the company's data is accessible only by paid subscription, they do offer some well-thought-out research via podcasts and their website.

S&P Global Inc. (https://www.spglobal.com/) is a leading provider of global market data offering a wealth of insightful research and market commentary, including sovereign credit ratings.

■ Websites: Economic Data

The American Petroleum Institute (https://www.api.org/) provides rig count data and other useful information for the energy sector.

The Chicago Mercantile Exchange (https://www.cmegroup.com) is one of the world's leading derivatives marketplaces. The website provides useful data and analysis of a wide range of derivatives on commodities, interest rates, equities, and currencies. Investors can use this information to create a WTI strip curve for analyzing the energy sector.

The Energy Information Administration (EIA) (https://www.eia.gov/) is an excellent resource to decipher the endless acronyms of the energy world from WTI to Mboe/d to OPEC to LNG.

The National Association of Realtors (https://www.nar.realtor) provides data relating to new home sales.

The Oil & Gas Journal (https://www.ogj.com/) brings in the pertinent articles from EIA, OPEC, and API, if you want a one-stop shop for energy sector information.

OPEC, the Organization for Petroleum Exporting Countries (https://www.opec.org/opec_web/en/), provides an insightful global perspective on oil supply and demand.

US Census Bureau (https://www.census.gov/) is a source for US economic data, including new building permit activity.

■ Websites: Regulatory Filings

AnnualReports (https://www.annualreports.com/) is a provider of 112,775 annual reports from 9,187 international companies.

EDGAR (https://www.sec.gov/edgar.shtml)—The US Securities and Exchange Commission created the EDGAR (Electronic Data Gathering and Retrieval) website to provide easy access to the financial statements filed by companies listed in the United States.

SEDAR (www.sedar.com) is the official Canadian site that provides access to most public securities documents and information filed by issuers with the 13 provincial and territorial securities regulatory authorities.

SEDI, The System for Electronic Disclosure by Insiders (SEDI) (www.sedi. ca), is Canada's online, browser-based service for the filing and viewing of insider reports as required by various provincial securities rules and regulations. SEDI replaces paper-based reporting and provides for an efficient disclosure process.

■ Websites: Investment Education

CFA Institute (www.cfainstitute.org)—In addition to administering the Chartered Financial Analyst designation (highly recommended for anyone interested in any investment-related career), CFA Institute provides free insightful articles related to investing through the CFA Institute Research Foundation.

Investopedia (https://www.investopedia.com/)—A leading provider of financial news: original studies, research, data analysis offering an abundance of investment dictionaries, advice, reviews, ratings, and comparisons of financial products. Includes an up-to-date news section covering the latest from corporations, global markets, and politics.

WallStreetPrep (https://www.wallstreetprep.com/)—Provides online courses and instructor-led bootcamps to prepare students and professionals for the demands of investment banking and corporate finance.

■ Social Media

RenMac—(@RenMacLLC) Follow Jeff DeGraaf and the team at RenMac on LinkedIn and Twitter for insightful, regular updates on the equity markets, including thoughts on where we are in the market cycle.

■ Company Checklist

Does the company generate similar or higher profits than its competitors?	
What is the competitive advantage that is driving higher growth and profitability?	
Is the company's competitive advantage sustainable?	
Is the company's revenue stream sustainable? Will it grow or shrink?	
Is the company an industry leader or laggard in research and development?	
Can the company successfully expand into new regions or closely related markets?	
Does the company have sound economic, social and governance policies?	
Is the management team experienced and focused, or are they untested or distracted?	
Will the company be able to service its debt if the economy weakens?	
Will management grow by acquiring? If so, how good is their acquisition track record?	
Does the compensation structure of management align with shareholder interests?	
Is the management team committed to returning excess cash to shareholders?	
Is the company attractively priced vs. competitors and in relation to its earnings power?	

Page numbers followed by *f* refer to figures.

INDEX